Understanding the IBM WebFacing Tool

A Guided Tour

Understanding the IBM WebFacing Tool

A Guided Tour

Claus Weiss and Emily Bruner

MC PRESS

Understanding the IBM WebFacing Tool: A Guided Tour
Claus Weiss and Emily Bruner

Published by MC Press Online, LP
IBM Press Associate Publisher: Tara B. Woodman, IBM Corporation
IBM Press Alliance Publisher: David M. Uptmor, MC Press

For information on translations and book distribution outside the United States or to arrange bulk-purchase discounts for sales promotions or premiums please contact:
MC Press
Corporate Offices:
125 N. Woodland Trail
Lewisville, TX 75077

Sales and Customer Service:
P.O. Box 4300
Big Sandy, TX 75755-4300

First edition
First printing: July, 2003
ISBN: 1-931182-09-4

Every attempt has been made to provide correct information in this book. However, the publisher, the editors, and the authors do not guarantee the accuracy of the book and do not assume responsibility for information included in or omitted from it.

The following are trademarks of International Business Machines Corporation in the United States, other countries, or both: DB2, Lotus, Tivoli, WebSphere, IBM, the IBM logo, IBM Press, and the e-business logo.

Rational, Rational Developer Network, and ClearCase are registered trademarks of Rational Software Corporation and/or IBM Corporation in the United States, other countries, or both.

Microsoft, Windows, Windows NT, and the Windows logo are trademarks of Microsoft Corporation in the United States, other countries, or both.

Java and all Java-based trademarks are trademarks of Sun Microsystems, Inc. in the United States, other countries, or both.

Intel, Intel Inside (logos), MMX and Pentium are trademarks of Intel Corporation in the United States, other countries, or both.

UNIX is a registered trademark of The Open Group in the United States and other countries, licensed exclusively through The Open Group.

Other company, product, and service names may be trademarks or service marks of others.

Acknowledgements

We want to thank the following people for their tremendous support:

Larry Schweyer for helping with the sample exercises

Maha Masri for supplying some of the exercises

Phil Coulthard for suggesting to write the book

Satish Gungabeesoon

George Farr

John Steinbacher

George Voutsinas

Melanie Steckham

Inge Weiss

Vadim Berestetsky

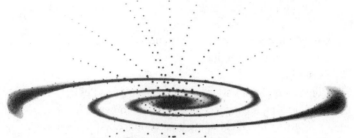

Contents

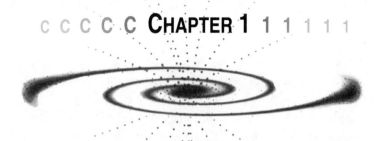

C C C C C **CHAPTER 1** 1 1 1 1 1

WebFacing Tool introduction

The goal of many iSeries programmers is to catch up with the latest technology and create Web-enabled graphical user interfaces for their iSeries programs. The WebFacing Tool is designed to convert your DDS-based user interface descriptions to Web-based user interfaces for use in an Internet browser. The conversion process generates JavaServer Pages (JSP) and XML files that replace the existing DDS code. The WebFacing Tool is one of the main components of IBM WebSphere Development Studio Client for iSeries (Development Studio Client). This chapter outlines Development Studio Client, and then covers WebFacing Tool concepts, to give you a general picture of WebFacing conversion and runtime activities. The chapter also explains how to install Development Studio Client, Version 5.0, and how to install the sample application included with this book, which you will use during most of the hands-on exercises.

WebSphere Development Studio Client

This book is based on WebSphere Development Studio Client Version 5.0, which is the second release of this product.[1] If you are still working with Development Studio

---

[1]Development Studio Client Version 4.0 was announced in June 2002, and shortly afterward delivered to customers. It is the follow-on product to WebSphere Development Tools for iSeries Version 5.1. The version of the WebSphere Studio Client products aligns itself with WebSphere Application Server. Development Studio Client is unique because it is shipped with an iSeries product called WebSphere Development Studio (WDS), which aligns itself with the OS/400 versions. So Development Client Studio Version 4 and Version 5 are working with OS/400, Version 5.1 and 5.2.

Client Version 4.0, you do not need to worry; the WebFacing Tool user interface has remained fairly consistent and you should be able to follow the exercises with no problems. I have added special remarks and special sections where I found the differences between the versions sufficient to confuse the reader.

Development Studio Client is not the first workstation-based product for the iSeries host or for AS/400 application developers. The first product was CoOperative Development Environment for AS/400 (CODE/400), released in 1992. IBM followed with a second product, VisualAge RPG, two years later. At that time both products were running on OS/2. In 1997, Windows versions of these products were released. In the year 2001, IBM consolidated the application development tools for iSeries and combined the host-based products, Application Development Tool Set (ADTS) and the RPG, COBOL, C, and C++ compilers, with a set of workstation-based application development tools. This new packaging of iSeries application development tools was intended to support the iSeries programmers with tools for both traditional applications and the new Web-based e-business applications. The workstation tools came on the market under the WebSphere brand with the name IBM WebSphere Development Tools for iSeries Version 5.1 (WDT). WDT included the following components:

1. CODE, a set of workstation-based tools that programmers could use for traditional iSeries application development, instead of green-screen–based tools such as Program Development Manager (PDM), Source Entry Utility (SEU), Screen Design Aid (SDA), and Report Layout Utility (RLU).

2. VisualAge RPG (VARPG), a tool for developing graphical user interface (GUI) client/server applications, featuring easy connectivity to the iSeries host and a low learning curve for RPG programmers.

3. VisualAge for Java (VAJAVA), a tool supporting the complete cycle of Java development for Java server and client applications.

4. WebSphere Studio, a tool for developing Web sites and e-business applications in conjunction with VAJAVA.

5. WebFacing, a tool to give traditional green-screen applications Web enablement along with an attractive graphical user interface.

That's right, the first release of WebFacing became available in WDT Version 5.1. At this time, IBM wanted to consolidate all application development tools for all platforms, and the team responsible for iSeries development tools decided to base a new generation of iSeries-specific tools on this platform. The framework for these new tools is called Eclipse, originally developed by IBM and then donated to the Open Source Consortium. The Eclipse framework is now managed by the Eclipse.org consortium.

The advantages of basing the iSeries development tools on a nonproprietary standard are manifold. First of all, you can reuse platform-independent tools without change. This applies to many iSeries-specific functions and components. Because these iSeries tools can act as plug-ins to an open-source framework, the tools' *behavior* and user interface is not platform specific, even if some of the *functions* are specific. For example, the iSeries unique perspective lists iSeries objects, but the Properties views of these objects are similar to those for other platform objects. This allows iSeries programmers to work with tools that programmers on other platforms use as well. It also means that other programmers can easily switch to iSeries development, since the tools behave the same way.

Development Studio Client Version 4.0 was the first implementation of this new tool base. The current version, 5.0, has many enhancements over Version 4.0 and gives you an even greater set of development tools:

1. The Remote System Explorer, which provides enhanced tools for traditional iSeries application development

2. The IBM WebFacing Tool, with its latest release fully integrated with Version 5.0 of WebSphere Application Server (WAS) and the Web project structure it requires

3. Web tools for developing e-business applications, with enhancements to support iSeries-specific features

4. Java tools for developing Java and Web applications for any platform

5. XML tools, for creating XML descriptions of interfaces to make them available in a nonproprietary format

6. Web services tools, for creating the descriptions of Web services

7. Many wizards that guide programmers through the creation of Web applications and help them get started even with a limited skill base in the Web environment

Figure 1.1 shows a graphical view of the Development Studio Client product and how it is packaged with an unlimited usage license inside WebSphere Development Studio.

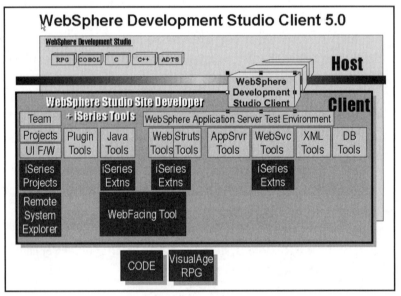

Figure 1.1: Product packaging of Development Studio Client Version 5

The Client section represents the Eclipse environment. All of the tools inside the Client box are plug-ins to the Eclipse framework. The Classic tools, CODE and VARPG, are positioned outside of the main section, since they are not plug-ins to Eclipse. They can be invoked from Eclipse-based tools but run outside of the Eclipse workbench. The lighter-shaded boxes in the Client section represent tools that are part of WebSphere Studio Site Developer (WSSD). The darker boxes represent the tools that the team in the Toronto Laboratory developed for iSeries application developers.

An advanced edition of Development Studio Client Version 5.0 is also available. WebSphere Studio Application Developer is the base for this edition. It provides the same end-to-end support for the creation and maintenance of J2EE applications and Web services. In addition, it provides extensive support for Enterprise JavaBeans (EJB) and for Java Message Service.

The advanced version of Development Studio Client also provides additional capabilities for the WebFacing Tool, including the ability to generate the run-time elements conforming to the Struts framework and to work with Print services. Some of the User Interface elements can also be generated as JSP custom tags.

This book will guide you through the WebFacing Tool, and it will also introduce other tools in the Development Studio workbench, for example, that you will use:

- The WebSphere Application Server (WAS) Test Environment, to run and test the WebFaced application inside the workbench without having to deploy to a server.

- Web Tools, to enhance the look of the initial Web page created by the WebFacing Tool.

- The Remote System Explorer, to change and re-create an RPG program to adapt it to the WebFacing environment. Typically, you do not have to adapt the RPG and COBOL programs for WebFacing, but sometimes it is handy to add extra functions that enhance the Web interface.

- The integrated iSeries Debugger, to help you debug your application.

The coverage will begin with a look specifically at the WebFacing Tool.

Basic concepts behind the WebFacing Tool

Before you use the WebFacing Tool, I want to explore some of the basic WebFacing concepts. In a nutshell, the tool converts a 5250 user interface application to a Web application. The following sections look at the components of a Web application.

Concept of a Web application

A Web application is ideally split into three distinct parts:

1. The user interface

2. The controller logic

3. The business model

For a Web application the user interface displays in a browser and is described in HTML tag language. In many cases, additional Java script logic executes in the browser, to enhance the user interface, since the basic HTML tag language can produce only a very rudimentary user interface.

The controller logic for the Web application is written in Java and runs on an application server. The controller logic determines which user interface components (Web pages) to display and what business logic to run depending on requests and input from the end user on the browser.

The business logic can run on any server platform and can be implemented in any programming language. In an iSeries shop the platform normally is an iSeries server and the programming language is RPG or COBOL.

Figure 1.2 shows a typical three-tier Web application environment.

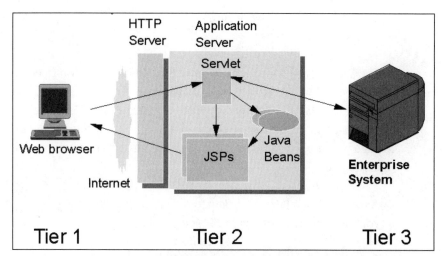

Figure 1.2: Graphical representation of a three-tiered Web application

The WebFacing Tool converts the green-screen user interface to a Web user interface. With this conversion, the original green-screen application runs as a Web application. The controller logic normally implemented in a servlet, which essentially decides which page is shown next, still resides in the original application. Therefore, the application is not a "true" Web application even though it behaves like one. Actually, the WebFacing run time is a servlet that acts as intermediary between the application and the user interface.

WebFacing conversion

To change the green-screen user interface of a host application into a Web application, the WebFacing Tool has to convert the DDS user interface description to an HTML user interface description. The browser then understands how to display the HTML tags and the data included from the application. Part of the WebFacing conversion process is the selection of the DDS source members that make up the application's user interface.

To reflect the dynamic nature of the 5250 user interface, the Web user interface description must be capable of supporting changes at run time. For example, output fields have to be able to add data at run time. Plain HTML does not support dynamic content, but JavaServer Pages do. JSP files consist of HTML tags that define the static content, and Java code for the dynamic pieces of the user interface. When a JSP file is requested, the Java code in the JSP file runs on the server, resulting in dynamic content of the page. The file is then sent as pure HTML to the browser and rendered as a Web page.

The WebFacing Tool needs another piece of information to be able to work in the Web environment. How is your application invoked in the 5250 environment? The command that invokes the application must be specified. The WebFacing Tool creates an index.html page that contains a link. Selecting this link from the index page will invoke routines in the WebFacing server and start the application on the iSeries host.

As you will see later on, you need to specify only a few things before you convert your application with the WebFacing Tool.

During conversion, the WebFacing Tool accesses the specified DDS source and creates the corresponding JSP files, and several other files, from your DDS source members. It places these files onto your workstation. Since the WebFacing Tool is a plug-in to the WebSphere Studio workbench, the information is stored in the workbench workspace. To specify the WebFacing work environment, you create a WebFacing project in the workbench before you start the conversion.

WebFacing run time

Now that I have explained what you have to do to convert your 5250 user interface, I will explain more about the WebFacing run-time environment.

The goal of WebFacing is to provide a more attractive user interface for an existing application without impacting its logic. Ideally, you should not need to touch the logic of your RPG, COBOL, CL, C, or C++ programs. Let's look at how the programs work today with their text-based user interface.

In your iSeries programs you use a workstation file to indicate that you want to display data in a user interface. The workstation files contain record formats, which describe the data buffer layout of your user interface. Essentially, all dynamic content of your user interface is described through the record formats, and at run time the data inside the record format is passed from the program to the user interface and vice versa. The data buffer definition in the record formats is the interface between your program logic and the user interface. In your programs, you communicate with the workstation file by writing the buffers when you display a screen and reading the buffers when you receive input from the user interface.

The requests to the workstation file are handled by the iSeries workstation manager, which takes the data in the buffer and surrounds it with 5250 control characters. It does this according to the DDS user interface description you provided for the record format and that is stored in a display file. The complete 5250 data stream with user interface definitions and data is sent to the 5250 terminal, which renders the 5250 data stream and displays the user interface parts with the data.

Figure 1.3 shows this process.

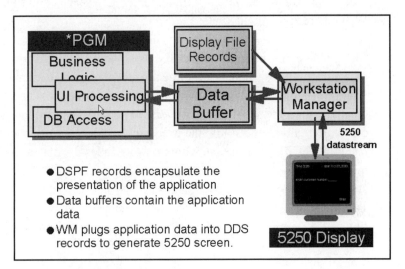

Figure 1.3: Interactive model

For a WebFaced application, this picture changes. The device that renders the user interface is a browser. The browser is sending requests to a Web server instead of a 5250 terminal that is directly connected to a workstation controller on an iSeries server.

The program itself still communicates with a workstation file, but the iSeries workstation manager itself is enhanced for the WebFacing environment. This change in the iSeries workstation manager has to be installed with a PTF. Please visit the WebFacing Web page for the latest PTF numbers for your specific iSeries OS/400 release.

The workstation manager enhancement enables it to sense whether an application is connected to a 5250 device or to the WebFacing server. If the application is invoked via the WebFacing server, the workstation manager does not create the 5250 data stream around the data it receives from the programs. Instead, it passes this data directly to the WebFacing server. The WebFacing server hands the data over to the WebFacing run time, which is implemented as a servlet and runs on the IBM WebSphere application server.

The WebFacing run time receives the workstation file data from the program in a data buffer. The WebFacing runtime also receives information on which record format to display. From this information, the run time invokes the corresponding JSP, created during the WebFacing conversion process. The JSP takes the data from the data buffer and inserts it into the user interface description from the conversion. The resulting HTML data stream, which now includes the data as well as the user interface description, is sent to the browser. The browser then renders the data stream and displays the data as a Web page.

Figure 1.4 shows the changed iSeries workstation environment for WebFaced applications.

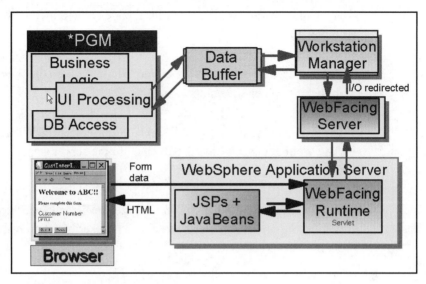

Figure 1.4: WebFacing model

Figure 1.5 shows the individual steps in the flow of a WebFaced application invocation.

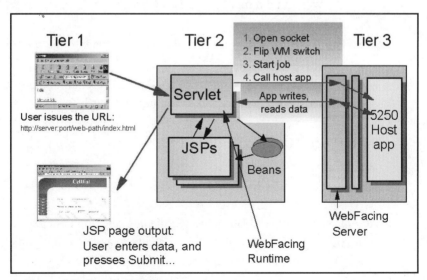

Figure 1.5: How it all works

1. The end user requests the index.html page created by the WebFacing conversion.

2. The end user clicks on the generated HTML link on the page to invoke the application he or she wants to run.

3. The request is send to the Web server and invokes the WebFacing run time. (The WebFacing run time is published to the server as part of the WebFacing project.)

4. The WebFacing run time connects to the specified iSeries host, and the WebFacing server receives the request. (I describe later how to start the server on the iSeries server.)

5. A job is created, and the command to invoke the application is run in that job.

6. The application writes a record format to the workstation file, and workstation manager handles this request.

7. The workstation manager passes the record format to the WebFacing server.

8. The WebFacing server sends the record format to the WebFacing run time.

9. The WebFacing run time invokes the JSP corresponding to the record format. The data from the program is included in the JSP.

10. The HTML stream including data is sent to the browser.

11. The browser renders the data stream and displays the Web page.

With this short introduction to the WebFacing development and run-time environment, you are ready to tackle basic WebFacing tasks. Before you try the exercises, however, I will explain how to install the sample Order Entry application on the iSeries host. You will use this sample application during most of the WebFacing exercises. After the iSeries application installation, I explain how to install the WebFacing Tool. Because the WebFacing Tool is not a stand-alone tool, I will tell you how to install Development Studio Client on your workstation. If you have already installed Development Studio Client, you can skip that section.

Installing the sample application and iSeries setup

To be able to complete the exercises, you need to install the sample application library that accompanies this book. The sample application comes in the form of a save file on a workstation CD. Before you put a new user interface on this sample application, you will get a look at the green screens featured in this application. From running through the screens you will get a good idea of how the application looks and behaves in its original version and what the differences are after it is converted with the WebFacing Tool.

Installing the sample library

For the installation, you will need access to an iSeries server running OS/400 V5R1 or higher. On your iSeries server, you need authority to create a save file in library QGPL, (or any other library you have access to), and you also need authority to create a new library.

In the examples throughout this book, I use an iSeries host with the host name of S400A, and I use a sample user ID and password WDSCLABxx. When going through the exercises on your host, replace S400A with your real iSeries host name, and use your own iSeries user ID and password when accessing the host at your location.

The CD that comes with this book is a workstation CD; the save file it contains has to be copied to the iSeries host and restored to a library.

Installing the sample library

This is an overview of the steps to install the sample library on your iSeries server. If you are familiar with these tasks you might want to skip the detailed instructions and just install the library WFLABXX with these three high-level steps:

1. Create a save file on the iSeries server.

2. FTP the save file wflabxx.sav from the workstation CD to this save file on the iSeries server.

3. Restore library WFLABXX from the save file.

Detailed instructions for installing the sample library

The following detailed instructions show you exactly how to complete the steps outlined in the previous section.

Start a 5250 emulator and use it to

- Sign on to your iSeries server.

- Create a save file named WFLABXX in library QGPL using the Create Save File (CRTSAVF) command:

```
crtsavf qgpl/wflabxx
```

(Instead of using QGPL you can select a library of your choice.)

To transfer the file from the CD to your iSeries host,

- Insert the CD into your workstation CD-ROM drive.

Establish a File Transfer Protocol (FTP) connection to your iSeries server:

- In a DOS command window type

```
ftp s400a
```

(Remember to use your own iSeries host name or IP address instead of S400A.)

- Press the **Enter** key.

When prompted in the DOS window,

- Enter your iSeries user ID and press the **Enter** key.

- Enter your iSeries password and press the **Enter** key.

After the FTP session is established, in the DOS window,

- Enter bin and press the **Enter** key (to make sure no character set–specific conversion occurs).

In the DOS window,

- Type

```
put x:/wflabxx.sav QGPL/WFLABXX
```

and press the **Enter** key. (*x* represents the CD-ROM drive letter; use the letter that corresponds to your workstation's CD-ROM drive. Also, use the library that contains the save file you created in the previous step, if it is not QGPL.)

After the file is copied, you are notified in the DOS window.

- Type quit and press the **Enter** key.

You may close the DOS window now and remove the CD.

The last step is to restore the library from the save file. Use your 5250 session in your emulator to restore library WFLABXX.

- Enter the following Restore Library (RSTLIB) command on the command line:

```
rstlib savlib(wflabxx) dev(*savf) savf(qgpl/wflabxx)
```

(Again, if you did not put the save file in the QGPL library, then use the other library name instead of QGPL.)

Once the WFLABXX library is created, you are ready to set up the job environment on your iSeries server and begin the exercises.

Setting up the job environment

To successfully perform WebFacing conversion, you will need to specify the WFLABXX library in your job's library list. My suggestion is to make sure it is automatically added when your user ID logs on. You can do this by changing your user profile's job description. Just add the library to the list of libraries in the job description that your user profile uses. If you do not want to change your user environment, create a separate user profile for these exercises and make the WFLABXX library the current library for this special user profile.

Setting up the WebFacing server on an iSeries box

The WebFacing run-time support on the iSeries host is a very straightforward process since the WebFacing server is part of OS/400 V4R5 and higher. This means that you do not incur any additional run-time cost for the WebFacing server. You might think that you do not have to take any action since the WebFacing server is part of OS/400. However, you still need to install the WebFacing server and update the iSeries workstation manager by installing PTFs. The latest PTF numbers are available on the WebSphere Development Studio Web site. The page that will get you there is:

ibm.com/software/awdtools/iseries

This is the main page for iSeries tools. (We hope that the URL will not change even if product names change.)

On this page, select the link to the IBM WebFacing Tool. On the WebFacing page, there is a link to the system requirements page that contains the latest PTFs for each of the supported OS/400 releases. This list often changes, so I will not list the PTFs here.

The WebFacing server is a normal TCP/IP server like the FTP and http servers. Its name is *WEBFACING.

After you have installed the OS/400 PTFs for WebFacing, you need to start the server with the iSeries command `strtcpsvr *Webfacing`. The WebFacing server by default is started on port 4004 on your iSeries host.

You are now ready to move on to the workstation setup instructions.

Installing Development Studio Client

WebFacing is a workstation tool that runs under the Microsoft Windows operating system. However, it is not a tool that you can install separately; you need to install the overall product that WebFacing is a part of. This overall product is called Development Studio Client. If you have not installed Development Studio Client yet, acquire the three CDs or the DVD and run the setup program. The CDs or the DVD are workstation media. Do not try to put them into your iSeries host optical drive. If you do not personally have the CDs or DVD, your company should have them.

If you have WebSphere Development Studio (WDS) installed on your OS/400 V5R1 or V5R2 system, you have a license for the Development Studio Client product. If you still have the predecessor of Development Studio Client, which is WebSphere Development Tools (WDT), then you can upgrade to the new product version by reordering it and specifying the following feature code: 5722-WDS FC 5903.

As mentioned before, I have based the exercise descriptions in this book on the newest version of WebSphere Development Client, which is Version 5.0. If you only have Version 4.0, you should be fine. The user interface of the WebFacing Tool is not very different, but where there are differences, I explain how to complete the tasks for both versions.

After installing the product, make sure that you obtain and install the latest fix pack/service pack. As I write this book the current information is as follows:

- For Version 5.0, obtain fix pack 5.0.1 (follow exactly the instructions on our Web site about how to install this fix pack).

- For Version 4.0, obtain service pack 4.

Assuming you have the required product installed on your workstation, you can now start with product configuration.

Setting up WebSphere Development Studio Client

When you use Development Studio Client, the product sets up a workspace on your local system to store all of your data and preferences. If you have used Development Studio Client before, you might want to start with a fresh workspace for the exercises in this book. If you have never used Development Studio Client, you can skip this section and go to the end of the chapter. I am assuming in the instructions for this book that you are starting with a fresh workspace. More specifically, the screen captures for the exercises were taken on a workstation with a fresh workspace.

If you want the instructions and the screen captures in this book to match your environment, you can reset your workspace. Resetting the Development Studio Client workspace will make your environment look like you are starting with a brand new installed product.

I suggest you leave your workspace as it is and accept that some of the instructions and figures in this book might be slightly out of sync with your actual working environment. If you are fine with this, then just this skip to the end of the chapter. If you want to reset your workspace, follow these instructions.

Resetting the Development Studio Client

I separated the workspace resetting instructions for Version 5.0 and Version 4.0 of Development Studio Client because the default workspace locations are different.

Warning: If you have already completed work on your system with Development Studio Client, be careful that you do not delete your workspace. Just rename it instead; this way you can always work with this workspace again.

Resetting Version 5.0

When you start the product, you might be prompted to specify a workspace location. If you see the workspace dialog, you just need to specify a different location and you are set.

However, if you elected to make this workspace the default location, then you can easily reset the workspace:

- Go to a command prompt window.

Change to the Application Development Client installation directory, with the default being *x:\Program Files\IBM\WebSphere Studio*, where *x* is the drive on which you installed Development Studio Client.

- Select the correct drive; key in *x:* (replace *x:* with the drive you installed Development Studio Client on).

- Press **Enter**.

- Select the **current directory**; key in **CD Program Files\IBM\WebSphere Studio**

- Press **Enter**.

Run the command to start Development Studio Client and reset the workspace. For the *standard* Development Studio Client edition, use the following command to invoke WebSphere Studio Site Developer:

- Key in **wssitedev –setworkspace**

For the *advanced* Development Studio Client edition, use the following command to invoke WebSphere Studio Application Developer:

- Key in **wsappdev –setworkspace**

This will bring up the workspace selection dialog shown in Figure 1.6.

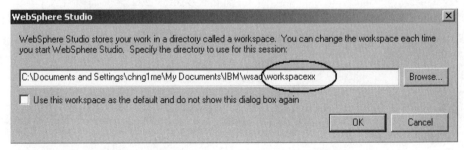

Figure 1.6: Dialog to reset workspace

- Specify a new workspace name so that Development Studio Client starts with this workspace. This will start Development Studio Client.

Tip: Do not select the check box to make this the default workspace, or else you will lose the ability to select the workspace when you start Development Studio Client.

To get back to the previous default of showing the Remote System Explorer perspective, open it by (refer to Figure 1.7)

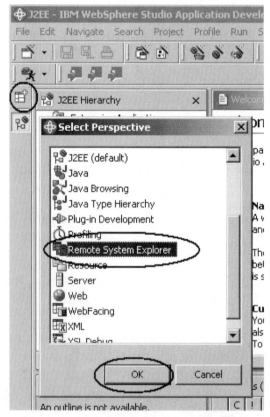

Figure 1.7: Opening the Remote System Explorer perspective

- Selecting the **Perspective icon** on the left workbench taskbar

- Selecting **Remote System Explorer** from the list

- Clicking the **OK** push button

The Remote System Explorer perspective opens.

You can now close the J2EE perspective by (refer to Figure 1.8)

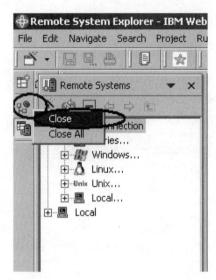

Figure 1.8: Closing the J2EE perspective

- Right-clicking on the **J2EE icon** on the taskbar

- Selecting the **Close** option from the pop-up menu

Now your Development Studio Client is reset to the way it appeared when you first used it.

In case you need your old Development Studio Client environment again later, just select your old workspace at startup.

If you just want to move a project from an older workspace to your current one—if, for example, you want to work on other projects while you complete the exercises in this book—you can use the import function in the workbench.

Resetting Version 4.0

To reset the workbench in Version 4.0, locate the Development Studio Client product folder on one of your local hard drives; by default, the name of the folder is WDSC. If you did not change the name during installation, look for this WDSC folder. Otherwise, look for the folder name you specified during install. Inside this product folder you will find the subfolder WSSD.

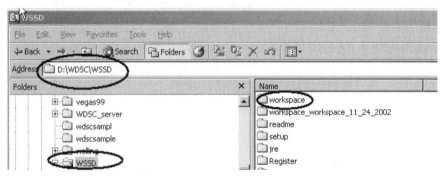

Figure 1.9: Sample of Windows Explorer with workspace directory in Version 4.0

In Windows Explorer, rename the workspace directory; in my sample in Figure 1.9: Sample of Windows Explorer with workspace directory in Version 4.0, the location is *D:\wdsc\wssd\workspace*.

Rename the workspace subfolder inside the WSSD folder; this will force Development Studio Client to re-create the workspace folder. When you start Development Studio Client, the workbench creates a new workspace folder if it cannot find an existing workspace.

If the file is locked and cannot be renamed, make sure that Development Studio Client is not still open. Make sure to close it now. If the file is still locked, the Java virtual machine might still be running; give it some more time to close down or go to the Windows task manager. In the processes list of task manager, locate the javaw.exe process, select it, and end the process. Now try renaming the workspace directory again.

In case you need your old Development Studio Client environment back, rename the workspace folder you used for the exercises in this book, and just rename the original workspace folder back to workspace.

Starting the Development Studio Client Workbench

Now go ahead and start Development Studio Client from the Start menu (see Figure 1.10).

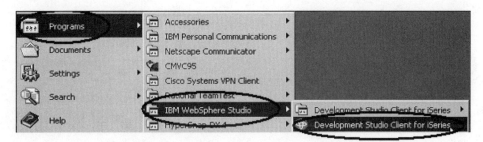

Figure 1.10: Windows Start menu with Development Studio Client shortcuts

You are all set to start with the exercises. Before you start using Development Studio Client and the WebFacing tool, first you will work with the 5250 screens of the Order Entry application to learn how they behave. Then you will start using the Web-Facing Tool.

Have fun and enjoy the modernization of your green-screen applications.

Exercise—A look at the green-screen user interface

In this exercise, you place the Order Entry sample application onto your iSeries server. The sample is on the CD that came with this book, and the installation and setup instructions are in Chapter 1.

Reviewing the 5250 application

You are ready to explore the sample WebFacing application. You will invoke the application from a 5250 session, work with the application's green screens and function keys, and test your user profile setup configuration. If you can run this application directly without changing the job environment on the iSeries system, then you should not encounter any problems during WebFacing conversion or with the Web-Facing server. If you do encounter problems, make sure that the library list for your job is set up correctly to include the WFLABXX library at job startup.

The goal of the exercise

The goal of this exercise is to explore the 5250 application before you use the Web-Facing Tool to convert it into a browser-based user interface. You will become familiar with the 5250 screens and the behavior of the application. After conversion with the WebFacing tool, you will easily be able to compare the 5250 with the Web user interface.

At the end of the exercise, you should be able to

- Invoke the application

- Know what screens the application provides

- Know how the application works in its 5250 environment

- Know what function keys are supported and what functions they enable

Scenario

In this scenario, you use a 5250 emulation screen to start the sample Order Entry application. In the application, the first screen prompts you for a customer number. You select a customer from a list of valid customers and then fill an order for this selected customer. To fill an order, you select a part from a special list and add it to the order by specifying the quantity. After you specify all parts and their quantities for this order, you complete the order by pressing function key 6 (F6). The application then prompts you for a new customer number to initiate the next order. At the beginning of this scenario, you work with the help panels provided by the application.

Starting the 5250 application

To start the Order Entry application you need a 5250 emulator on your workstation. Start a 5250 emulation screen.

Signing on to the iSeries system and calling the order entry application

On the 5250 emulation screen,

- Enter the user ID and password that you set up in the previous chapter. Once you have logged in, the emulator starts a job that has the WFLABXX library in its library list.

On the command line of the 5250 screen,

- Invoke the Order Entry application by typing CALL ORDENTR.

The application starts, displaying the first panel as shown in Figure 2.1. This first screen prompts for a customer number. You can type the customer number directly or you can press function key 4 to display a window that shows a selection list of existing customers.

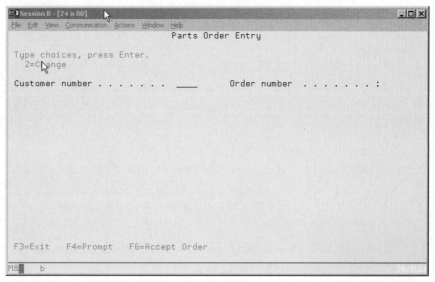

Figure 2.1: Order Entry application first panel

Before you begin the order entry process, explore the Help. This application uses User Interface Manager (UIM) help. Keep in mind that you will use the WebFacing Tool to convert these UIM help panels along with the Display File source. To understand the results of the UIM help conversion, I suggest you navigate through the Help in the 5250 environment so that you will have a basis of comparison when you view the Help in the browser.

Using online help

■ Move the cursor to the Customer number entry field.

■ Press **function key 1 (F1)**.

Panel group help is displayed, as shown in Figure 2.2.

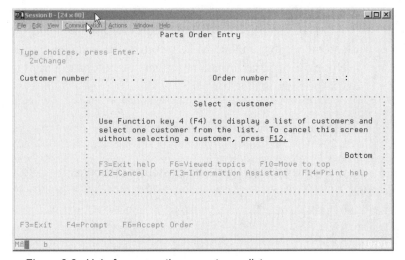

Figure 2.2: UIM help panel for customer number

■ To view additional help, move the cursor underneath the 1. in the Help area
and press the **Enter** key.

Figure 2.3 shows a sample of the panel that appears.

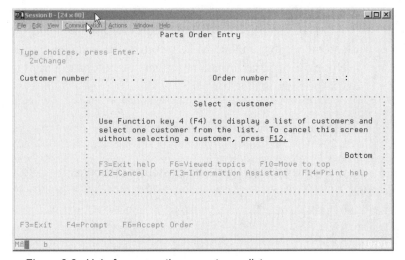

Figure 2.3: Help for requesting a customer list

■ Press **function key 12** to return to the Customer number field help.

■ To view additional help for the second choice, move the cursor underneath the 2. in the Help area and press the **Enter** key.

Now you see detailed help for keying in the customer number, as shown in Figure 2.4.

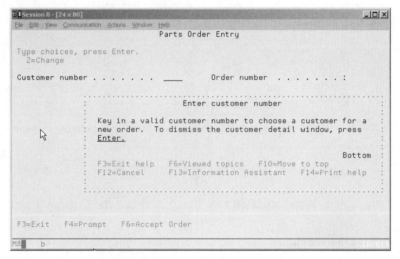

Figure 2.4: Detailed help for specifying a valid customer number

■ Press **function key 12** to exit the Help for the Customer number field.

On the main help panel in the Select Customer - Help area,

■ Press **function key 2** to view the extended Help.

Figure 2.5 shows the extended Help for the Customer number field.

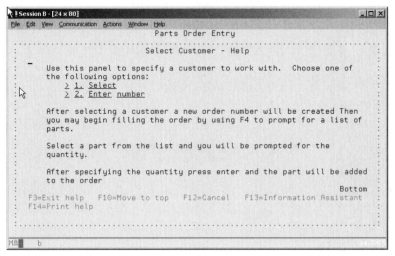

Figure 2.5: Extended Help panel for customer number

■ Press **function key 12** to exit the extended Customer number field Help.

■ Press **function key 12** again to exit the Customer number field Help.

On the application customer number input panel,

■ Move the cursor near the Order number field.

■ Press **function key 1.**

Context-sensitive help for this area is displayed, as shown in Figure 2.6.

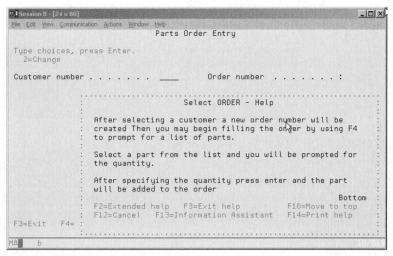

Figure 2.6: Help for Order number

■ Press **function key 12** to exit the Order number field Help.

Selecting a customer

Now that you can see how the Help panels function in this application, you are ready to specify a customer for this order. You can specify a valid customer number, or you can select from a list of valid customers. I want you to use the selection list because that choice makes use of the WINDOW DDS keyword, so that you can see how the WebFacing Tool converts a DDS window.

■ Press **function key 4** to display the customer selection list.

A list of customers displays, as shown in Figure 2.7.

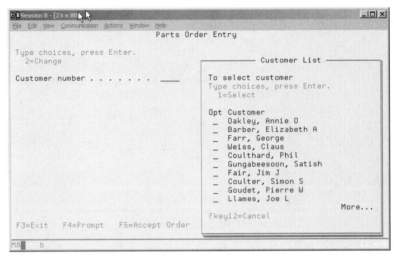

Figure 2.7: Customer list panel

■ Select a customer by typing **1** in the Options field.

■ Press the **Enter** key to proceed.

You will return to the initial panel, but now it is filled with detailed data for the selected customer, as shown in Figure 2.8. Notice that the application assigns an order number as well. You can now order a quantity of parts.

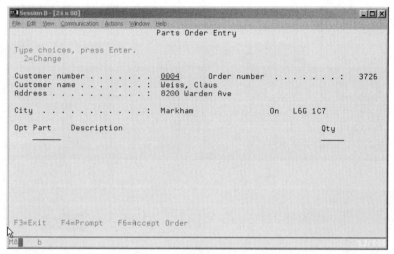

Figure 2.8: Order entry panel with detailed customer data

Filling the order

Selecting a part is similar to selecting a customer. You can type the part number directly or select the part from a selection list. I want you use the parts selection list as you used the customer selection list in the last exercise.

On the order entry panel,

■ Press **function key 4** to view a list of available parts.

A parts list displays, as shown in Figure 2.9.

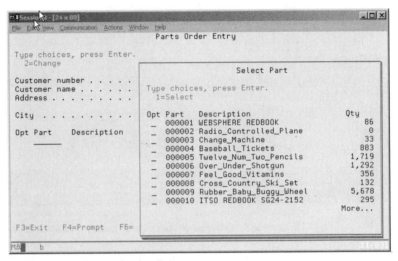

Figure 2.9: Part selection list

■ Select a part that has a large quantity by typing **1** in the Options field.

Back on the order screen, the part appears in the order on the top line of the parts list, as shown in Figure 2.10.

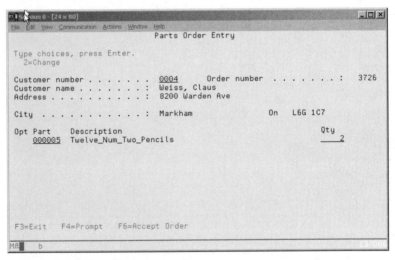

Figure 2.10: Specify parts quantity

To order a certain quantity of this part,

- Change the Quantity field to a value, for example, 2, as shown in Figure 2.10.

- Press the **Enter** key to add the part and quantity to the order.

The detailed order line for this part, with a specified quantity, is now part of this order, as shown in Figure 2.11.

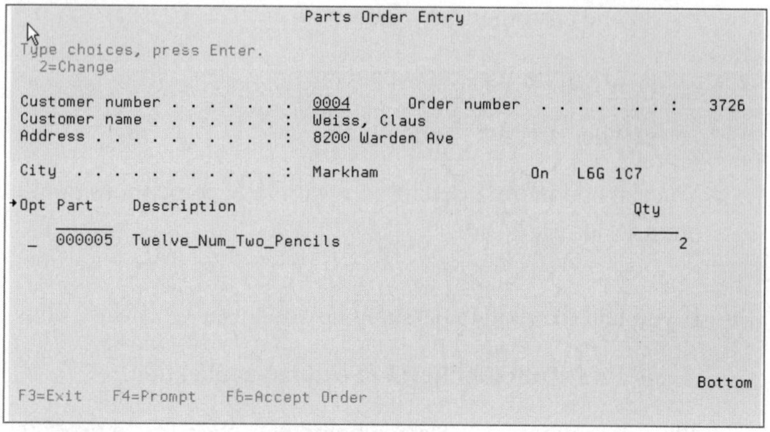

```
                           Parts Order Entry
 Type choices, press Enter.
   2=Change

 Customer number . . . . . . .  0004     Order number  . . . . . . . :   3726
 Customer name . . . . . . . :  Weiss, Claus
 Address . . . . . . . . . . :  8200 Warden Ave

 City  . . . . . . . . . . . :  Markham              On   L6G 1C7

 Opt Part      Description                                   Qty

 _   000005  Twelve_Num_Two_Pencils                                 2




                                                              Bottom
 F3=Exit    F4=Prompt    F6=Accept Order
```

Figure 2.11: One item added to order

To practice adding more parts to your order, repeat the following three steps as many times as you would like:

1. Press **function key 4** on the order panel to go to the parts list.

2. Select a part from the parts list.

3. Specify the part's quantity.

When you feel the order is complete, go to the next task.

Completing the order

On the order entry panel,

- Press **function key 6** to accept the order.

Once you accept the order, it is added to the database. You return to the starting screen of the application and can begin a new order.

Upon completing this exercise, you have worked with all panels in this application:

1. The start order entry panel

2. Several help panels

3. The customer list window

4. The full order entry panel

5. The parts list window

You can add more orders if you want to become more familiar with the application, but it is not necessary.

If you feel that you understand how the user interface of this application works,

■ Press **function key 3** to exit the application.

You are now ready to place a brand new Web-based user interface onto this application.

Analysis

You have completed the exercise: a look at the green-screen user interface. Here is what you did:

1. Started the order entry application

2. Used the help panels in the application

3. Selected a customer from the customer selection window

4. Selected parts from the parts selection window

5. Specified a quantity of parts for the order

6. Completed the order

7. Exited the application.

In the next chapter, you will create a WebFacing project.

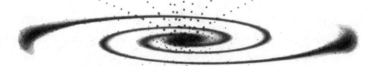

Exercise—Creating a WebFacing project

A WebFacing project contains information unique to WebFacing, such as the source to be converted. It also follows the formal directory structure of a Web project, and it conforms to the Java 2 platform Enterprise Edition (J2EE) Web application standard. Before you can create a Web user interface for the Order Entry application, you need to create a WebFacing project.

The goal of the exercise

The goal of this exercise is to practice using the WebFacing project wizard inside the WebSphere Development Studio Client workbench to create a new WebFacing project. You can then use this WebFacing project to facilitate the conversion of your DDS source and to test the generated output.

At the end of the exercise, you should be able to

- Start the Development Studio Client workbench

- Start the WebFacing Tool project wizard

- Step through the project wizard pages

- Provide the correct input to the project wizard and create the project

- Browse through the new project

Scenario

To create a WebFacing project, you identify the project information, such as the DDS source member names to be WebFaced. The WebFacing Tool stores this information in a workspace on your workstation. This exercise guides you through the process of identifying the DDS and Panel Group source members you want to convert with the WebFacing Tool. It also shows you how to specify part of the run-time information you will need later when running the WebFaced application.

Before you start

To run this exercise you need WebSphere Development Studio Client for iSeries Version 5.0 or 4.0 installed on your workstation. Short instructions on how to install the product are provided in Chapter 1.

The figures in this book show sample user interface snapshots based on a workspace that is brand new. If you have already used the product, your environment will be slightly different, and you need to adjust for that fact when following my instructions or comparing my screen shots with your real desktop environment.

Starting the Development Studio Client workbench

From the Start menu (refer to Figure 3.1),

■ Click: **Start → Programs → IBM WebSphere Studio → Development Studio Client for iSeries**.

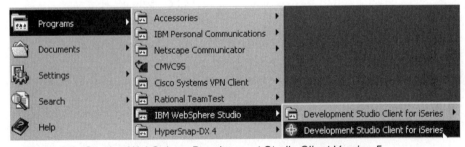

Figure 3.1: Starting WebSphere Development Studio Client Version 5

A dialog as shown in Figure 3.2 appears, asking you for the workspace location (unless you used Development Studio Client before and selected not to show this dialog again). The workspace contains all the information about your Development

Studio projects. You can accept the default or you can use a separate workspace to store the work related to the WebFacing exercises in this book. You can create a new workspace at any time if, for example, you prefer not to mix these exercises with your real development.

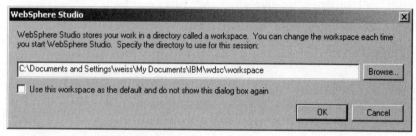

Figure 3.2: Dialog for workspace selection

■ Click the **OK** push button.

After a few moments, the workbench opens, and a window similar to the one shown in Figure 3.3 appears on your desktop.

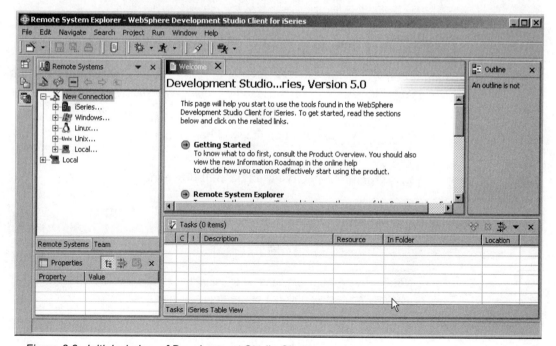

Figure 3.3: Initial window of Development Studio Client

Note: If you did not reset the workbench, or you are working with the base edition of Development Studio Client or Development Studio Client Version 4.0, your environment will differ slightly from the screen captures in this book.

Opening the WebFacing perspective

Each perspective in Development Studio Client is customized with special views and tools to aid you in the tasks you want to perform. When you first open the workbench, the Remote System Explorer (RSE) perspective is active by default, In this perspective, you can work with iSeries objects, specify connections to iSeries servers, and use the interface as a programming environment similar to the green-screen environment of Program Development Manager (PDM). Although the Remote System Explorer is fundamental to Development Studio Client, it is not suited to WebFacing tasks. This is why you need to use the WebFacing perspective.

To create a WebFacing project, you first need to open the WebFacing perspective (see Figure 3.4):

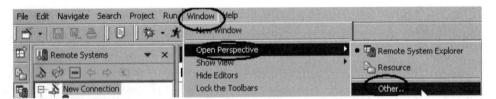

Figure 3.4: Workbench menu structure for opening a perspective

- Select the **Window** item on the workbench menu bar.

- Select **Open Perspective** from the pull-down menu.

- Select the **Other** option from the submenu.

Note: Version 4.0 users, instead of using the *Window* option on the menu bar, use the Perspective option: **Perspective → Open → Other**.

A dialog similar to Figure 3.5 displays.

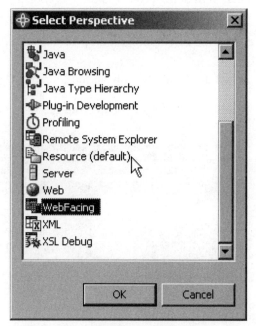

Figure 3.5: Select Perspective dialog

- Select **WebFacing** from the list.

- Click the **OK** push button.

The workbench now displays the WebFacing perspective and opens the WebFacing Projects view on the left-hand side of your workspace. You are ready to create a WebFacing project.

Creating a WebFacing project

To create a WebFacing project in the workbench,

- Select the **File** option on the workbench menu bar to display the File menu.

- Select the **New** option from the File menu.

- Select **WebFacing Project** from the submenu, as shown in Figure 3.6.

Figure 3.6: Menu structure to create a new WebFacing project

This invokes the WebFacing project wizard.

Completing the WebFacing Project page

In the WebFacing project wizard you first see the WebFacing Project page (Figure 3.7).

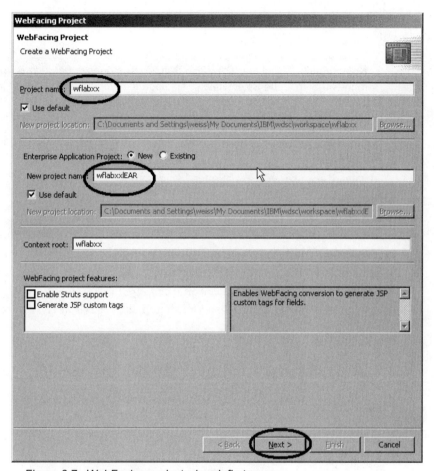

Figure 3.7: WebFacing project wizard, first page

Note: The Figure 3.7 screen capture was taken using the advanced edition of Development Studio Client. If you are not using the advanced edition, you do not see the two WebFacing project features listed in the bottom left of this page.

- Type the project name, **wflabxx**.

- Change the Enterprise Application Project name to **wflabxxEAR**. This creates a unique application file for this WebFacing project.

- Click the **Next** push button.

The J2EE Setting page opens.

Note: Version 4.0 users: The J2EE Setting page does not appear in your environment. Skip to the Select display file source members to convert page.

On this page, you can specify the J2EE level you want the WebFacing Tool to use when creating WebFacing project files. Development Studio Client Version 5.0 is designed for use with WebSphere Application Server (WAS) Version 5.0. However, you can still use WAS Version 4.0 or earlier when you deploy. In real-life development, if you use WAS Version 5.0, then I recommend you select J2EE level 1.3. If you are using a previous version of WAS in your environment and are planning to deploy the WebFaced application to this version, then I recommend you select J2EE level 1.2. This is because older versions of WAS do not support level 1.3 J2EE. In this exercise you will use the WebFaced application in the WebSphere Test environment, which is version 5.0, so you should select J2EE level 1.3 (see Figure 3.8).

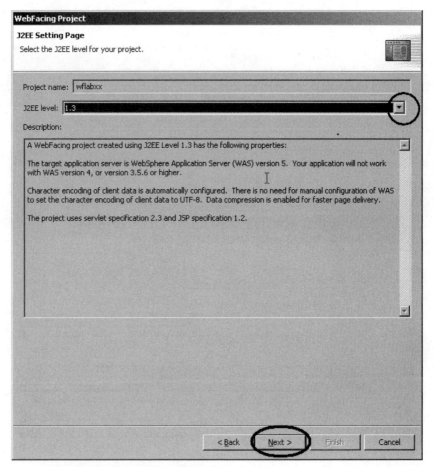

Figure 3.8: Page to select J2EE level

■ Click on the little arrow beside the J2EE level combination box.

■ Select **1.3** from the list.

■ Click the **Next** push button.

The Select display file source members to convert page opens as shown in Figure 3.9.

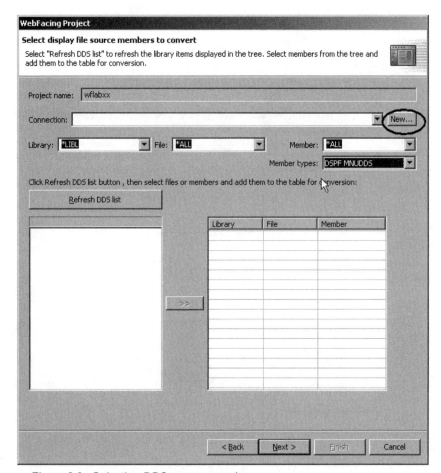

Figure 3.9: Selecting DDS source members

Selecting display file source members to convert

On the third page of the WebFacing project wizard you need to specify the name of
the iSeries server that contains your display file DDS source. You also need to specify the source members you want to convert. Specifically, the WebFacing Tool needs
to know these names:

- Server name

- Library name

- Source file name

- Member name

Tip: You need to identify members for all record formats your application uses. If
you miss one, then your user interface will show a *Page not found* error if that
particular record format is requested at run time.

First you need to specify the iSeries server name where the Data Description Source
(DDS) is located. To do this, you configure a connection to the server.

Creating a new connection in Development Studio Client

Because you are starting with a new workspace, you need to specify a connection to
an iSeries server.

- Click the **New** push button (on the right side of the page beside the
  Connection combination box) as shown in Figure 3.9.

The New personal profile dialog opens as shown in Figure 3.10.

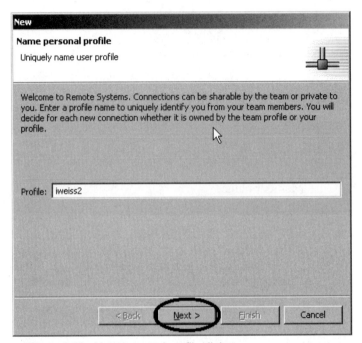

Figure 3.10: New personal profile dialog

- Accept the default profile name.

- Click the **Next** push button.

On the Remote iSeries System Connection page, as shown in Figure 3.11,

- Enter the iSeries Host name.

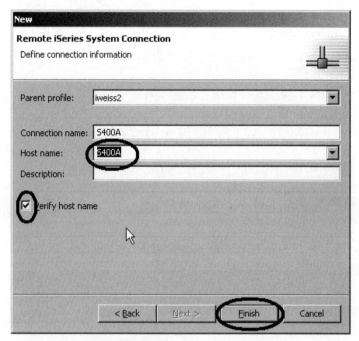

Figure 3.11: New connection dialog, second page

Important: This is your iSeries server name; do not use the one in Figure 3.11, unless your system is named S400A.

To keep things simple, the Connection name combination box is filled automatically with the same name.

Note: Version 4.0 users: Enter your user ID in the user ID entry field. Use the same ID that you used in the emulation session when you ran the Order Entry application from the green screen. Make sure to also use this ID during conversion and when testing the application.

- Check the Verify host name check box.

- Click the **Finish** push button.

The connection is created and can be reused by all tools in the workbench. The connection wizard also tests whether the iSeries host can be reached. If the test is successful, you will see the Select display file source members to convert page.

- Check that your iSeries server is selected in the Connection combination box.

- Make sure that ***LIBL** is selected in the Library combination box.

- Click the **Refresh DDS list** push button.

A user ID and password dialog opens, as shown in Figure 3.12.

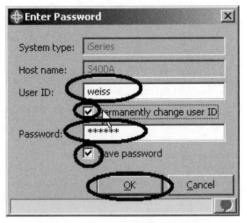

Figure 3.12: Log-on dialog to access iSeries server

- Type your user ID. Use the same user ID that you used when running the Order Entry application earlier in this book.

- Check the **Permanently change user ID** check box.

- Type your password.

- Check the **Save password** check box.

- Click the **OK** push button on the Enter Password dialog.

A connection to the iSeries server is established. The library list of your iSeries job is displayed in the tree view list, on the WebFacing project wizard page as shown in Figure 3.13.

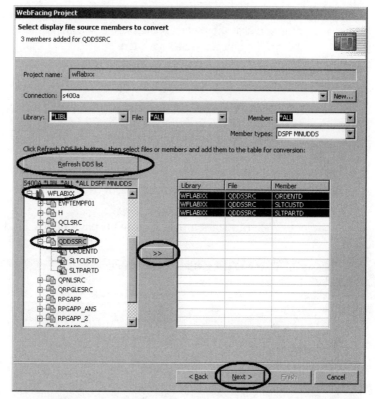

Figure 3.13: WebFacing project wizard, showing expanded library WFLABXX

■ Select the **WFLABXX** library from the list.

■ Expand it by clicking the plus sign **(+)** beside the library name.

■ Expand **QDDSSRC**, and select all members from the list by holding down the Shift key.

- Click the >> push button in the middle of the page to copy the selected members over to the list of members to be converted.

Note: To move all members in a source file, you can select the source file icon itself and click the **>>** push button. This will add all members in a source file to the list of members to be converted.

- Click the **Next** push button at the bottom of the page to proceed to the next page of the wizard.

The WebFacing Tool now knows which DDS members to convert for this project. The conversion has not yet taken place, but the information is stored for future use.

The Select UIM source members to convert page opens, as shown in Figure 3.14.

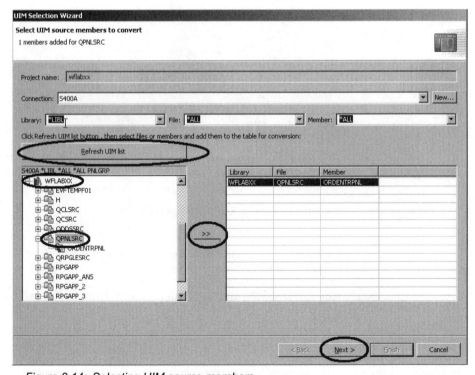

Figure 3.14: Selecting UIM source members

You now need to identify the panel group source containing the help information for the Order Entry application.

- Click the **Refresh UIM list** push button.

- Expand the **WFLABXX** library.

- Select the **QPNLSRC** source file from the expanded list (of the WFLABXX library).

- Click the >> push button in the middle of the page to copy all members over to the list of members to be converted.

There is only one panel group member in this source file: ORDENTRPNL.

- Click the **Next** push button at the bottom of the Select UIM source page, to proceed to the next page of the wizard.

Completing the Specify CL commands page

You will now provide the information that the WebFacing wizard uses to create the initial index.html page. This is the page that will invoke the Order Entry application.

Do you remember what you typed on the command line to start the Order Entry application in the 5250 emulation session during the first exercise in Chapter 2? It was *CALL ORDENTR.*

Why is this important? The WebFacing run-time environment needs to know the invocation command for your application in order to send this invocation command to the iSeries server and start your application from the browser.

The page shown in Figure 3.15 is the WebFacing project wizard page where you specify the necessary information.

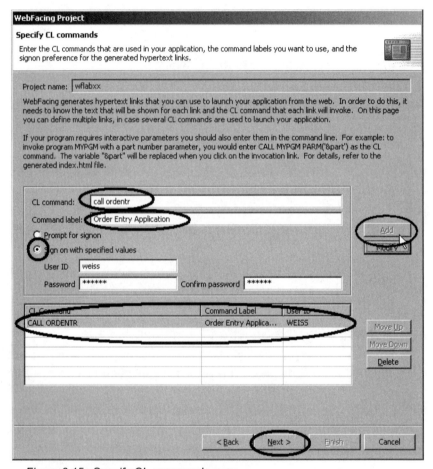

Figure 3.15: Specify CL commands page

- Type **CALL ORDENTR** into the CL command entry field.

- Type **Order Entry Application** into the Command label entry field.

Tip: If you do not type anything into the Command label field, the CL input is copied into this entry field

---

■ Select the **Sign on with specified values** radio button.

Setting this radio button automatically applies the user ID and password you specified when connecting to your iSeries server. You will use this setup for testing purposes, to make life easier for you when starting the Order Entry application, so that you do not have to specify authentication information. You do not need to worry about security in your production environment because you can easily change the authentication, as I will show you later in the book.

■ Click the **Add** push button on the right side of the page.

Note: Make sure the text and command you typed into the entry fields are shown in the list at the bottom of the page.

■ Click the **Next** push button at the bottom of the wizard page.

Choosing a Web style

On the wizard page shown in Figure 3.16, you can select a Web style for your converted screens.

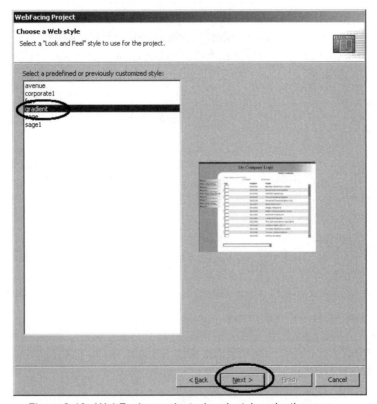

Figure 3.16: WebFacing project wizard, style selection page

- Select **gradient** from the list of available styles.

- Click the **Next** push button.

Completing the WebFacing Project information

On the page shown in Figure 3.17, you have the choice to create the project and convert the source in one step, or only create the WebFacing project. At this point, you only need to create the WebFacing project. Conversion is part of the next exercise.

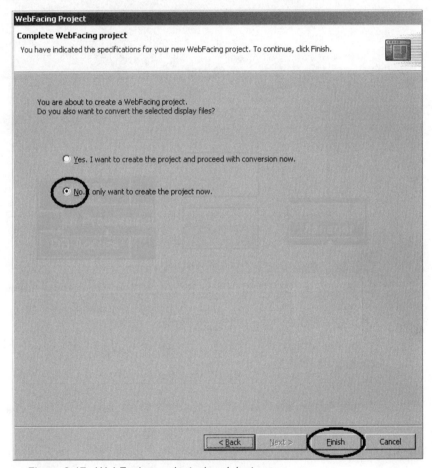

Figure 3.17: WebFacing project wizard, last page

■ Select the **No, I only want to create the project now** radio button.

■ Click the **Finish** push button.

The workbench takes a few moments to create the WebFacing project. Eventually, your new WebFacing project displays in the WebFacing Projects view as shown in Figure 3.18.

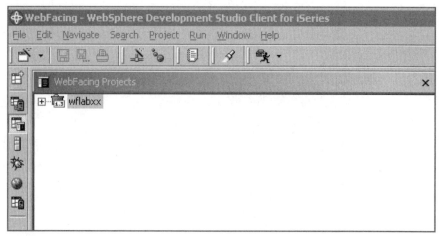

Figure 3.18: WebFacing Projects view with wflabxx project icon

The WebFacing project environment

Notice that the WebFacing project icon indicates which J2EE level the project will use.

If you expand the wflabxx project, you will notice that a couple of nodes have been added to this WebFacing project:

- The display file source members to use for WebFacing conversion.

- The panel group source members to convert

- The CL command that will invoke the Order Entry application

- The style to use for the converted screens.

When you expand the nodes in the tree view of your WebFacing project, you can see the information that is captured for this project.

■ Expand the nodes by clicking on the plus sign (+) beside them.

Figure 3.19 shows the expanded WebFacing project tree view.

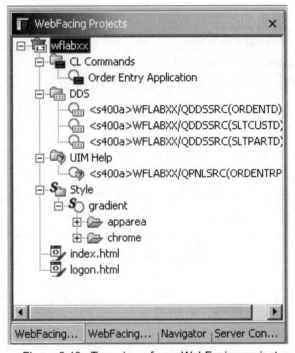

Figure 3.19: Tree view of new WebFacing project

Tip: If you need to add source members to the WebFacing project later on, right-click the **DDS** or **UIM Help** icon and select the **Add** menu option from the pop-up menu; this will launch the WebFacing wizard and display the correct dialog.

You are now ready to convert and run your application.

Analysis

You completed the exercise Creating a WebFacing Project. Here is what you did:

- You started Development Studio Client.

- You launched the WebFacing project wizard.

- You completed the pages of this wizard to create a new WebFacing project called wflabxx.

- You added the following information to the WebFacing project:
  - The DDS display file source members to use for the WebFacing conversion
  - The UIM panel group source members to convert
  - The CL command information, which will be used in the initial index.html page to start the Order Entry application
  - The Web style to use for the resulting Web pages

- You inspected the WebFacing project, to verify all information entered in the WebFacing project wizard.

You are ready to move on. In the next chapter, you will convert and run your application.

Converting selected source members

WebFacing conversion creates JSP files, XML files (for record format layouts), and several other files needed for the Web application you are creating with the Web-Facing Tool.

The goal of the exercise

The goal of this exercise is to practice the conversion of a WebFacing project. In this case, you will use the wflabxx project that you created in the previous exercise (Creating a WebFacing Tool Project). In the previous exercise, you specified all of the information necessary for the WebFacing Tool to successfully convert your application. Now you will do the conversion itself.

On the WebFacing Project icon you will select the convert option, to begin the conversion, and you will work with the conversion logs to check the results.

At the end of this exercise, you should be able to

- Use the WebFacing Tool to select specific source members for conversion

- Use the WebFacing Tool to start the conversion process

- Analyze the conversion logs

Scenario

You have already created a WebFacing project in Development Studio Client. In this project, you specified which display file source and panel group source to convert, and in which iSeries server these source members are located. The WebFacing Tool will use this information during the conversion process. In this exercise, you will also specify whether you want to convert *all* source members belonging to this project or *selected* ones only.

A word regarding security: You do not have to log on to the iSeries server during conversion because your user ID and password were stored during the WebFacing project setup and will be reused here.

Converting iSeries source members to Web files

WebFacing conversion is performed inside Development Studio Client. If the product is not already up and running, open it now from the Start menu.

Selecting the project and source members

If a WebFacing perspective displaying your project is not visible, you need to

- Open the WebFacing perspective.

Tip: Check the sidebar of the workbench for the WebFacing perspective icon. If you find it, click the icon to switch to the WebFacing perspective. Icons show perspectives that are open but not presently active. It is good practice to avoid having too many instances of the same perspective open. If you restrict yourself to one open instance of a perspective, you will improve the performance of the workbench. It is good to keep this in mind since there is no limit set to the number of perspectives you can have open. Figure 4.1 shows the icons on the sidebar of the workbench. In this instance, the Remote System Explorer perspective is active.

Figure 4.1 shows the workbench with four perspectives open:

 1. The WebFacing perspective

 2. The Remote System Explorer perspective

 3. The Java perspective

 4. The Web perspective

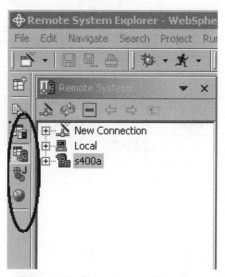

Figure 4.1: Open perspectives on workbench sidebar

 To switch to the WebFacing perspective, which is already open but not active, select its icon from the sidebar.

 Tip: You can open a new perspective by clicking the **Open a perspective** icon at the top of the sidebar.

To begin conversion in the WebFacing perspective,

- Select the WebFacing project you worked on in the previous exercise, **wflabxx**.

- Expand this project by clicking **the plus sign (+)** beside its icon in the WebFacing Projects tree view.

You should see a DDS folder in the expanded tree. If you do not see a DDS folder, you might be in the Navigator view and not in the WebFacing Projects view (see Figure 4.2).

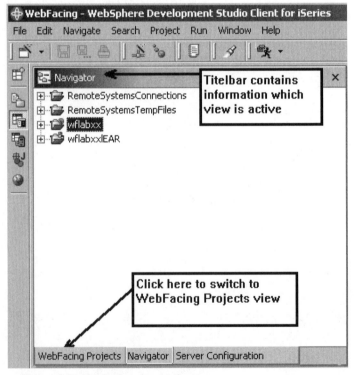

Figure 4.2: Navigator view active

If the view title bar is not WebFacing Projects, locate the WebFacing Projects tab at the bottom of the view, and click it once. Now the WebFacing Projects view is active and you should be able to find the DDS folder.

- Expand the DDS folder so that you can see all three of the members that you selected in the Chapter 3 exercise, Creating a WebFacing Tool Project, as shown in Figure 4.3.

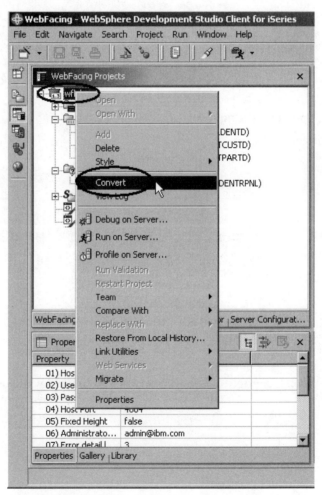

Figure 4.3: WebFacing project ready to convert

Starting the WebFacing conversion

From here you can select individual members or a collection of members to convert.

In this exercise you will convert all of your DDS and panel group members by choosing the WebFacing project icon as the starting point for the conversion. Later on in the book, you will have the opportunity to convert just a single source member.

- Right-click the **wflabxx project icon**.

- Select **Convert** from the pop-up menu.

The conversion process begins. This will take some time; be patient.

A progress dialog displays, indicating what members are being converted, as shown in Figure 4.4.

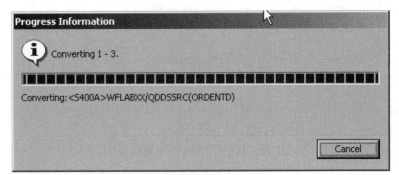

Figure 4.4: Conversion progress dialog

When the progress dialog disappears, WebFacing conversion has finished.

Analyzing the conversion logs

Notice the conversion log in the right pane, as shown in Figure 4.5.

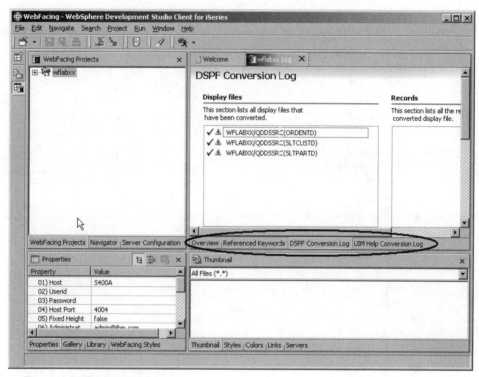

Figure 4.5: Conversion log

The bottom of the log displays the following tabs:

- Overview

- Referenced Keywords

- DSPF Conversion Log

- UIM Help Conversion Log

The Overview page

The Overview page (Figure 4.6) contains information about the overall conversion process for a WebFacing project.

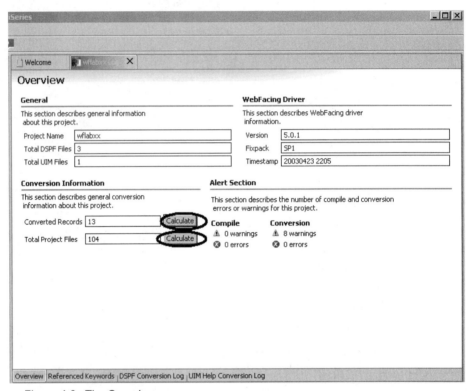

Figure 4.6: The Overview page

The information on this page is divided into four areas:

1. The *General* section contains the project names and the number of members converted.

2. The *WebFacing Driver* section has information on the WebFacing driver level used for the conversion. This might be useful in case you talk to IBM service and they request this information.

3. *Conversion Information* has two Calculate push buttons that you can use in case you are interested in some statistical data about your WebFacing conversion.

4. *Alert Section* is the most important section, since it tells you how successful the conversion has been. In case any errors are shown, use the detail pages to check the impact of these errors. Check the warnings as well; they might clue you in to why the behavior of a WebFaced application differs from the original.

The Referenced Keywords page

The Referenced Keywords page (Figure 4.7) shows two lists: on the left side a list of the converted members, and on the right side the keyword contained in a selected member and the WebFacing support for this keyword.

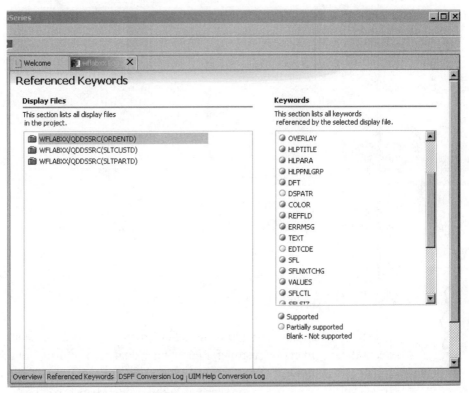

Figure 4.7: The Referenced Keywords page

Selecting a member in the left list will show all keywords used in this member and their WebFacing support status. If you need more detail on these keywords, check the WebFacing help. The WebFacing help under the Reference topic has a DDS Support tables section that provides more detailed information for many keywords.

The DSPF Conversion Log page

The DSPF Conversion Log page (Figure 4.8) lists all the display file members converted in the left-side list and shows the individual record format names in a given selected member.

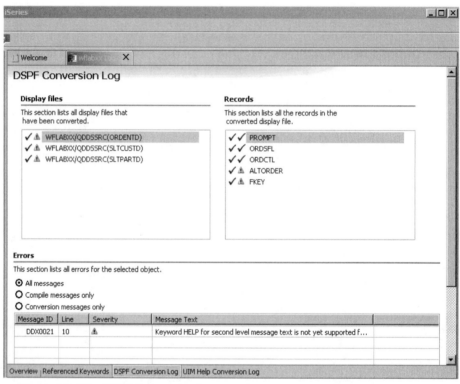

Figure 4.8: The DSPF Conversion Log page

Selecting a member on the left side will display the record formats inside the member and the conversion results for each individual record format in the right-side list. It will also display any file-level keyword problems in the message list at the bottom. If you select a specific record format in the right-side list, detailed messages for this record format are displayed in the message list.

The UIM Help Conversion Log page

The UIM Help Conversion Log page (Figure 4.9) is very similar to the DSPF Conversion Log page; similar information is displayed here for UIM help members instead of DDS display file members.

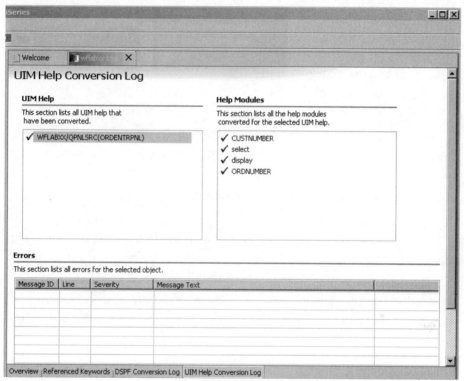

Figure 4.9: The UIM Help Conversion Log page

Navigation through the page is the same as for the DSPF Conversion Log page.

You have now converted the DDS display file and panel group source. Click each tab to see more details about the conversion

Analysis

The first important step to move your application to the Web is complete. The DDS source and panel group source are now available in a form a browser understands. The conversion itself is fairly easy, because you already created the WebFacing project. Once the project exists, the WebFacing Tool has all the information readily available for conversion. If you have to alter the original source later on, you can easily reconvert the project.

You have completed the exercise Converting Selected Source Members. Here is what you did:

- You selected the WebFacing project to convert, including all DDS source members and all panel group source members that are part of this project.

- You started the WebFacing conversion process.

- You analyzed the conversion logs to ensure that no serious errors occurred during conversion.

You are ready to move on. In the next chapter, you will run your application with its new user interface. Proceed to the exercise Running the Web-enabled Application.

Running the Web-enabled Application

Now that you have converted your source members, you are ready to test the Web-Faced application. To run your application, you would typically need to copy all of your Web project files to a WebSphere Application Server (WAS) environment. Luckily, a WebSphere Application Server test environment is imbedded in Web-Sphere Development Studio Client. The WAS test environment makes it much easier for you to test your WebFaced application because you do not need to work with a WAS console and deploy to a remote environment. Later on, I will show you how to copy all the necessary application files to a production environment for the various versions of WAS.

In real-life application development, you would test thoroughly in the test environment, then export the WebFacing project files to a remote WAS for final testing before moving the Web-enabled application to your production WAS environment. For now, using the test environment on your workstation until you are sure that your WebFaced application is ready for public use will simplify testing tremendously.

The goal of the exercise

The goal in this chapter is to practice testing your Web-enabled application in the WAS test environment. In the WebFacing perspective, you will specify that you want to run your project in the Development Studio Client test environment. From the initial Web page, you will select the link created by the WebFacing Tool to invoke the WebFaced Order Entry application.

At the end of this exercise, you should be able to

- Set up the WebSphere Application Server test environment

- Run the Web application in the WebSphere Application Server test environment

- Select the link on the invocation Web page to invoke the RPG application

- Step through the Web-enabled application using the HTML-based user interface

Scenario

When you converted the user interface for your Order Entry application, the Web-Facing Tool created a complete Web application that you can run in an application server. The WAS test environment and the Web project in the workbench are completely integrated so that you no longer need to publish (copy) your files to a production environment to test the application. You will use the index.html file, created by WebFacing conversion, as the default page for this Web application.

When the application is up and running, you will perform the same actions that you did in Chapter 2 (navigation through the green-screen panels of the Order Entry application). The difference is that you will navigate through the new WebFaced user interface.

Opening the index.html page

Follow these steps to display the index.html page for your Web-enabled application:

- Select your WebFacing project icon in the WebFacing perspective.

■ Right-click the **wflabxx** project as in Figure 5.1.

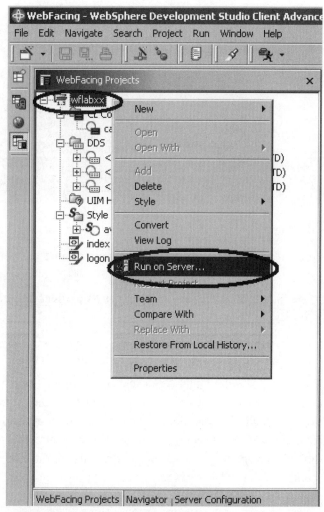

Figure 5.1: Pop-up menu for WebFacing project icon with Run on Server selected

■ Select **Run on Server** from the pop-up menu.

A Server Selection dialog appears as shown in Figure 5.2.

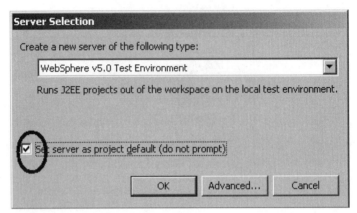

Figure 5.2: Server Selection dialog

To prevent this dialog from appearing every time you select **Run on Server**,

■ Select the check box **Set server as project default (do not prompt)**.

■ Click on the **OK** push button.

You have just initiated the WAS test environment. After a few moments, the browser opens in the right pane of the workbench. Be patient; it takes time for the application server to load. The minimum memory requirement for running the WAS test environment is 768 MB according to the IBM announcement letter for Development Studio Client Version 5.0. Eventually, you will see the index.html page appear in the workbench's built-in browser.

Note: Version Development Studio Client Version 4.0 users will also notice that the active perspective is now the Server perspective.

Figure 5.3 shows the browser inside the workbench with the index.html page displayed.

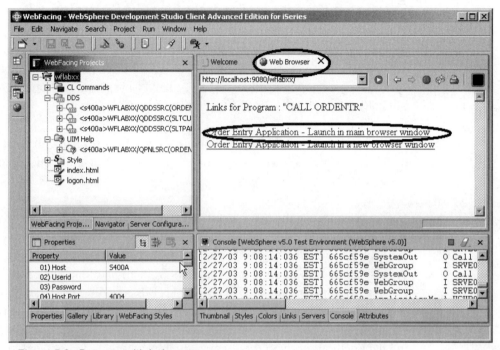

Figure 5.3: Browser with index page

Tip: To enlarge the browser window to the size of the workbench window, double-click on the browser title bar. To reduce it to its original size, double-click on the enlarged browser window's title bar.

Setting up the test environment for WAS Version 4.0

You have a choice of running WAS Version 4.0 or Version 5.0 in the WAS test environment. If you have followed my instructions using Development Studio Client Version 5.0, then you are already running WAS Version 5.0, in which case you can skip this topic and move on to the topic titled "Continuing for both Development Studio Client Version 4.0 and 5.0" on page 85.

If you decided to use WAS Version 4.0, or if you are working with Development Studio Client Version 4.0, you will need to follow the steps under this topic to set up WAS correctly.

Before you can use the WAS Version 4.0 test environment for your WebFaced application, you need to change the default application server settings. WebFacing applications are generated with support for UTF-8, a Unicode encoding to enable the display of Web pages with characters from any national language in the world. Because WAS Version 4.0 does not use UTF-8 encoding by default, you need to enable UTF-8 through the WAS administrative console. You need to perform this setup once for each server instance. In WAS Version 5.0, you can send the encoding parameter directly to the server, which is why you do not need to specify the UTF-8 encoding.

If you are using WAS Version 4.0 or Version 3.5.6 on your remote server, you need to set up your remote WAS environment as well. The WebFacing help documentation provides detailed setup information for these environments, so I will not go through the remote server WAS setup in this book.

If you are working with WAS Version 4.0, in the test environment,

- Switch to the Navigator view by clicking the **Navigator** tab in the WebFacing Projects view (Figure 5.4).

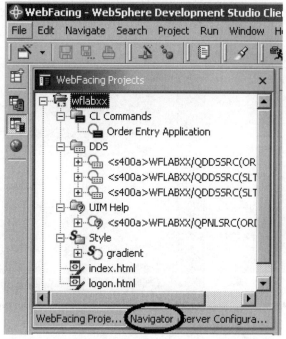

Figure 5.4: WebFacing Projects view with Navigator tab highlighted

■ Expand the **Servers** folder in the Navigator view, as shown in Figure 5.5.

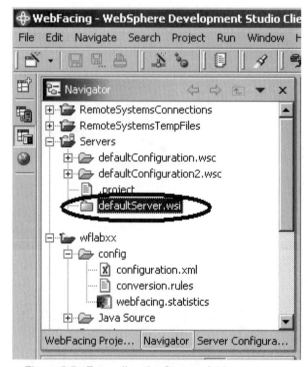

Figure 5.5: Expanding the Servers folder

■ Double-click the **defaultServer.wsi** file.

Note: For Development Studio Client Version 4.0 users, this file has the name *defaultInstance.wsi* in your environment.

The WebSphere 4.0 Test Environment properties dialog is displayed, as shown in Figure 5.6.

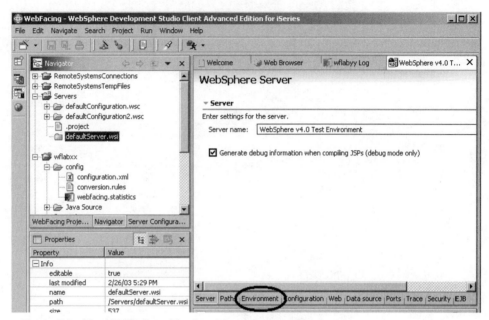

Figure 5.6: The WebSphere Version 4.0 properties dialog

■ Click the **Environment** tab; as shown in Figure 5.6.

The Environment Options page displays as shown in Figure 5.7.

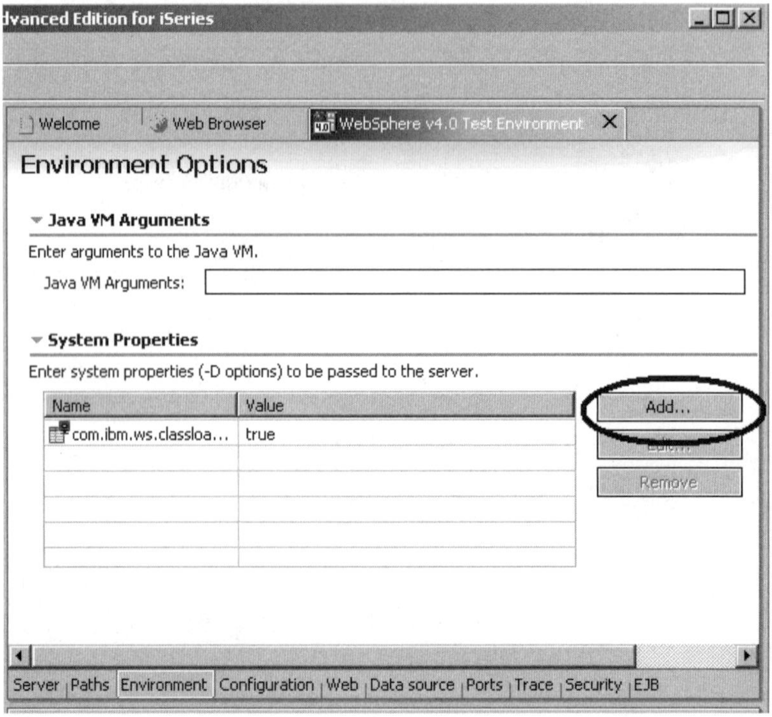

Figure 5.7: The Environment Options page

■ Click the **Add** push button.

In the Add System Property dialog that appears, as shown in Figure 5.8,

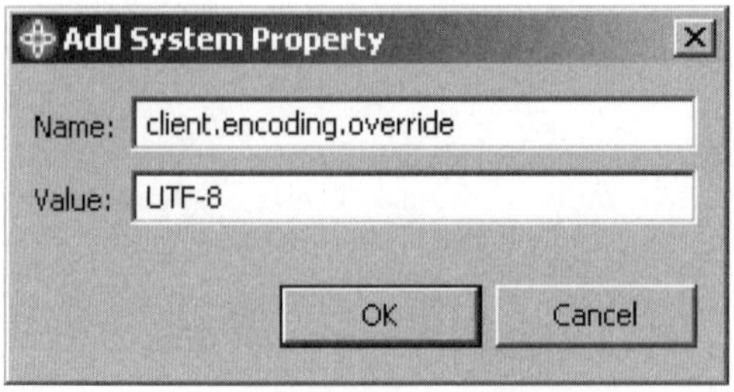

Figure 5.8: Add System Property dialog

■ Enter **client.encoding.override** in the Name entry field.

■ Enter **UTF-8** in the Value entry field.

Tip: Make sure that you use exact spelling and that you enter the upper- and lowercase characters exactly as shown. Using a different case will cause problems later on when you run the application.

■ Click the **OK** push button.

Back in the workbench (Figure 5.9),

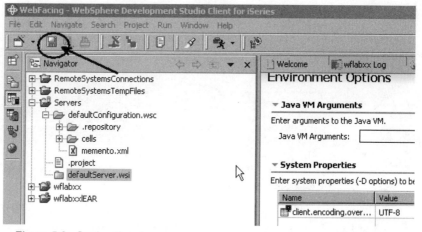

Figure 5.9: Saving the changes

■ Select the **Save** icon on the toolbar or use the **File → Save** option on the menu bar to save the changes.

The user interface you use to change the class loader setup depends on whether you work with Version 4.0 or 5.0 of Development Studio Client. I describe the steps for both environments separately. In Development Studio Client Version 5.0,

■ Click the **Configuration** tab.

■ Select **MODULE** in the Module visibility combination box, as shown in Figure 5.10.

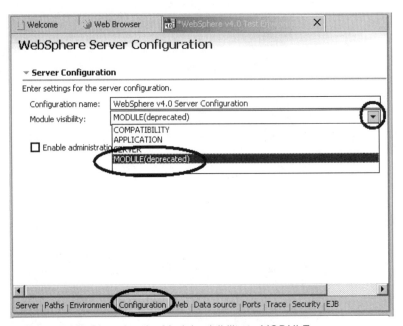

Figure 5.10: Changing the Module visibility to MODULE

■ Save this setting by clicking the **Save** icon on the toolbar or select the **File → Save** option from the workbench menu bar.

In Development Studio Client Version 4.0,

■ Expand the **defaultConfiguration.wsc** folder in the Navigator view under the Servers folder.

■ Double-click the **server-cfg.xml** file.

In the dialog that appears, as shown in Figure 5.11.

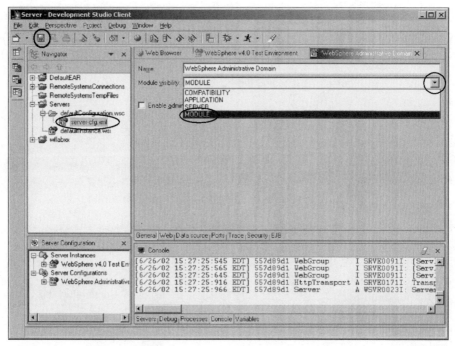

Figure 5.11: Module visibility

- Click the down-arrow button in the Module visibility combo box.

- Select **MODULE** from the selection list in the combo box.

- Save this setting by clicking on the **Save** icon on the toolbar or select the **File → Save** option from the workbench menu bar.

Continuing for both Development Studio Client Version 4.0 and 5.0

Close the editor windows and browser windows that have been opened in the workbench. It is important to close the browser window so that the browser discards cached information.

■ Click the **X** push button on the editor's Windows title bar, as shown in Figure 5.12.

Figure 5.12: Closing the editor dialogs

The application server is now set up. To apply these changes to the server setting, you need to restart the application server.

At the bottom of the workbench on the right side,

■ Click the **Servers** tab, as indicated in Figure 5.13.

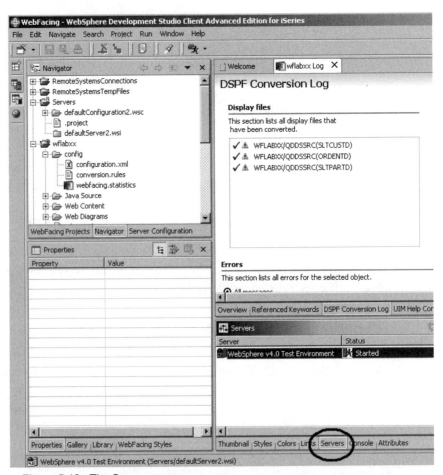

Figure 5.13: The Servers page

■ Right-click the **Server instance** in the Servers list, as shown in Figure 5.14.

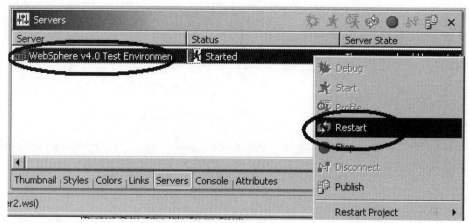

Figure 5.14: Pop-up menu for application server

■ Select **Restart** from the pop-up menu.

After the Console view displays a message that the server is open for e-business, you can go back to the WebFacing Projects view in the WebFacing perspective of the workbench.

■ Right-click the **wflabxx** project

■ Select **Run on Server** from the pop-up menu.

The index.html page displays in the browser window.

Running the Web application

In the browser window as shown in Figure 5.3, the WebFacing Tool creates two links for the Order Entry application automatically.

1. The top link uses the current browser session with all available toolbars and buttons.

2. The second link invokes a new browser session for the application. This new browser session displays only the window frame, without any of the browser menus or toolbars. This second link was added because many WebFacing users felt that the normal browser window could overwhelm some end users by offering too many capabilities, such as the Back button on the toolbar.

■ In your browser pane, click the top **Order Entry Application** link.

Tip: For Development Studio Client Version 4.0 users, you have to click the link twice. The first click gives the browser focus, and the second click sends the click event.

After a few moments, the first application page appears in the browser, as shown in Figure 5.15.

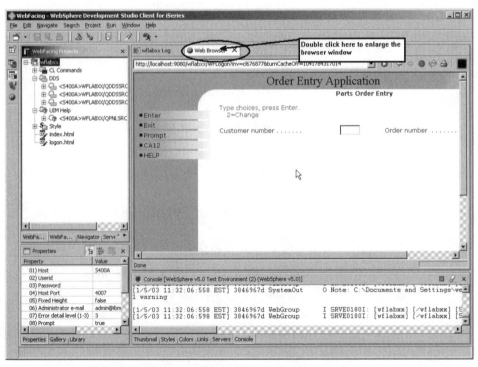

Figure 5.15: First application page in browser window

If you find the response time a bit slow, keep in mind that the first time the JSP file is requested, it has to be compiled into a servlet. If you run the application a second time, you will see improved performance because the servlet already exists. This is normal application server behavior.

Using the new interface, you can perform the same actions as in Chapter 2 to examine the results of the WebFacing conversion. This will give you a sense of how the default conversion changes your original application. You will then have a chance to improve the conversion results.

The one area that you cannot test in the built-in browser is the Help documentation support. If you press the F1 key in the internal browser, you will see an error message, as shown in Figure 5.16. You will have to start the application from an external browser. I will show you how to do this at the end of the chapter.

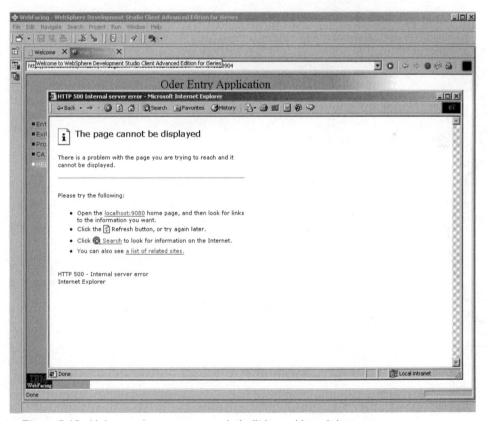

Figure 5.16: Help panel error message in built-in workbench browser

■ Click the **Prompt** push button, or press **function key 4** to view the selection list window, shown in Figure 5.17.

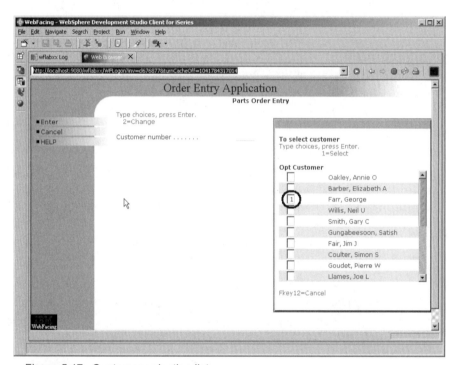

Figure 5.17: Customer selection list

■ Select a customer from the subfile.

■ Press the **Enter** key.

You will return to the Order Entry Application screen, shown in Figure 5.18.

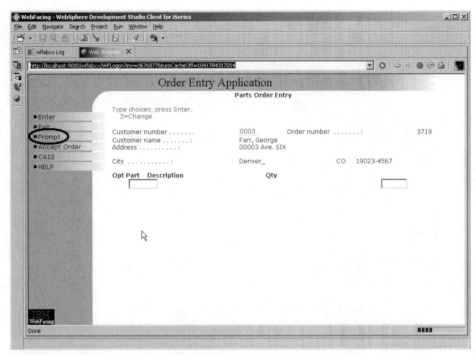

Figure 5.18: Order Entry Application screen with customer details

■ Click the **Prompt** push button or press **function key 4** to display the parts selection list, as shown in Figure 5.19.

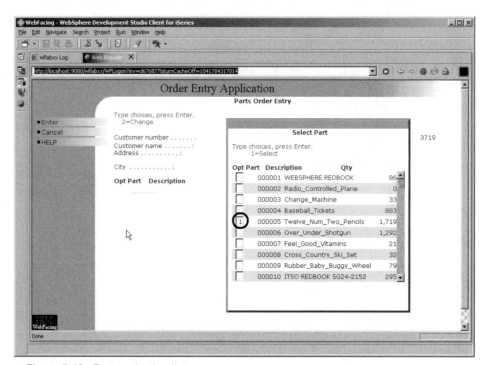

Figure 5.19: Parts selection list

■ Select a part.

■ Press the **Enter** key.

On the Order Entry Application screen (Figure 5.20),

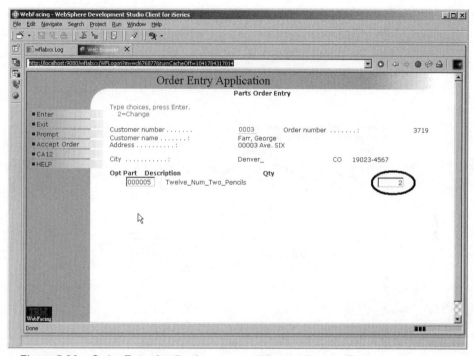

Figure 5.20: Order Entry Application screen with quantity specified

■ Enter a number in the Qty box.

■ Press the **Enter** key.

Continue ordering one or two more parts.

■ Press **function key 6** to accept the order.

The application works in the same manner as in the 5250 environment, except that now you can navigate through the application with an Internet browser–based user interface.

Testing the Help documentation support

As I mentioned, the Help documentation support works only when you run the application in an external browser. Start Internet Explorer on your desktop and type in the following URL: *http://localhost:9080/wflabxx/*. You could also copy and paste it from the internal browser URL bar.

Internet Explorer displays the index.html page as shown in Figure 5.21.

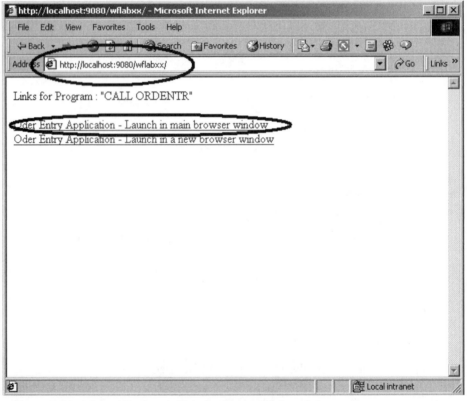

Figure 5.21: Internet Explorer with index.html *page for wflabxx*

■ Click the first link on this page.

The application opens in the browser. To view the Help,

■ Press the **F1** key.

Another browser window opens with the help information, as shown as in Figure 5.22.

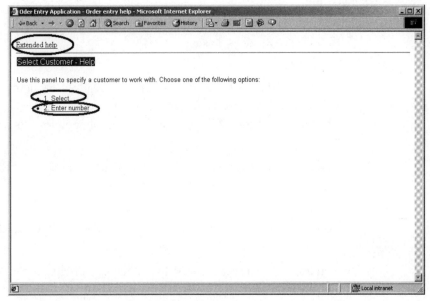

Figure 5.22:   Help panel in browser

Now try the following links:

- ■ Select

- ■ Enter number

- ■ Extended help

Your UIM-based Help panels are all available in the WebFaced application.

Close the Help browser window and press F3 to end the application.

Analysis

You have completed the exercise Running the Web-enabled Application. Here is what you did:

■ You set up the WAS test environment.

■ You selected the **Run on Server** option for the WebFacing project, which started the WAS test environment and opened a browser in the workbench. This browser showed the default index.html page for this project.

■ You selected a link on the index.html page to invoke the Web-enabled application.

■ You used the Web-enabled application as you did in Chapter 2.

■ You used an external browser to test the UIM help panels.

You are ready to move on. In the next chapter, you will improve the look of your Web-enabled application. I will guide you through the customization and enhancement of your application. Proceed to the exercise Changing the Web User Interface.

Changing the Web User Interface

To enhance the results of the WebFacing Tool, IBM added a new function to the CODE Designer tool called Web settings. CODE Designer is the GUI-based screen design tool for 5250 panels. With this tool, you can change aspects of the user interface related to the WebFacing conversion process. CODE Designer stores the Web setting information as comment lines in the DDS source. When you convert the application using the WebFacing Tool, these DDS source comment lines are picked up and applied to the new user interface.

Tip: You cannot use Screen Design Aid (SDA) on DDS source members that have been customized through Web settings. This restriction is imposed because SDA changes the location of or deletes comment lines, which would invalidate the WebFacing Web settings.

The goal of the exercise

The goal of this exercise is for you to change the user interface of your Web-enabled application with CODE Designer. In the WebFacing perspective, you will select a DDS source member to work with, start CODE Designer to open this DDS member, use Web settings in CODE Designer, and then reconvert the DDS member.

At the end of this exercise, you should be able to

- Access DDS source from the WebFacing perspective using CODE Designer

- Use Web settings to change the Web-enabled user interface

- Reconvert the altered DDS display file source member

Scenario

You want to improve the user interface generated by the WebFacing Tool. In particular, you want to improve the customer selection subfile. Currently, the Web user interface you use to select a record from this subfile does not behave the way you would like, because you need to key a 1 into the options column to select a record. This mimics exactly how the green screen works. However, you would like it to behave more like a Web user interface, where you select an item by clicking on a link.

When you use Web settings in CODE Designer, you enhance the user interface but you do not change the underlying function of the application. I will show you how to use Web settings capabilities in CODE Designer to make the necessary modifications.

You will change the second column in the customer selection subfile, which contains the customer name, from a simple text output field to a link. When the user clicks on this new customer name link, the correct information is sent to your program. You might ask, what is the correct information? What is your program expecting? It is expecting a 1 in the subfile Options field for the selected customer record. The Web-Facing conversion will add logic to the user interface, so that the Options field is filled with a 1 and the Enter key event is invoked when the user clicks the link.

Accessing DDS display file source

Since you will use the WebFacing perspective to invoke CODE Designer, you begin this exercise using Development Studio Client in the WebFacing perspective.

- Start WebSphere Development Studio Client and open the WebFacing perspective if it is not up and running already.

In the WebFacing perspective, make sure that you are in the WebFacing Projects view and not the Navigator view (as indicated by the tabs at the bottom of the view—see Figure 6.1).

■ Expand your project in the tree-view by clicking on the plus sign (+) beside the wflabxx WebFacing project icon, as shown in Figure 6.1.

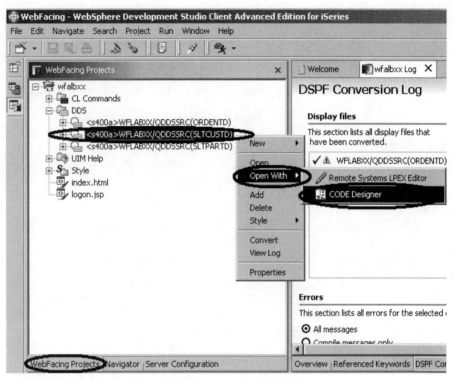

Figure 6.1: Pop-up menu for DDS source member

Complete the following steps to open CODE Designer:

■ Expand the **DDS** folder.

■ Right-click the **SLTCUSTD** source member inside the DDS folder.

■ Select the **Open With** option from the pop-up menu

■ Select the **CODE Designer** option from the submenu.

Figure 6.1 shows the menu structure.

CODE Designer loads the DDS member (this might take a few moments). CODE Designer opens and displays your DDS member (Figure 6.2):

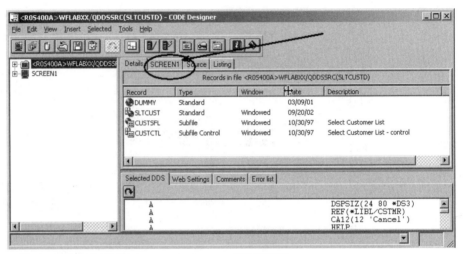

Figure 6.2: CODE Designer select group SCREEN1

■ Select the **SCREEN1** tab on the notebook. The arrow in Figure 6.2 points to the tab.

You should now see a dialog similar to Figure 6.3:

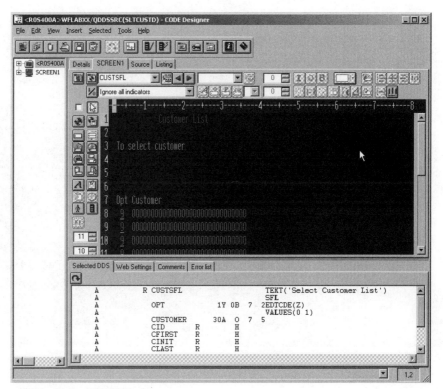

Figure 6.3: CODE Designer

As you can see, you are working with the green-screen image in CODE Designer. Do you recognize the screen? It is the customer selection list. This is the screen I want you to change so that it looks more like a Web page to the end user after WebFacing conversion.

■ Click the second column of the first row in the subfile (the Customer name field) as shown in Figure 6.4.

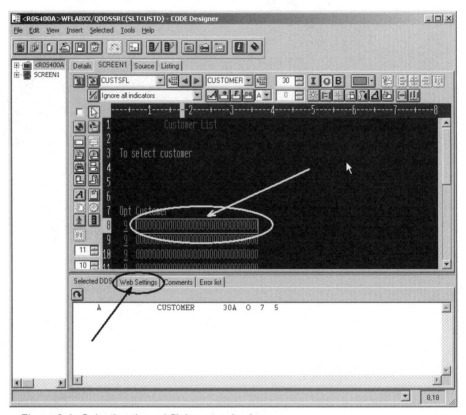

Figure 6.4: Selecting the subfile's second column

Applying Web Settings

Work with the notebook underneath the design window, and locate the Web Settings tab as shown in Figure 6.4.

■ Select the **Web Settings** tab by clicking it.

The Web Settings page in the CODE Designer window should look similar to Figure 6.5.

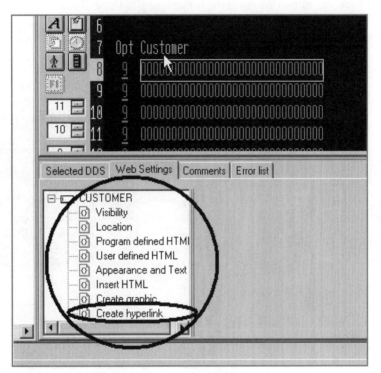

Figure 6.5: Web settings list for CUSTOMER field

■ On the Web Settings page, locate the list that shows the different Web settings available for the CUSTOMER field.

If some of the Web settings are missing,

- Scroll down to the bottom of the list and select **Create hyperlink** (see Figure 6.6).

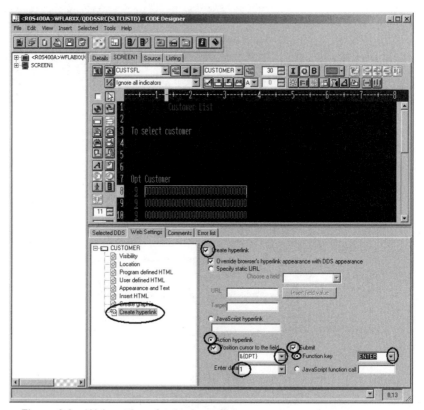

Figure 6.6: Web settings for the hyperlink

- Select the **Create hyperlink** check box to the right of the list.

- Select the **Action hyperlink** radio button.

- Select the **Position cursor to the field** check box.

- From the combination box underneath, select the **&{OPT}** value.

- Change the string value in the Enter data combination box to 1. This indicates that you want the application to enter a 1 in the Options field when the user clicks the hyperlink.

- Select the **Submit** check box.

- Select the **Function key** radio button.

- Select **Enter** from the **Function key** combination box.

Just to review, the information you specified will change your application user interface (upon WebFacing reconversion) in the following ways:

- The Customer name cells in the subfile are generated so that they appear as links in the browser window.

- At run time, when the link is clicked, a 1 is placed in the Options field. Also, a submit request is initiated to generate the equivalent of pressing the Enter key.

The basic task I wanted you to accomplish is complete, but the user interface now has an Option column that does not belong there. Also, the instructions on the page about how to select a customer are incorrect. Before you test this new feature, I want you to fix these inconsistencies with Web settings as well.

Hiding the Options column

On the design pane, you need to select the Options field to indicate that you want to work with it.

- Click the **Opt** column on the first record in the subfile to select it, as shown in Figure 6.7.

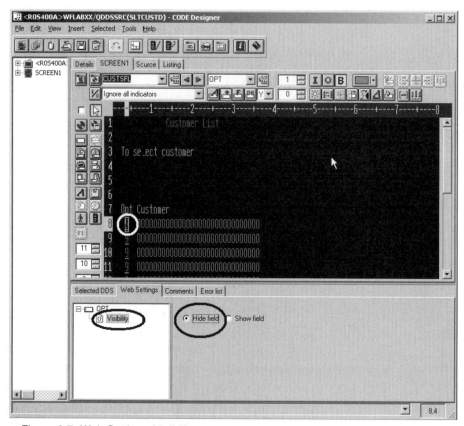

Figure 6.7: Web Settings *Visibility page*

On the Web Settings page,

- Click **Visibility** in the Web Settings list box.

- Select the **Hide field** radio button.

Now this column in the subfile will be hidden.

Hiding the Opt heading

You need to hide the heading for the Options field. Because the heading is located in the subfile control record, and not the subfile record, you need to give focus to a different record format in the design screen.

It might seem confusing that two record formats display in this view instead of one. To clear up this confusion, let me explain more about CODE Designer's features. When you use your iSeries green-screen interface, the screens are normally composed of multiple record formats, which are assembled by the RPG or COBOL program to present the real screen to your end user. For working in the design stage, CODE Designer has added the notion of a *group* to make it easier for you to understand how the screens you create from record formats will look at run time. A group resembles the run-time grouping of record formats for you at development time. You can assemble several record formats in a group, essentially mimicking what happens at run time with your record formats.

In this sample, I have already assembled the following three record formats into a group called SCREEN1:

- CUSTSFL

- CUSTCTL

- SLTCUST

To view a list of record formats belonging to a group, expand the combination box at the top of the design window as shown in Figure 6.8.

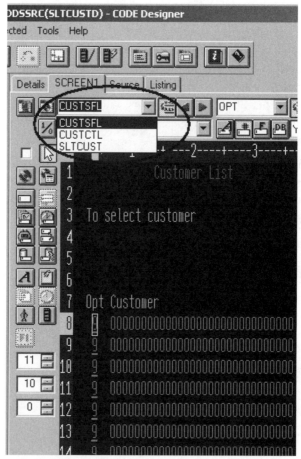

Figure 6.8: Group SCREEN1 and list of record formats

Only one record format in a group is active at any time. The active record format name is listed in the top field of the combination box. Also, all parts of the active record format are shown in regular density in the design window, but the inactive record format content is dimmed. You see this effect very clearly in Figure 6.8.

Until now you have been working with the subfile record format CUSTSFL, but now you need to clean up the subfile control record format CUSTCTL and make it the active record format. In other words, you need to give the record format *focus*.

To shift focus to another record format,

- At the top of the design pane, click the **arrow**, as shown in Figure 6.9, until CUSTCTL has focus.

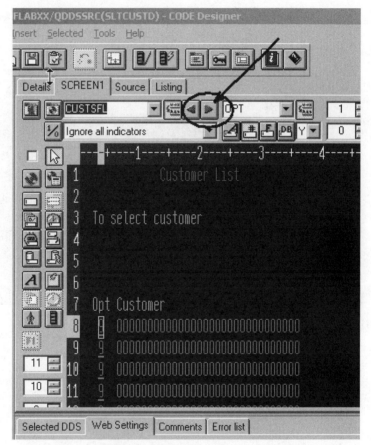

Figure 6.9: CODE Designer switching record formats in a group

The top pane of the design window is now highlighted, and the bottom one has only half the intensity. As mentioned before, the highlighted area is the one you can work with. Figure 6.10 shows the subfile control record in focus. You need to clean up the subfile control record format, beginning with hiding the Opt heading.

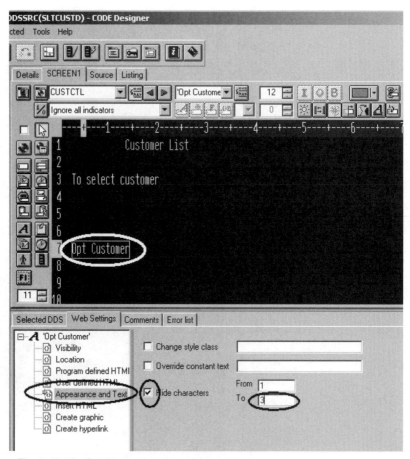

Figure 6.10: Subfile control record format in focus

- On the design pane, select the **Opt Customer** constant.

- On the Web Settings page, select **Appearance and Text** from the list box.

- Select the **Hide characters** check box.

- Specify **1** in the From field.

- Specify **3** in the To field.

Hiding the Select instruction

Now you need to remove the instructions on the panel that guide the user to put a 1 into the Options field. You do not have to give focus to a different record format since this constant is also located in the CUSTCTL record format.

On the design page in CODE Designer (Figure 6.11),

- Select the constant **1=Select** in the design area.

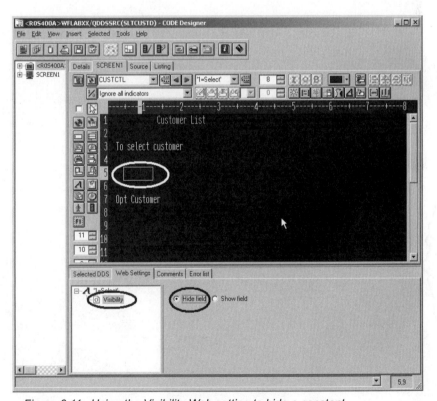

Figure 6.11: Using the Visibility Web setting to hide a constant

On the Web Settings page,

- Select **Visibility** from the list box.

- Select the **Hide field** radio button.

Changing the instruction (Type choices, press Enter)

You need to add new instructions for the WebFaced page, so that the end user knows to click the link to select a customer. Note that you cannot just change the 5250 constant, because you might still use this screen in a 5250 environment. You have to use Web settings to apply this change to the Web user interface only. Complete the following steps to change the instructional text:

- Select the instruction constant **Type choices, press Enter** on the design page, as shown in Figure 6.12.

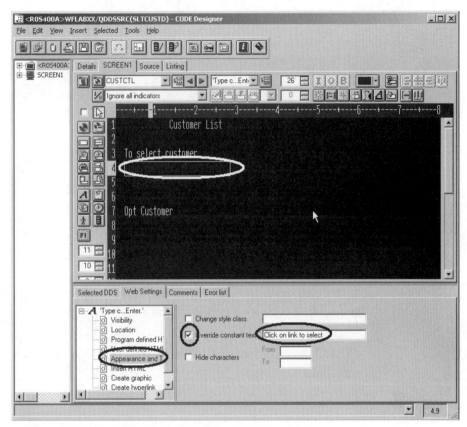

Figure 6.12: Changing the instructions with Web settings

On the Web Settings page,

- Select **Appearance and Text** from the list box.

- Select the **Override constant text** check box, and type the following new text in the field to the right of the check box: **Click on link to select**.

Now all Web settings are in place and you can save the source and reconvert this DDS member.

Closing CODE Designer and reconverting the DDS member

- Click the **X** button at the top right corner of the CODE Designer window.

- Specify **Yes** to save when prompted.

You are finished with CODE Designer.

- Go back to the WebFacing perspective in the Development Studio Client workbench (Figure 6.13).

- Select your **wflabxx** project in the WebFacing Projects view.

- If you cannot see the DDS folder as part of the wflabxx project, expand the project by clicking on the plus sign (+) in front of its icon.

- Expand the DDS folder, if it is not expanded already, to show all members in this folder.

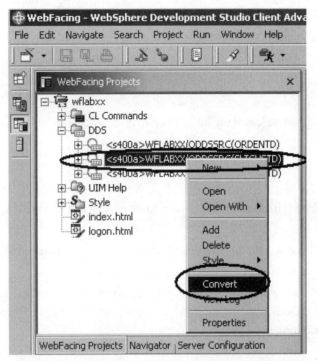

Figure 6.13: WebFacing Projects view, pop-up menu for DDS source member

- Select the member **SLTCUSTD** (the one you just changed).

- Right-click the **SLTCUSTD** member icon.

- Select **Convert** from the pop-up menu.

Only this member will be converted. A conversion report displays when the conversion is finished. Now you can test the new user interface.

Running the Web application

To verify the new user interface in your application,

- Right-click your **wflabxx** project in the WebFacing Projects view.

- Select **Run on Server** from the pop-up menu.

- Go to the browser pane and click the **Order Entry Application** link.

You will see the first screen of your application; nothing has changed there.

- Click the **Prompt** push button, or press **function key 4**.

As shown in Figure 6.14, the customer selection window appears and the Customer fields display as links. Also notice that the text is changed and the Option column is no longer visible.

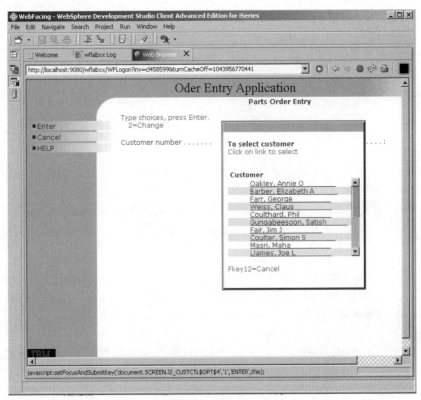

Figure 6.14: Customer selection window with links

- Select a customer from the list by clicking on the link.

- Go through the same steps as in Chapter 2.

Analysis

You have completed the exercise Changing the User Interface. Here is what you did:

- You used CODE Designer to access a DDS source member.

- You used Web settings in CODE Designer to change the Web user interface.

- You used the following Web settings: create hyperlink, visibility, appearance, and text.

- You reconverted the changed DDS.

Note that your green-screen user interface has not changed. If you invoke the application in its green-screen format, it will look like the original user interface. The Web settings affect only the WebFaced user interface.

You are ready to move on. You have improved the look of your application, but there are more improvements you need to make. In the next exercise I will show you how to improve the style of your Web application. Proceed to the exercise Changing the Style of the Web Interface.

Changing the Style of the Web User Interface

You can change the user interface of your Web-enabled application by using the WebFacing Properties Style dialog. This project-level feature applies changes to all the pages in your project. In this exercise, I want you to change the text color and font for all highlighted fields. When you finish that task, you will learn how to locate the Cascading Style Sheet .css file to see where the changes are stored.

The goal of the exercise

The goal of this exercise is to practice changing a style so that you can tailor the Web interface to your needs. You will open the Properties Style dialog, create a new style, change style settings, specify the new style to use for this project, and refresh the project with the new style.

At the end of this exercise, you should be able to

- Create a new style using the WebFacing Properties Style dialog

- Use the field-level properties pages to change the look of your Web pages

- Change the project to use a different style

- Work directly with the Cascading Style Sheet .css file

Scenario

You want to change how the WebFacing Tool maps some of the display attributes to colors and text styles. To give the Web user interface a better look, you need to change the default WebFacing style rules that govern how certain 5250 parts are displayed in a browser. In this chapter, you will learn how to change the style rules for highlighted fields.

Invoking the Properties Style dialog

In this exercise, you will use the WebFacing Tool's Properties Style dialog to tailor your Web user interface. You will change the style rules for highlighted fields in the 5250 panels so that the font is larger in the Web user interface.

■ Start WebSphere Development Studio Client and open the WebFacing perspective, if it is not up and running already (see Figure 7.1).

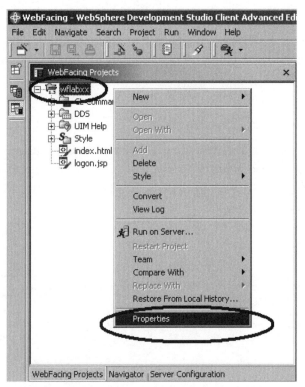

Figure 7.1: WebFacing project with pop-up menu

■ Right-click your **wflabxx** project.

■ Select **Properties** from the pop-up menu.

The WebFacing project Properties dialog opens as shown in Figure 7.2.

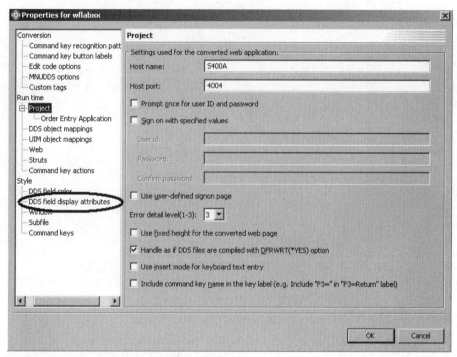

Figure 7.2: WebFacing project properties

■ Under Style in the tree view at the left side of the dialog, click **DDS field display attributes,** as shown in Figure 7.2.

The DDS field display attributes page opens on the right side of the dialog as shown in Figure 7.3.

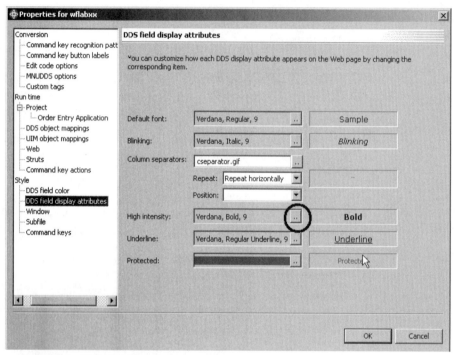

Figure 7.3: DDS field display properties

■ Click the push button to the right of the High intensity combination box.

The Font dialog opens as shown in Figure 7.4.

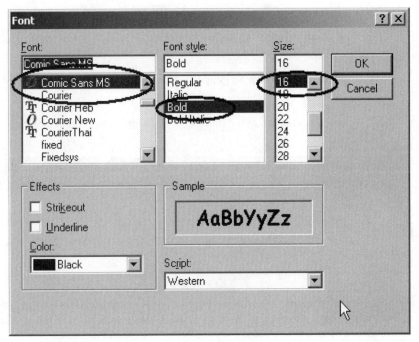

Figure 7.4: Font dialog

- In the Font box, select **Comic Sans MS**.

- In the Font style box, select **Bold**.

- In the Size box, select **16**. This changes the font size and appearance for parts that have the high-intensity attribute active.

Tip: Do not try to change the color in this dialog because the color settings here are not applied. Later in this chapter I will show you how to change the color.

- Click the **OK** push button.

Running the Web application

Let's check the new style in your application:

- Right-click your **wflabxx** project in the WebFacing Projects list.

- Select **Run on Server** from the pop-up menu.

- Go to the browser pane and click the **Order Entry** link.

You will see the first screen of your application. Notice the different font and font size of the text; these are the highlighted areas of your 5250 screen.

Execute the prompt for the customer. The customer selection screen contains highlighted text and this text displays in font Comic Sans Serif at size 16, as shown in Figure 7.5.

Tip: If the text still displays in the old fonts, most likely the browser has cached the page. You need to close the browser window and restart the application. This will invoke a new instance of the browser without cached content.

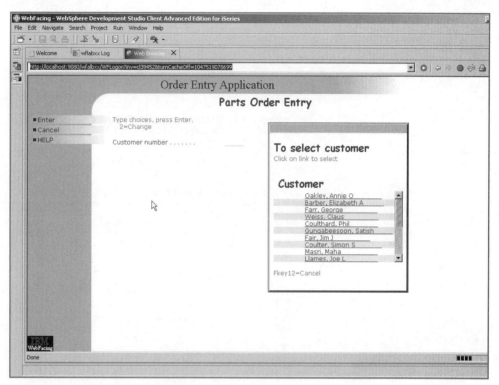

Figure 7.5: New highlight attribute mapping and non-CUA command key description

Unfortunately, the Font dialog contains a bug that hinders you from using the dialog to change the font colors. Therefore, I will show you how to directly change Web-Facing style classes.

Changing styles directly

In addition to working with properties in the WebFacing project, you can change the applied styles directly in the Cascading Style Sheet .css file that the WebFacing Tool uses. I will explain where to find this file in the WebFacing Project structure and how to navigate inside the file. In Chapter 17, I explain how to create your own style sheet classes and use them in a WebFaced user interface.

Locating the cascading style sheet file

In the WebFacing perspective, switch to the Navigator view.

- Click the **Navigator** tab as shown in Figure 7.6.

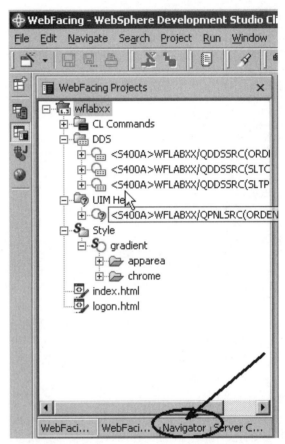

Figure 7.6: The Navigator tab in the WebFacing perspective

In the Navigator view,

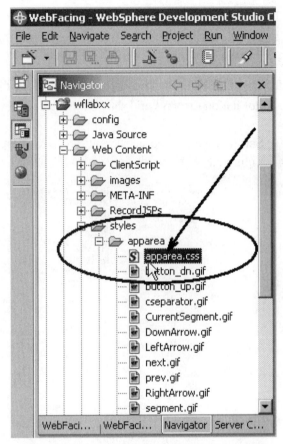

Figure 7.7: Navigator view with apparea.css file

■ Locate the *apparea.css* file in the WebFacing project as shown in Figure 7.7. This file is located in the following directory hierarchy:

```
wflabxx/Web Content/styles/apparea/
```

Tip: For Version 4.0 users, the directory structure is slightly different:

```
wflabxx/webApplication/styles/apparea/
```

■ Double-click on the *apparea.css* file icon in the tree view to open an editor for this file.

Changing the WebFacing highlighted style class

The editor dialog displays and shows the style source.

■ Scroll down the source file until you reach the .wf_hi class as shown in Figure 7.8.

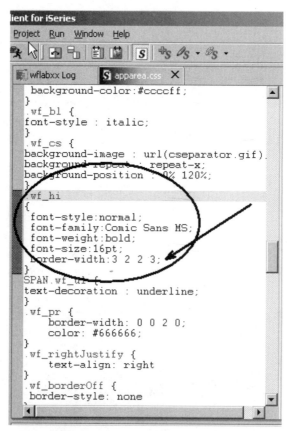

Figure 7.8: Editor dialog with apparea.css source located at the .wf_hi class

You can see the changes from the previous exercise applied here. The WebFacing Tool created style sheet classes for the different 5250 parts and attribute combinations. These items are stored here.

Each of the lines starting with a dot contains a style class name. The statements inside the curly brackets after the style class name describe the attributes of the class itself. For this WebFacing .css file, the class names are self-describing. For example, .wf_hi defines how a part that has the highlighted attribute active is displayed in the browser, and .wf_cs describes the column separator.

You can change the display characteristics for any of the 5250 attributes. For example, to change the color attribute of the *highlighted* class, complete the following steps:

■ Position the cursor at the end of the last line of the .wf_hi class before the ending curly (}) bracket, as shown in Figure 7.8.

■ Press the **Enter** key to insert a line.

■ Insert the color attribute you want to use, for example,

```
color: #ffff99;
```

as shown in Figure 7.9.

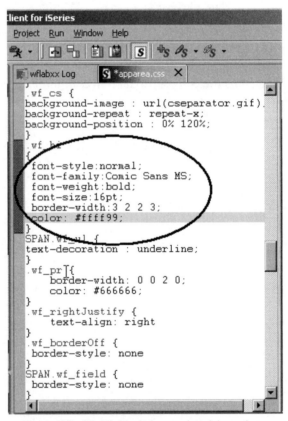

Figure 7.9: Highlighted class color changed

Tip: Do not forget the semicolon at the end of the item to delimit the line.

■ Save the change by clicking the save button in the workbench.

For Version 5.0 users, a nice feature is available in the Style sheet editor. You can view the changes you have made to a class directly in the editor without actually invoking the page and showing it in a browser. Look at the right side of the workbench beside the editor as shown in Figure 7.10.

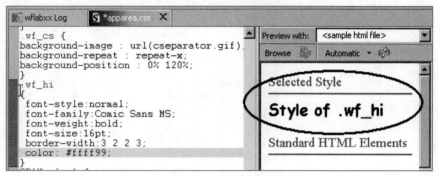

Figure 7.10: Style change example in Style sheet editor

If you are wondering what color is represented by the hex code ffff99, you can find out easily. You can see on a small sample to the right how the text appears after you apply the style.

Look into the area underneath the editor in the workbench as shown in Figure 7.11.

Figure 7.11: Color tab example

■ Select a color from the color palette.

The corresponding hex number appears in the dialog as shown in Figure 7.11.

Tip: Instead of a hex number you could use a color name such as yellow to set a color for a style class.

To see the changes you have made to the interface, run the application again.

Running the Web application

Close the Style sheet editor and the browser if they are still open.

- Close all open editors or views by clicking the **X** in the right upper corner of each one.

Now you can check the new style attribute in your application:

- In the WebFacing perspective, right-click your **wflabxx** project in the WebFacing Projects list, or Navigator view.

- Select **Run on Server** from the pop-up menu.

- Go to the browser pane and click on the **Order Entry** link.

You will see the first screen of your application. Notice the different color of the text in the highlighted areas of your 5250 screen.

Execute the prompt for the customer. The customer selection screen shows the same changed attribute. Remember that style changes are applied to all screens of the application as shown in Figure 7.12.

Tip: If the text is still showing the old colors, most likely the browser has cached the page. You need to close the browser window and restart the application. This will invoke a new instance of the browser without cached content.

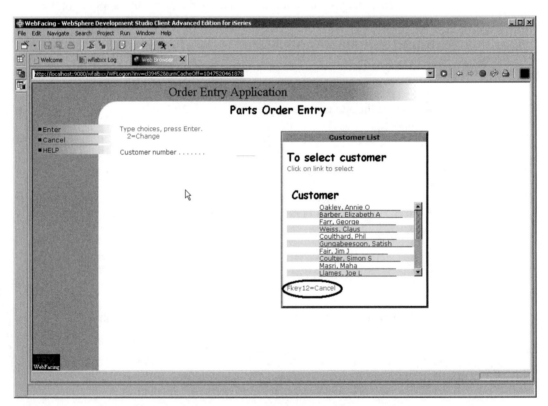

Figure 7.12: New color attribute applied to highlighted style class

You might not have noticed it before, but there is still a command key description at the bottom of the customer selection window as shown in the circle in Figure 7.12. As you may have guessed, you will fix this in the next exercise.

Analysis

You have completed the exercise Changing the Style of the Web User Interface. Here is what you did:

■ You used the WebFacing properties dialog to change the style for WebFaced highlighted fields.

■ You applied a new font style and a larger font size.

■ You tested these changes to verify that they were applied to all screens, making sure that the WebFacing Tool applied the changes without a reconversion of the DDS source. This is because style changes are directly applied at run time and do not require reconversion.

■ You edited the Cascading Style Sheet file directly with the Style sheet editor to change the color attribute of the WebFacing highlighted style class.

■ You saved and tested the application to make sure that the changes were applied on the application screens.

You improved the Web user interface and are ready to move on to the next chapter, where you will enhance the way the WebFacing Tool handles command key labels.

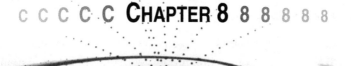

Adding command key rules and labels

The WebFacing Tool creates push buttons for all action function keys, or command keys, on a record format. The tool uses the available descriptions to add labels to the push buttons. While working with your application, you might notice that most command key descriptions that appear at the bottom of the original panels in the sample Order Entry application have been removed from the WebFaced user interface and have also been added to the push buttons.

The removal happens automatically if the command key descriptions follow the common user interface access (CUA) rules (for example, F3 = Exit). The missing descriptions might cause a problem because the WebFacing Tool does not have a string to place in the push button labels on the Web page. If the descriptions do not follow the CUA rules, they are not deleted, but you can supply your own rules to force deletion. On the other hand, your user interface contains enabled command keys without any visible descriptions for the keys. For example, command key 3 (for ending an application) or command key 12 (for canceling a task) are typically enabled for these tasks, but your user interface does not display descriptions for them at the bottom of the panel. Instead, the tool only inserts, for example, "CA12" for an active command key 12 in the push button label.

However, you can supply the WebFacing Tool with the command key description rules you use in your user interface, and the WebFacing Tool applies these rules to recognize your specific command key descriptions. You specify labels for these common command keys in the conversion properties so that the WebFacing Tool can label the push buttons correctly.

The goal of the exercise

The goal of this exercise is to practice adding your own command key recognition rules to WebFacing conversion properties. You will also add command key labels for command keys that do not have labels in the DDS source. You will use the WebFacing conversion properties dialogs, work with command key recognition patterns, and work with command key labels to repair the deficiencies in the WebFaced user interface. You apply the new WebFacing conversion properties when you reconvert the user interface.

At the end of this exercise, you should be able to add non-CUA command key prefixes to the conversion recognition patterns and add commonly used command key labels to the WebFacing conversion properties.

Scenario

The Order Entry application contains one screen that does not follow the CUA rules for command key descriptions. As mentioned in the last exercise, this screen is the customer selection list window. By default, the WebFacing Tool will not recognize these command key descriptions and will not delete them.

The main screen in the Order Entry application has a command key enabled with no associated description. As a result, the WebFacing Tool places a default string in the push button label representing this command key.

In this exercise, you learn how to enable the WebFacing Tool to deal with these common green-screen environments.

Working with command key description patterns

The prefix for the command, or function, key description in the SLTCUST record format is: Fkey=, as shown in Figure 8.1.

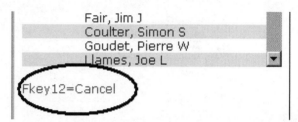

Figure 8.1: Function key description on customer selection panel

This pattern does not follow the CUA rules normally employed by iSeries user interfaces. In turn, the WebFacing conversion process does not recognize this pattern and does not hide it. Therefore, you have to add this prefix pattern to the WebFacing Tool conversion rules in the WebFacing Properties dialog.

In the WebFacing Projects view of the WebFacing perspective,

- Right-click your **wflabxx** icon.

■ Select **Properties** from the pop-up menu, as shown in Figure 8.2.

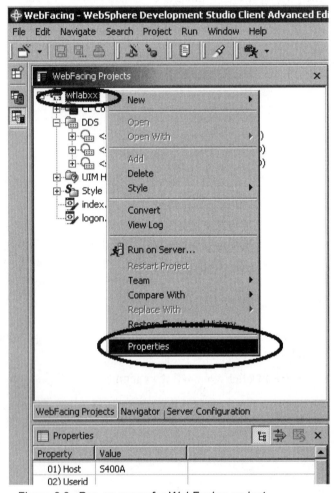

Figure 8.2: Pop-up menu for WebFacing project

The Properties for wflabxx dialog opens as shown in Figure 8.3. In the left-hand list of this dialog,

■ Select the **Command key recognition patterns** node.

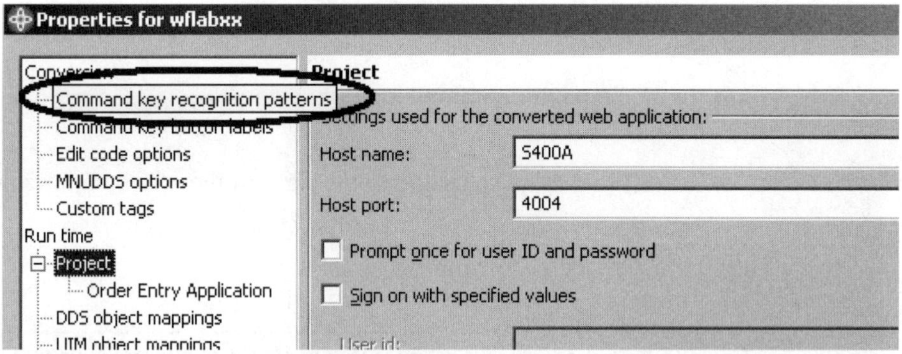

Figure 8.3: WebFacing Properties dialog

In the Command key recognition patterns dialog, the right pane switches to the associated dialog, as shown in Figure 8.4.

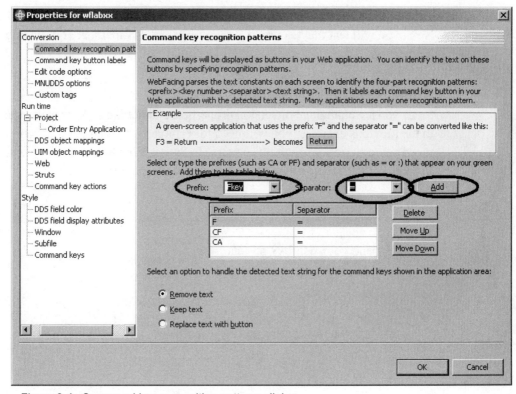

Figure 8.4: Command key recognition patterns dialog

- In the Prefix combination box, enter **Fkey**

- In the Separator combination box, enter **=**

- Click the **Add** push button to the right of these two combination boxes.

The additional rule is now part of this style.

Tip: The default conversion action is to remove the text from the bottom of the panel. You can change this by selecting a different action using the three radio buttons at the bottom of the dialog.

- Click the **OK** push button.

Next, you will test this feature by converting the DDS member and running the application.

Converting the application

Since you are changing conversion properties, and not the style properties as you did in the previous exercise, you will need to reconvert any member that contains command key descriptions with this pattern. In the sample Order Entry application, the SLTCUSTD member is the only one that uses this pattern.

In the WebFacing Projects view,

- Expand your **wflabxx** project.

- Expand the **DDS** folder.

- Right-click the **SLTCUSTD** member icon.

- Select **Convert** from the pop-up menu.

After conversion, examine the change.

Running the Web application

Now you can see how the new rule is applied to your Web-enabled application.

- Right-click your **wflabxx** icon in the WebFacing Projects list.

- Select **Run on Server** from the pop-up menu.

- Switch to the browser pane and click the **Order Entry** link.

You will see the first screen of the sample application.

- Click **Prompt** or press F4.

The customer selection list window opens as shown in Figure 8.5.

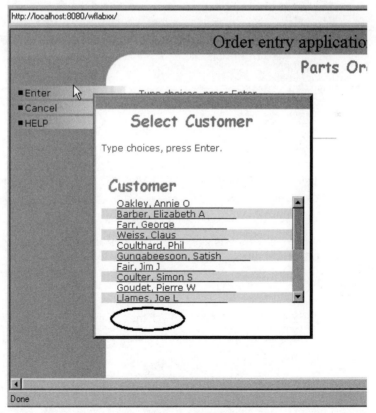

Figure 8.5: Customer selection window without command key label

Notice that the command key text "Fkey12=Cancel" no longer appears at the bottom of the window, as shown by the empty circle in Figure 8.5.

Replacing command key text with a push button

If you had selected the radio button **Replace text with button** on the Command key recognition patterns dialog shown in Figure 8.4, the outcome would look like Figure 8.6.

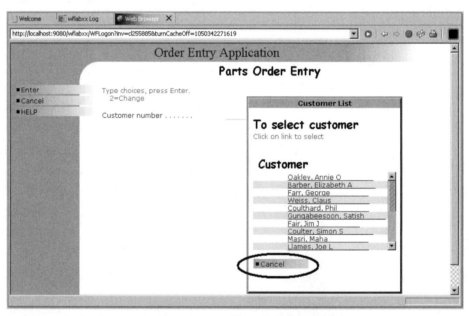

Figure 8.6: Customer selection window with push button added

Instead of removing the command key text from the bottom, WebFacing conversion would add a push button with text to the Web page. This rule would be applied to all record formats that contain command key text.

■ Select a customer or cancel by pressing F12 to return to the application's main panel, as shown in Figure 8.7.

Back on the Order Entry Application panel, you can see that the push button for F12 does not have a description. Its label shows CA12. The next exercise shows you how to repair the label.

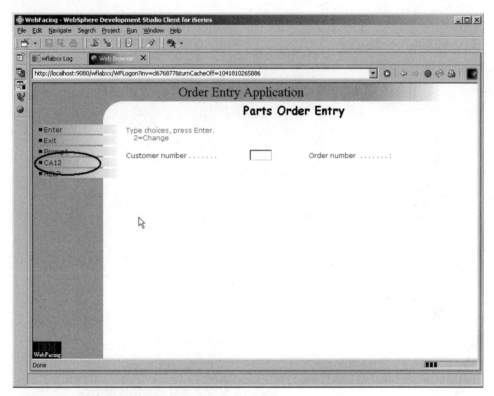

Figure 8.7: Missing label for command key CA12

Now that you know how to change the command key recognition patterns in the WebFacing Tool, the next scenario demonstrates a slightly different situation. As mentioned at the beginning of the chapter, you should learn how to add text to frequently used command keys that do not contain a text description in the DDS source.

Adding command key button labels

The WebFacing Tool allows you to specify command key descriptions for command keys that are commonly used in your application but are not described in your DDS source or on your screens. As a result, the conversion process can automatically change the push button labels on the Web pages to the correct text.

You will add the description Cancel to the WebFacing conversion properties so that the push button shows the label Cancel instead of CA12.

In the WebFacing Projects list,

■ Right-click your **wflabxx** project.

■ Select **Properties** from the pop-up menu, as shown in Figure 8.8.

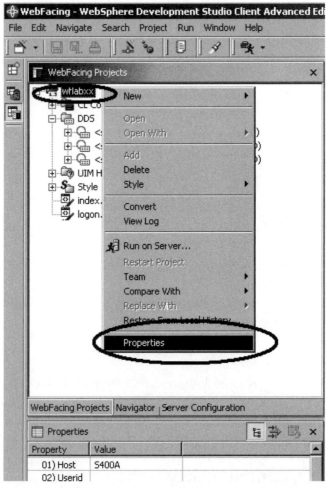

Figure 8.8: The Properties menu option for the WebFacing project

The Properties for wflabxx dialog opens.

In the list on the left side of this dialog, as shown in Figure 8.9,

> ■ Select **Conversion → Command key button labels.**

A dialog opens on the right side of the properties dialog.

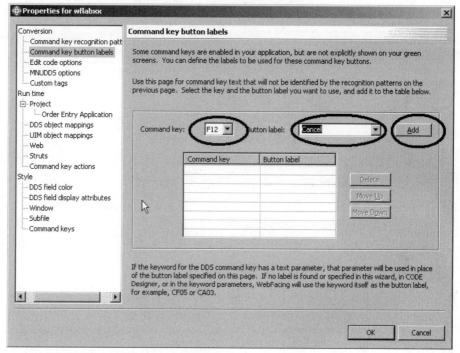

Figure 8.9: Command key button labels

> ■ In the Command key combination box, select **F12.**

> ■ In the Button label combination box, select **Cancel.**

> ■ Click **Add** (to the right of these two combination boxes).

The additional label is now part of the WebFacing conversion properties for this project.

- Click the **OK** push button at the bottom of the Properties dialog.

In the next section, you can test this feature.

Converting the application

Convert the application in the workbench:

- Expand your **wflabxx** project.

- Expand the **DDS** folder.

- Right-click the **ORDENTD** member icon.

- Select **Convert** from the pop-up menu.

After conversion, examine the change.

Running the Web application

Now you can look at the new label for the F12 push button in your Web-enabled application.

- Right-click your **wflabxx** project.

- Select **Run on Server** from the pop-up menu.

■ Go to the browser pane and click the **Order Entry** link.

■ Check that the Cancel push button on the first page now displays the correct label as shown in Figure 8.10.

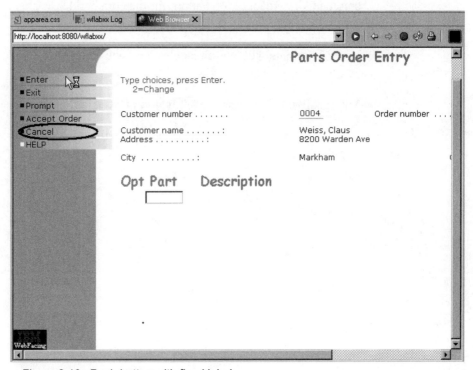

Figure 8.10: Push button with fixed label

Analysis

You have completed the exercise Adding Command Key Rules and Labels. Here is what you did:

- In the Command key recognition patterns page, you changed the Fkey12 command key recognition pattern for the command key label on the customer selection window.

- In the Command key button labels page, you changed the undefined F12 command key label.

- You reconverted and ran the application to verify the changes.

You are ready to move on. Next, you will continue to enhance the style of your Web-enabled application.

Working with additional style properties

In this exercise, you will enhance your Web user interface to make it even more user friendly in a Web environment. You will use the WebFacing Tool style properties dialog that you used in Chapter 7. Because styles are applied on a project level, your enhancements are applied to all Web pages in your project. Specifically, you will learn how to apply changes to windows, push buttons, and subfiles.

The goal of the exercise

The goal of this exercise is to use style properties to further improve the user interface. You will work with style settings and verify the changes by refreshing the style and running the application.

At the end of this exercise, you should be able to perform the following actions in the additional pages of the style properties dialog:

- Work with the window properties page

- Work with the scrollbar/subfile properties page

- Work with the command key look properties page

Scenario

Although you have improved the Web user interface so that the green-screen style is not as apparent as it is after basic WebFacing conversion, you can still add extra refinements to your Web pages. I will show you how you can do this with the Web-Facing Tool style properties.

Start the WebFacing style properties dialog

First, you will use the WebFacing style properties dialog to tailor your Web user interface.

You will apply changes to the window layout of your screens, thus changing the sub-file appearance, and you will enhance the command key push button appearance.

- Start WebSphere Development Studio Client and open the WebFacing perspective, if it is not up and running already.

- In the WebFacing Projects view, right-click your **wflabxx** project.

- Select **Properties** from the pop-up menu.

The project properties dialog opens as shown in Figure 9.1.

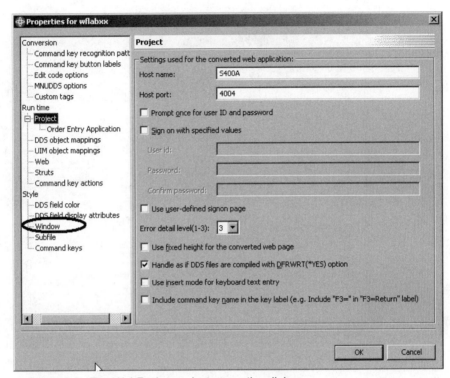

Figure 9.1: The WebFacing project properties dialog

■ Under Style in the tree view on the left side of the dialog, select **Window**.

The window properties page opens on the right pane of the dialog as shown in Figure 9.2.

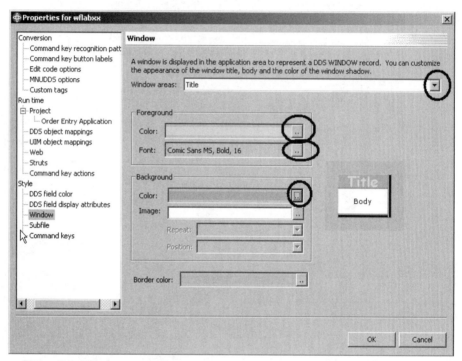

Figure 9.2: Window properties page

- Select **Title** in the combination box at the top of the page.

In the Foreground group box,

- Click the push button to the right of the Color combination box.

In the color selection dialog,

- Click **Yellow.**

- Click the **OK** push button in the color selection dialog.

Back in the Foreground group box,

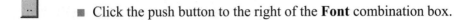 ■ Click the push button to the right of the **Font** combination box.

In the Font dialog,

　　■ Select font **Comic Sans MS**, size **16**.

　　■ Click the **OK** push button in the Font dialog.

In the Background group box,

　　■ Click the push button to the right of the Color combination box.

In the color selection dialog,

　　■ Click **Green**.

　　■ Click the **OK** push button in the color selection dialog.

Back in the window properties page,

- Select **Body** in the combination box at the top of the page as shown in Figure 9.3.

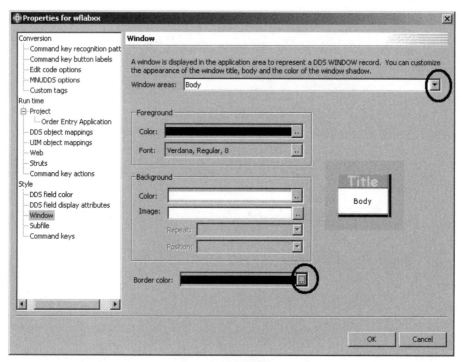

Figure 9.3: *Window properties page with* Body *selection*

In the Border color combination box at the bottom of the page,

- Click the push button to the right of the combination box.

In the color selection dialog,

- Select **Blue**.

- Click the **OK** push button in the color selection dialog.

Changing the appearance of the subfile

- Back in the properties dialog, under Style in the tree view on the left side, select **Subfile**.

The subfile properties page opens on the right pane of the dialog, as shown in Figure 9.4.

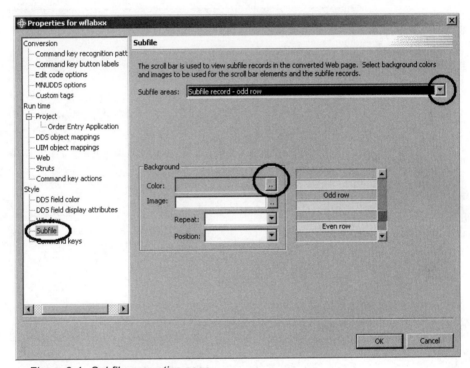

Figure 9.4: Subfile properties page

- Select **Subfile record - odd row** in the combination box at the top of the page.

In the Background group box,

- Click the push button to the right of the Color combination box.

In the Color chooser dialog,

- Select a light yellow color.

Tip: If you are interested in the hex value of certain colors as they are used in the style classes, the Color chooser displays the hex values. In Figure 9.5, the hex value is FFFFCC.

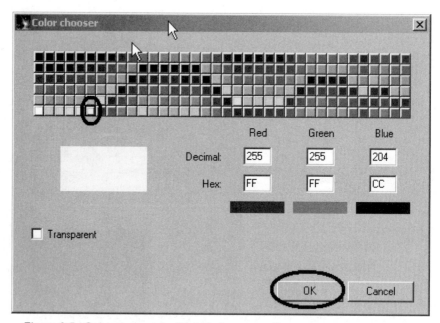

Figure 9.5: Color chooser for WebFacing properties

- Click the **OK** push button in the Color chooser dialog.

Back on the properties dialog,

- Select **Subfile record - even row** in the combination box at the top of the page, as shown in Figure 9.6.

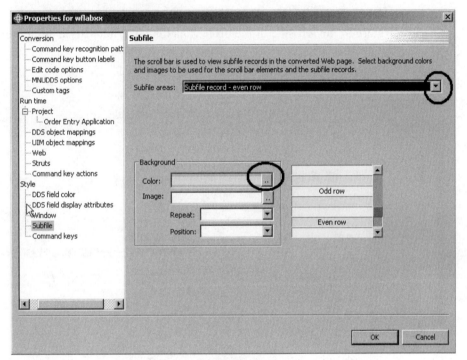

Figure 9.6: Properties page for subfile even rows

In the Background group box,

- Click the push button to the right of the Color combination box.

In the Color chooser dialog,

- Select a light green color.

- Click the **OK** push button.

Now at run time the odd and even records will be displayed with different background colors.

Next, you will customize the appearance of the command key push buttons.

Customizing the appearance of command keys

Return to the left side of the properties dialog. Under Style in the tree view,

■ Select **Command keys**.

The command keys properties page opens on the right pane of the dialog, as shown in Figure 9.7.

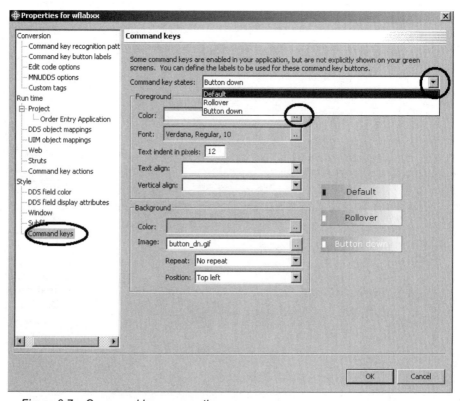

Figure 9.7: Command keys properties page

In the Foreground box, change the color for all three states of the buttons:

■ Default

■ Rollover

■ Button down

Your customizations are complete.

■ Click the **OK** push button in the properties dialog.

Running the Web application

Now you can see the new look of your application.

■ Right-click your **wflabxx** project.

■ Select **Run on Server** from the pop-up menu.

■ Run the application.

■ Click **Prompt**.

The application window in Figure 9.8 shows different colors, and the subfile records are also colored. The command key push buttons change color, depending on the state they are in.

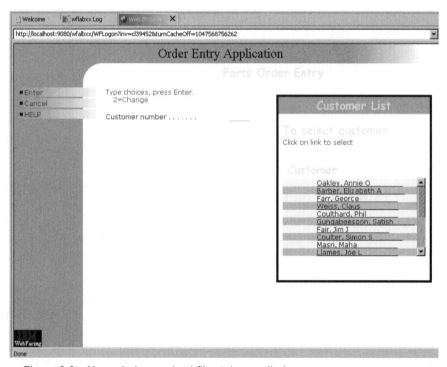

Figure 9.8: New window and subfile styles applied

Analysis

You completed the exercise Working with Additional Style Properties. Here is what you did:

- You opened the style properties dialog and worked with three different properties.

- You verified the changes by running the application.

You are ready to move on. Next, you add authentication support to this application so that users must identify themselves through a sign-on dialog at run time. Proceed to the exercise Adding Authentication.

Adding authentication

In this exercise, you will change the run-time behavior of your application. Instead of using the default user ID and password (the one you used when you selected the members to convert your DDS source), you will now force the user to provide his or her own sign-on information. You just have to remove the user ID and password from the CL command properties. I will also show you how to use your own authentication dialog.

The goal of the exercise

The goal of this exercise is to secure your application by making authentication mandatory before anyone can invoke the application.

Right now, the user ID and password are saved inside the application. You will remove the user ID and password information to force authentication, and then you will verify by running the application again.

At the end of this exercise, you should be able to

- Understand authentication support in the WebFacing Tool

- Secure your application by forcing authentication before the application is invoked

■ Remove the default user ID and password

■ Add your own authentication dialog

Scenario

Up to this point, you have avoided mandatory sign-on to a server when testing your Web-Faced application, since your user ID and password are set as the default. Now you need to move the application into production and you need the WebFaced application to prompt the users for sign-on information.

This exercise demonstrates how to enable authentication support and how to use your own authentication dialog instead of the default WebFacing dialog.

Using the project properties dialog

In this section, you use the CL command run-time properties page to remove the default user ID and password information.

■ In the WebFacing Project view, right-click your **wflabxx** project.

■ Select **Properties** from the pop-up menu.

Providing run-time properties for the project

The Properties for wflabxx dialog opens as shown in Figure 10.1.

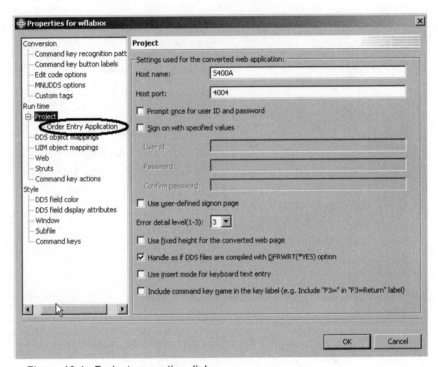

Figure 10.1: Project properties dialog

Under Run time in the tree view on the left side of the dialog,

■ Select **Order Entry Application**.

The Order Entry Application properties dialog displays, as shown in Figure 10.2.

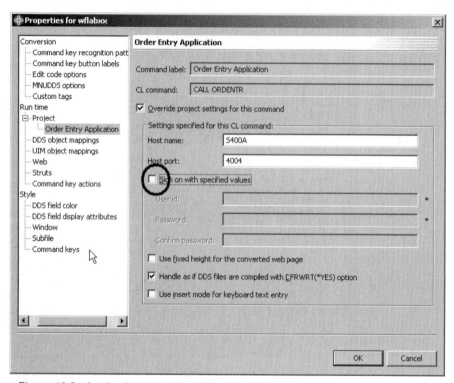

Figure 10.2: Application properties page

- Deselect the **Sign on with specified values** check box.

- Click the **OK** push button at the bottom of the dialog.

You return to the WebFacing project view.

You have changed the authentication behavior for this link, in this application. In this WebFacing project only one link exists, but imagine if there were multiple entry points in your application, such as a menu. If that were the case, you could specify a different authentication behavior for each link.

Tip: If you have multiple links in a WebFacing project and you want the authentication to be the same for each link, you can specify an authentication rule on the project level. In this case, you would specify the desired authentication behavior in the *project* properties page instead of the application properties page.

Running the Web application

As before, run your application in the WAS test environment.

- ■ Click the **Order Entry** link.

You will see the authentication dialog. If the authentication dialog does not display, you need to restart the application server.

You restart the server by using the Servers view in the bottom right area of the workbench (see Figure 10.3):

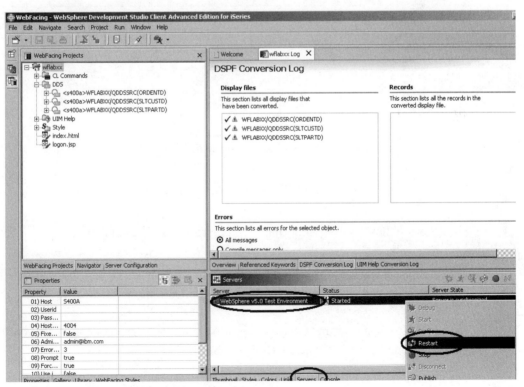

Figure 10.3: Restarting the WAS test environment

■ Select the Servers view by clicking the **Servers** tab.

■ Select **Restart** from the pop-up menu.

After a short while, the Server console displays a message that the server is ready for business.

■ Run the application.

Now you should see the authentication dialog as shown in Figure 10.4.

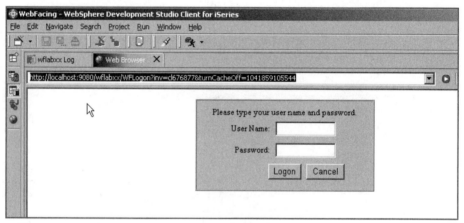

Figure 10.4: WebFacing Tool authentication dialog

■ Specify your **User Name** and **Password**.

■ Click the **Logon** push button on the authentication dialog.

The application runs as it did before, as long as the job environment for the user ID you specified is set up correctly for this application.

Next I will show you how to use your own authentication dialog, instead of the one provided by the WebFacing Tool.

Using your own sign-on dialog

If you do not like the sign-on dialog that comes with the WebFacing Tool, you can use your own dialog and instruct the WebFacing run time to invoke yours instead of the default. A WebFacing project comes with a sample logon.html file, which you can modify to a style that you prefer in your environment. In this section I show you how to modify the dialog. Afterward, I show you how to specify that you want to use your own sign-on dialog.

Changing the logon.html file

In the WebFacing Projects view,

- Expand the **wflabxx** project node, if it is not already expanded.

A logon.html file displays beneath the project, as shown in Figure 10.5. This file is a sample that displays how the default WebFacing logon dialog is built, but it is there for you to customize. The file comes with the HTML tags that you need if you want to incorporate the WebFacing logon *function*, but not the *appearance*, into your own environment. You can copy these HTML statements into your own HTML page.

Figure 10.5: WebFacing Projects view with logon.html file

Note: If you use the Struts run time, in the advanced edition of the product, the WebFacing Tool uses the logon.jsp file and not the logon.html file. Therefore, you would use logon.jsp during this exercise instead of logon.html.

Using Page Designer to add a heading to the Logon page

You will use a different Development Studio Client workbench tool to make the dialog more attractive. This tool is called Page Designer.

To invoke Page Designer (refer to Figure 10.6),

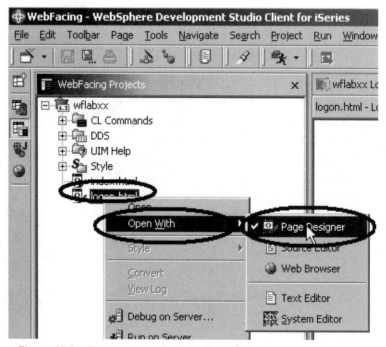

Figure 10.6: Pop-up menu for logon.html file

- Right-click **logon.html** in the WebFacing Projects view.

- Select **Open With** from the pop-up menu.

- Select **Page Designer** from the pop-up submenu.

Page Designer opens on the upper right-hand side of the workbench as shown in Figure 10.6.

First I want you to add your company name as a dialog heading. In the Page Designer window, click on the **Design** tab, as shown in Figure 10.7, to make sure you are on the Design page.

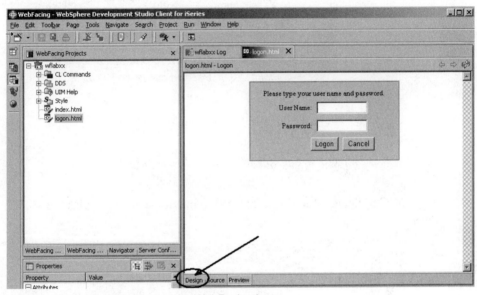

Figure 10.7: Page Designer with WebFacing logon

- Click in the logon dialog just before the string **Please type your user name and password**, as shown in Figure 10.8.

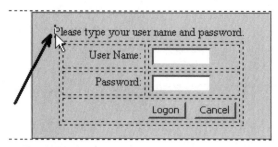

Figure 10.8: Position cursor and click

- Select **Insert** from the workbench menu bar.

- Select **Paragraph** from the pull-down menu.

- Select **Heading2** from the submenu as shown in Figure 10.9.

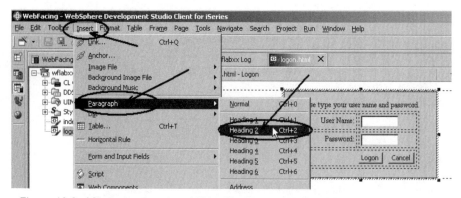

Figure 10.9: Menu structure to add Heading2 tag to logon dialog

A box opens on top of the dialog.

■ In the box, enter your company name.

If you have a company name that takes up more than one line, you can widen the logon box:

■ Move the cursor on top of any of the black rectangles on the side of the logon frame. The cursor shape will change to a two-headed arrow, as shown in Figure 10.10.

■ Drag the side of the frame to make it wider or narrower.

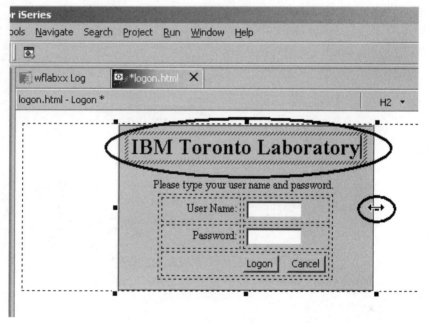

Figure 10.10: New logon dialog, with cursor shape changed to drag-enabled

You might also want to change the color of your new logon dialog. In the next section, I will show you how to change the color and then test the new dialog.

Using Page Designer to change the background color of the Logon page

In Page Designer,

- Right-click the background of the logon frame.

- Select **Attributes** from the pop-up menu as shown in Figure 10.11.

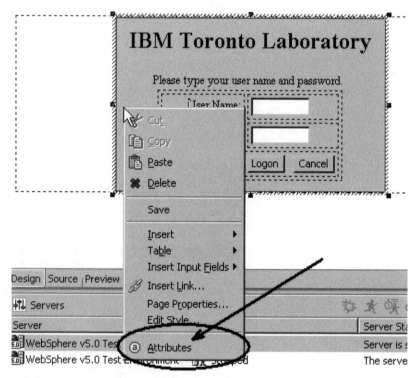

Figure 10.11: Pop-up menu in Page Designer

You will see an Attributes editor display in the lower right area of the workbench, as shown in Figure 10.12.

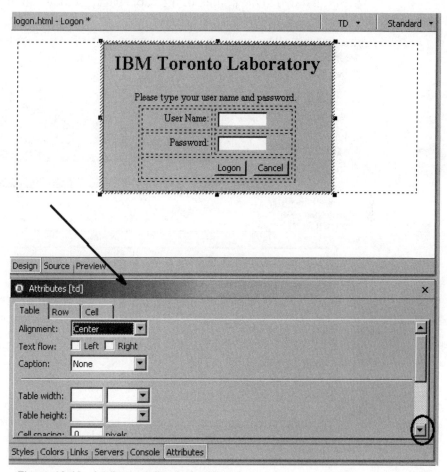

Figure 10.12: Attributes editor in workbench

In the Attributes editor,

- Scroll down to the bottom of the Table page, as shown in Figure 10.13.

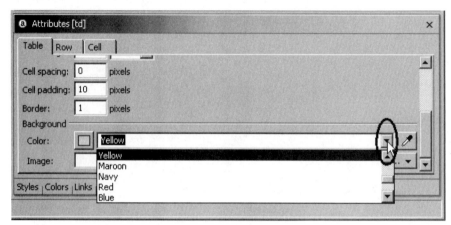

Figure 10.13: Selecting yellow for background color of logon dialog

- Select the **arrow** on the Color combination box to open the list.

- From the list of colors, select **Yellow**, or whatever background color you like, for your logon page.

 Tip: You could use the color picker push button to point to an area on your desktop that has a good color, and then click on that area to apply the color.

Now your logon frame has an attractive background color. Accordingly, the color in the Page Designer window has been adjusted.

To verify how the logon page will look in a browser, you can preview the change.

■ Select the **Preview** tab in Page Designer, as shown in Figure 10.14.

Figure 10.14: Logon page in Preview mode

Another view in Page Designer is the Source view, which displays the source for your page in an editor.

■ Click on the **Source** tab.

The HTML source editor displays the current page source, as shown in Figure 10.15.

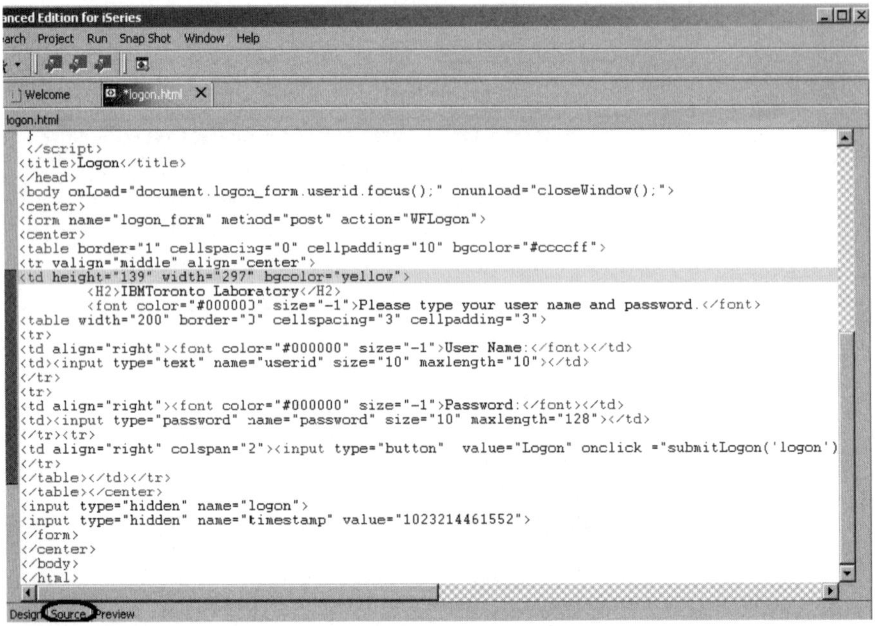

```
         }
         </script>
         <title>Logon</title>
         </head>
         <body onLoad="document.logon_form.userid.focus();" onunload="closeWindow();">
         <center>
         <form name="logon_form" method="post" action="WFLogon">
         <center>
         <table border="1" cellspacing="0" cellpadding="10" bgcolor="#ccccff">
         <tr valign="middle" align="center">
         <td height="139" width="297" bgcolor="yellow">
              <H2>IBMToronto Laboratory</H2>
              <font color="#000000" size="-1">Please type your user name and password.</font>
         <table width="200" border="J" cellspacing="3" cellpadding="3">
         <tr>
         <td align="right"><font color="#000000" size="-1">User Name:</font></td>
         <td><input type="text" name="userid" size="10" maxlength="10"></td>
         </tr>
         <tr>
         <td align="right"><font color="#000000" size="-1">Password:</font></td>
         <td><input type="password" name="password" size="10" maxlength="128"></td>
         </tr><tr>
         <td align="right" colspan="2"><input type="button"  value="Logon" onclick ="submitLogon('logon')
         </tr>
         </table></td></tr>
         </table></center>
         <input type="hidden" name="logon">
         <input type="hidden" name="timestamp" value="1023214461552">
         </form>
         </center>
         </body>
         </html>
```

Figure 10.15: Source editor window in Page Designer

If you wanted to invoke the WebFacing logon action from a different dialog, you would need to copy the source into your file.

The file name for your WebFacing logon page must be logon.html. This is the file the WebFacing run time sends to the browser.

In Chapter 20 I show some alternatives to control the invocation of your WebFaced applications.

You are ready to test the new logon page.

- Save your Page Designer changes by clicking the **Save** push button on the work-bench toolbar as shown in Figure 10.16.

Figure 10.16: Save push button in workbench toolbar

- Close Page Designer by clicking the **X** on its window bar as shown in Figure 10.17.

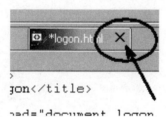

Figure 10.17: Closing Page Designer

Changing the WebFacing properties to use a different Logon page

In the WebFacing Projects view,

- Right-click your **wflabxx** project.

- Select **Properties** from the pop-up menu.

The project properties dialog displays, as shown in Figure 10.18.

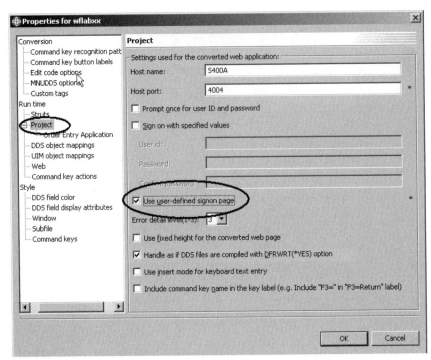

Figure 10.18: WebFacing project properties dialog

In the project properties dialog,

- Select the **Use user-defined signon page** check box.

- Press the **OK** push button at the bottom of the properties page.

Now you can try out the new logon page.

Running the Web application

As before, run your application in the WAS test environment.

- Click the **Order Entry** link.

You will see the new authentication dialog (see Figure 10.19).

If the new authentication dialog does not appear, you need to restart the WebSphere test environment as described earlier in this chapter. Some of the files might be cached and therefore need to be reloaded in order to display updates.

Figure 10.19: The new logon dialog

- Specify your **User Name** and **Password**.

- Click the **Logon** push button on the authentication dialog.

The application will run as before, as long as the job environment for the user ID you specified is set up correct for this application.

Analysis

You have completed the exercise Adding Authentication. Here is what you did:

- You removed the default user ID and password information from the Order Entry application.

- You ran the application and provided authentication where requested.

- You worked with Page Designer to produce your own logon page by changing the default WebFacing logon page.

- You tested your new user-defined logon page.

You are ready to move on. In the next chapter, you will learn about display file mappings. If source member names and display file names do not match, you need to let the Web-Facing run time know about these name differences. Proceed to the exercise Display File Mapping.

Display file mapping

In the 5250 environment, the record formats that describe the user interface exist inside the display files. At run time, your system resolves the record format requested by a program by searching for the display file in a fully qualified library or in a library in the library list. In the WebFacing Tool, this works differently. The WebFaced application does not use a display file located in the native OS/400 system, so a different way of resolving record formats is required.

Until now, the mapping of your record formats at run time has been successful because I used the default name when creating the display file, which is the member name of the DDS source member. The WebFacing Tool assumes at run time that this default has been used. Therefore, the WebFacing run time can easily find the correct .jsp file that represents the requested record format.

You need to examine the files that the WebFacing Tool created during conversion of the Order Entry application. Figure 11.1 shows the directory structure of your Web-Facing project in the Navigator view.

You can see that the created folder structure is a duplicate of the DDS source environment structure, used by the Order Entry application. The library name, source file name, and member name are all part of this structure. The .jsp file has the name of the record format itself. When running the application, WebFacing run time uses this structure to find the correct record format requested by the program.

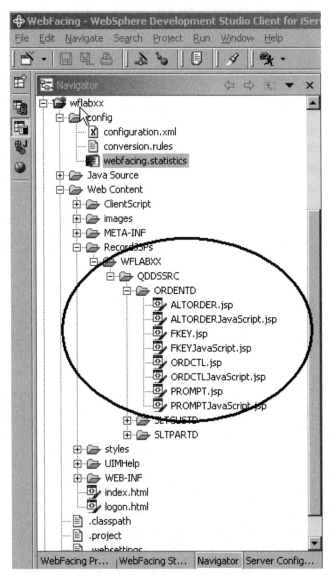

Figure 11.1: WebFacing project folder structure

As mentioned before, this works as long as the run-time environment reflects the development environment. However, this is not always the case. To give you more flexibility to reflect your real run-time environment, you can specify mapping rules with the WebFacing Tool.

This exercise shows you how to specify a mapping rule for a display file, when the display file does not have the same name as the source member from which it was created.

The goal of the exercise

The goal of this exercise is to apply a mapping rule for a display file created with a name other than the default name of its associated source member.

You will change the properties for your WebFacing project and define a new mapping rule.

At the end of this exercise, you should be able to

■ Change the command used to invoke the application

■ Explain how record format mapping is performed in the WebFacing Tool

■ Change the WebFacing mapping rules

Scenario

First you need to change the command to invoke the sample WebFaced application. In the wflabxx library, shipped with this book, I have included another program. This program is identical to the program you have been using until now, except that it uses a different display file name for the customer selection list.

First you will run this program, which tries to access display file ZSLTCUSTD instead of SLTCUSTD. To put you in an end user's position, you will receive a run-time error, telling you that the corresponding ZSLTCUSTD.jsp could not be found.

You will then change the WebFacing mapping rules to reflect the real run-time environment.

Changing the invocation command

The Invocation (.invocation) file contains the command your program uses to start your application. When you created this project, you specified the command CALL ORDENTR. Now you will change this to invoke program ZORDENTR instead. Program ZORDENTR will call program ZSLTSCUSTR, and it will use display file name ZSLTCUSTD, which does not have a corresponding ZSLTCUSTD.jsp file.

In the Development Studio Client workbench,

- Open the WebFacing perspective if it is not open already.

- Make sure you are in the Navigator view, as in Figure 11.2.

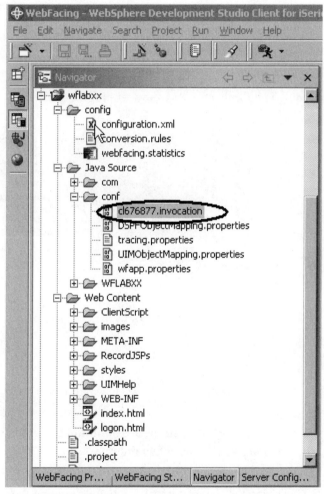

Figure 11.2: WebFacing project with .invocation file

■ Expand your **wflabxx** project.

■ Expand the **Java Source** directory.

■ Expand the **conf** directory.

■ Locate the .invocation file.

■ Double-click the **.invocation** file icon.

A source editor displays, as shown in Figure 11.3.

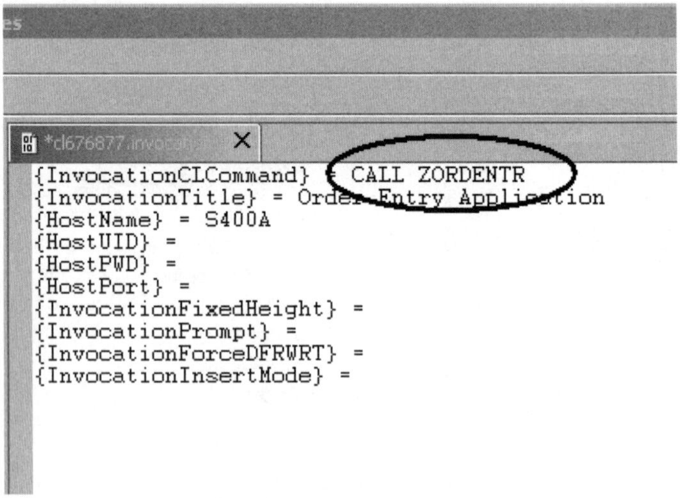

Figure 11.3: Editor window with .invocation file

■ Change the **InvocationCLCommand** to CALL ZORDENTR, by adding a Z to the name of the called program.

By changing the .invocation file, you are changing the invocation information for this application.

Now save the .invocation file and run the Order Entry application:

- Select the **File** menu option in the workbench.

- Select the **Save clxxxx.invocation** menu option from the File menu, or use the Save push button on the workbench toolbar, as shown in Figure 11.4.

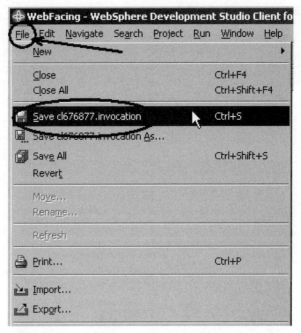

Figure 11.4: Workbench File menu structure

- Close the .invocation editor window.

Before you start the Order Entry application, you need to restart the WebSphere test environment, to pick up the change you made.

Select the **Servers** tab from the bottom of the workbench window, as shown in Figure 11.5.

■ Right-click the application server you are using.

■ Select **Restart** from the pop-up window.

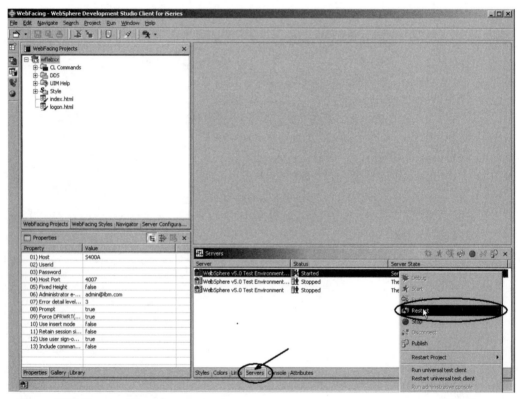

Figure 11.5: Servers tab and pop-up menu

The console will display a message that the server is open for e-business, as shown in Figure 11.6.

```
pTransport A SRVE0171I: Transport http is listening on port 9,080.
pTransport A SRVE0171I: Transport https is listening on port 9,443.
ConnectorC A ADMC0026I: RMI Connector available at port 2809
erve      A WSVR0001I: Server server1 open for e-business
```

Figure 11.6: Console view with server confirmation message

In the WebFacing perspective,

■ Right-click the **wflabxx** project.

■ Select **Run on Server** from the pop-up menu.

■ Click the **Order Entry** link to start the application in the browser.

■ When the first screen displays, press **F4**.

You will see the error message shown in Figure 11.7.

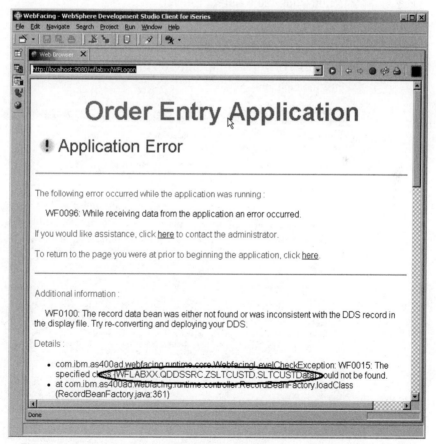

Figure 11.7: WebFacing run-time error message, when .jsp file cannot be found

Program ZORDENTR is calling another program that is requesting a record format in display file ZSLTCUSTD instead of SLTCUSTD (the default). The WebFacing run time is looking for the .jsp file in folder ZSLTCUSTD. This folder does not exist, since the member name at conversion was SLTCUSTD.

You will fix this by changing the mapping properties.

■ Close the browser window.

Changing the WebFacing mapping rules

In the WebFacing Projects view (make sure you are not in the Navigator view),

■ Right-click the **wflabxx** project.

■ Select **Properties** from the pop-up menu.

■ Select **DDS object mappings** on the properties dialog, as shown in Figure 11.8.

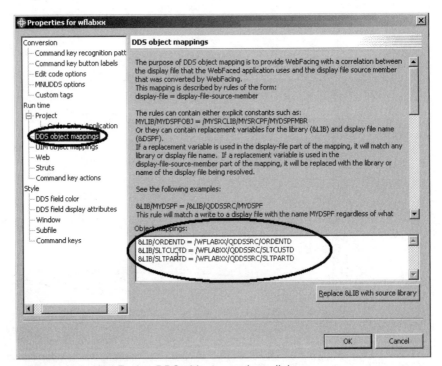

Figure 11.8: WebFacing DDS object mappings dialog

The DDS object mappings dialog displays. At the bottom of the dialog, you can see the default rules that are applied for a WebFacing project. You need to change one of the rules to reflect the fact that the display file has a different name than the DDS source member. This will enable the WebFacing run time to find the corresponding .jsp file.

The text in this dialog explains what kind of rules you can supply to reflect your run-time environment, to ensure that the WebFacing run time applies the correct mappings to find the correct record formats in your environment.

Change the second line in the list box at the bottom of the dialog to point to display file ZSLTCUSTD from source member SLTCUSTD, as shown in Figure 11.9.

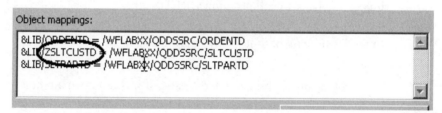

Figure 11.9: Changed mapping rule for member SLTCUSTD

Now the WebFacing run time knows that it has to look into folder SLTCUSTD when it receives a request for a record format in display file ZSLTCUSTD.

■ Press the **OK** push button on the Properties dialog.

Now you can test this change.

Running the Web application

As before, run your application in the WAS test environment. First, however, you need to restart the server as described earlier in this chapter.

In the WebFacing perspective,

■ Right-click the **wflabxx** project.

- Select **Run on Server** from the pop-up menu.

- Click the **Order Entry** link.

- Press **F4** on the first panel to see the application function properly again.

The WebFacing run time now finds the record format in folder SLTCUSTD because the mapping rule points the program in the right direction.

Changing the invocation command back

In order to work with the remaining exercises in the book, you need to change the invocation back to call program ORDENTR.

In the Development Studio Client workbench,

- Open the WebFacing perspective if it is not open already.

- Make sure you are in the Navigator view.

- Expand your **wflabxx** project.

- Expand the **Java Source** directory.

- Expand the **conf** directory.

- Locate the .invocation file.

- Double-click the **.invocation** file icon.

In the source editor,

- Change the **InvocationCLCommand** to CALL ORDENTR, by removing the Z you added during this exercise from the name of the called program.

Now save the .invocation file and run the Order Entry application:

- Select the **File** menu option in the workbench.

- Select the **Save clxxxx.invocation** menu option from the File menu, or use the **Save** push button on the workbench toolbar.

- Close the .invocation editor window.

Before you start the Order Entry application, you will have to restart the WebSphere test environment to pick up the change you made.

Analysis

You have completed the exercise Display File Mapping. Here is what you did:

- You ran a program that used a display file name that did not match the member name, creating a run-time error for a missing .jsp file.

- You used the run-time properties to change the display file mapping to the actual display file name.

- You restarted the application server and ran the application again. This time it worked.

You are ready to move on. Next, you will delete a WebFacing project.

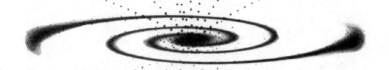

Deleting WebFacing projects

It is supposed to be very easy to delete a WebFacing project, but there is some unexpected behavior in this environment that you need to be aware of, so I have devoted a separate chapter to this subject. Because you need to create a project in order to delete it, the chapter has grown from a simple description of deleting a project into a bit more.

Creating and deleting WebFacing projects is a very straightforward process. After creating and deleting a project, you would expect to be able to run other projects with no problem. However, if you share an EAR file, you might receive error messages during setup or when you run an application in the WAS test environment. This chapter shows you how to handle publishing and run-time errors, and how to recover from these error situations.

Some of the behavior in the WAS test environment depends on the fixpack level of Development Studio Client you are using. I am using Level 5.0.1 for this exercise. If you are on a different level, some of the messages might be different in your environment.

The goal of the exercise

The goal of this exercise is to create and delete a WebFacing project and then deal with any subsequent problems. Afterward all your projects will work again without any server startup or run-time problems.

At the end of this exercise, you should be able to

■ Create a new WebFacing project using an existing EAR file

■ Delete a WebFacing project

■ Recover from initialization errors in WAS if there are undeleted files in the Web project structure

■ Recover from publishing errors

Scenario

You want to create a WebFacing project that shares an EAR file with another WebFacing project; that is, you want to add the project to an existing EAR file. You then decide to delete the WebFacing project.

When you create or delete a WebFacing project, some of the information in the shared EAR file is not synchronized. This can cause startup problems when you try to run Web applications in the test environment. In this exercise, you will learn how to recover from these problems.

Creating a project

In order to preserve the WebFacing project you have created in the previous exercises, I want you to create a similar WebFacing project just to be able to delete it.

Create a new WebFacing project with the name wflaba:

■ Use the **WebFacing Project** menu option as shown in Figure 12.1: New project list to create new WebFacing project1.

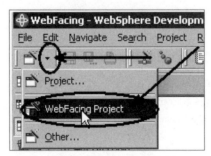

Figure 12.1: New project list to create new WebFacing project

In the WebFacing Project wizard (Figure 12.2),

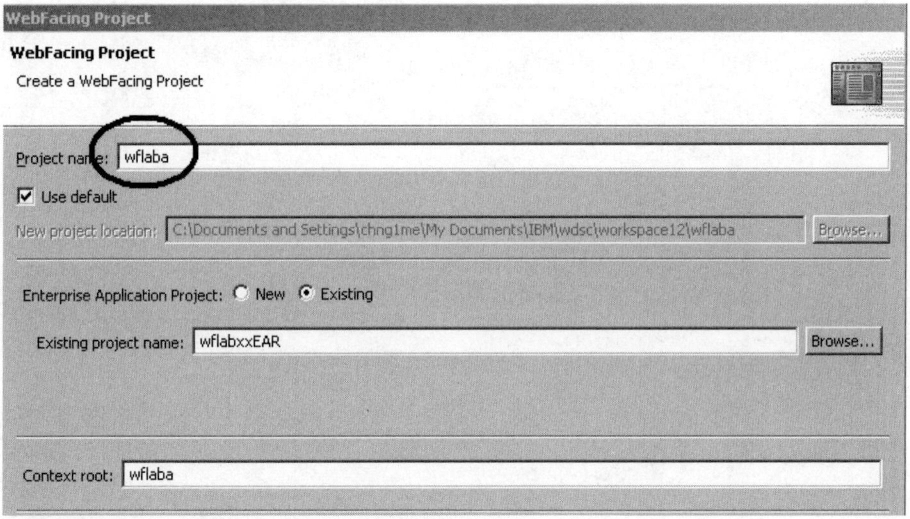

Figure 12.2: Specify project name and EAR name

■ Specify **wflaba** as the project name.

■ Specify use of the existing **wflabxxEAR** as the EAR file project name.

■ Click the **Next** push button to proceed to the next page.

■ Select JSP level **1.3**.

■ Click the **Next** push button to proceed to the next page.

On the Select Display File Source Member page (Figure 12.3),

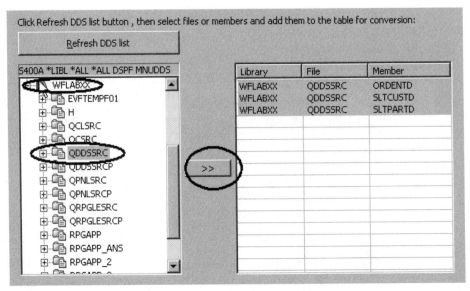

Figure 12.3: Selecting DDS source members

■ Click the **Refresh DDS list** push button.

In the list box,

■ Expand your **iSeries** connection.

■ Expand your **wflabxx** library.

■ Select the **QDDSSRC** file in the wflabxx library.

■ Click the >> push button to select all members in QDDSSRC.

■ Click the **Next** push button to proceed to the next page.

Skip the Select UIM source members page by

- Clicking the **Next** push button.

On the Specify CL commands page (Figure 12.4),

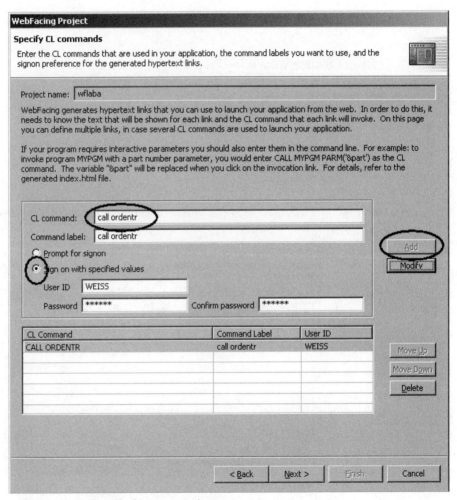

Figure 12.4: Specify CL commands page

- Enter **call ordentr** in the CL command entry field.

- Select the **Sign on with specified values** radio button.

■ Click the **Add** push button.

■ Click the **Next** push button to proceed to the next page.

On the Choose Web Style page,

■ Click the **Next** push button (to choose the default style).

On the Complete WebFacing Project page,

■ Select the **Yes, I want to create the project with conversion now** radio button.

■ Click the **Finish** push button.

You might get a Repair Server Configuration error message as shown in Figure 12.5.

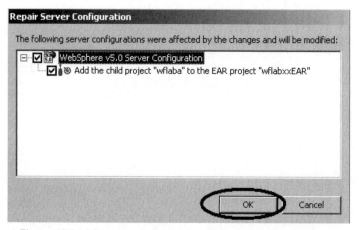

Figure 12.5: Message dialog to repair server configuration

■ Click the **OK** push button on the message dialog.

The WebFacing project is created and conversion begins.

Once conversion is finished, you can run your application. In the WebFacing Projects view,

- Right-click the new **wflaba** project.

- Select **Run on Server** from the pop-up menu.

In the browser you might get the error message "The page cannot be found" (see Figure 12.6). You will then have to restart the application server.

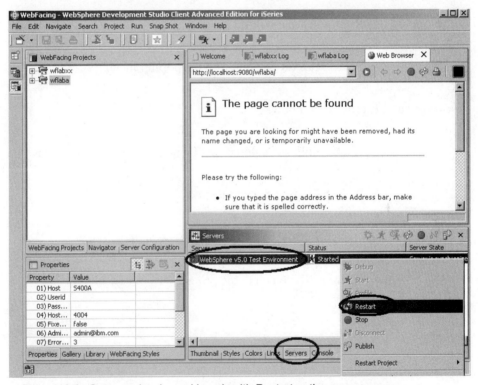

Figure 12.6: Servers view in workbench with Restart option on pop-up menu

- Select the **Servers** tab.

In the Servers view,

- Right-click the server you are using.

- Select the **Restart** option from the pop-up menu.

- Close the browser.

After the server has started, go to the WebFacing Projects view.

- Right-click the **wflaba** project.

- Select **Run on Server** from the pop-up menu.

In the browser window,

- Click a link on the index.html page, to run the application.

- Press **F3** to exit the application.

- Close the browser by clicking the **X** on its window bar.

Now you are ready to delete the project.

Deleting the WebFacing project

In the WebFacing Projects view (Figure 12.7),

Figure 12.7: Select Delete option from pop-up menu

■ Right-click the **wflaba** project.

■ Select **Delete** from the pop-up menu.

A message box displays as shown in Figure 12.8.

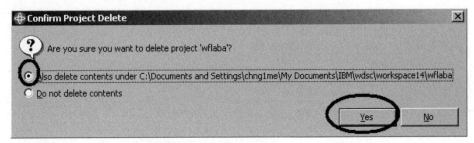

Figure 12.8: Delete confirmation message box

■ Select the **Also delete contents under . . .** radio button.

■ Click the **Yes** push button.

The Repair Server Configuration dialog (Figure 12.9) will appear.

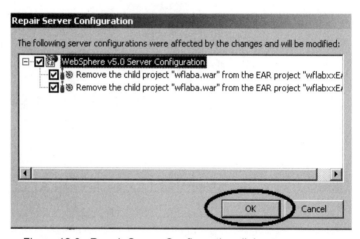

Figure 12.9: Repair Server Configuration dialog

■ Leave the default selections.

■ Click the **OK** push button.

The WebFacing project wflaba is deleted. If you switch to the Navigator view, as shown in Figure 12.10, you will notice that the wflabxxEAR file still exists. This is necessary since the wflabxx project also uses the EAR file. An EAR file can contain information about multiple projects, so it is not safe to delete it when only one project is deleted. An EAR file will not be deleted when a project gets deleted, even if it is the only project that actually uses the EAR file.

Tip: If your EAR file contained only information from the deleted WebFacing project, then it would be easiest for you to delete this EAR file. That way you do not have to worry about synchronizing your Web Server environment.

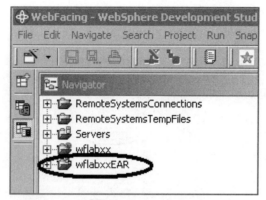

Figure 12.10: Navigator view with
wflabxxEAR

Now you will work with the original project again.

Run the application in Development Client Version 5.0. In the WebFacing
Projects view,

- Right-click the original **wflabxx** project.

- Select **Run on Server** from the pop-up menu.

You will see an error message in the browser: "The page cannot be found."

- Restart the application server.

You might get an application server error message that the server did not start
correctly (Figure 12.11).

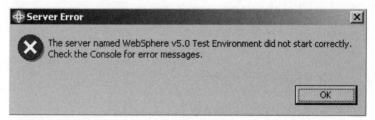

Figure 12.11: Message dialog that server did not start correctly

- Click the **OK** push button.

Removing the WAR file from the module list

Go to the Navigator view (Figure 12.12).

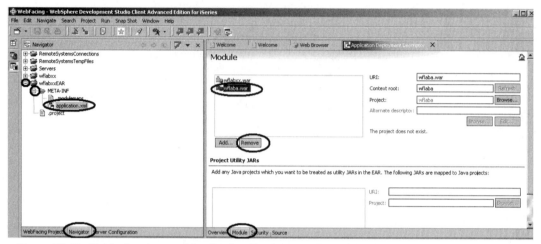

Figure 12.12: Navigator view and Application Deployment Descriptor

- Expand the **wflabxxEAR** node.

- Expand the **META-INF** node.

- Double-click the **application.xml** file.

An editor window opens with the Application Deployment Descriptor file.

- Click the **Module** tab.

- Select the leftover **wflaba.war** file from the list of modules.

- Click the **Remove** push button.

- Save the file.

- Close the edit window.

- Right-click the **wflabxx** project icon.

- Select the **Run on Server** option from the pop-up menu.

Your project is now working; you had to remove the WAR file from the module list.

Handling the publishing failure message

Sometimes you may receive a "Publishing failed" error message that requires some action to get you going again. Here I describe the necessary steps.

You may see a dialog telling you that publishing has failed, as shown in Figure 12.13.

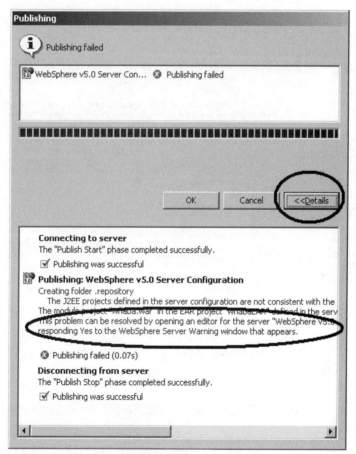

Figure 12.13: Publishing error

■ Click the **Details** push button.

The details text tells you how to fix this error. The circled area in Figure 12.13: Publishing error13 indicates the relevant section in the error message.

To fix this problem,

- Click the **OK** push button on the error dialog.

- Switch to the Navigator view.

In the Navigator view,

- Locate and expand the **Servers** folder.

- Double-click the **.wsi** server file, as shown in Figure 12.14.

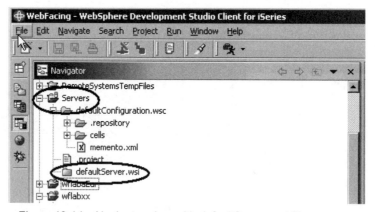

Figure 12.14: Navigator view with defaultServer.wsi file

An editor should open, where you can edit the server properties. Before the editor opens, however, you receive a warning as shown in Figure 12.15.

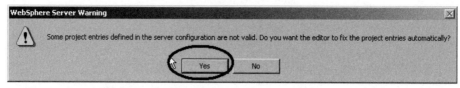

Figure 12.15: Warning that configuration problems exist

- Click the **Yes** push button to repair the problem.

The editor opens after the repair is completed, and you do not need to take any further action.

- Close the editor by clicking on the **X** of its window bar.

A message displays, as shown in Figure 12.16, telling you that the configuration has been changed.

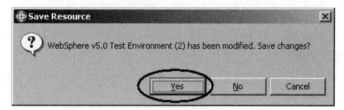

Figure 12.16: Save confirmation message

- Click the **Yes** push button to confirm and save.

When you return to the workbench,

- Select the **Servers** tab at the bottom of the workbench window, as shown in Figure 12.17.

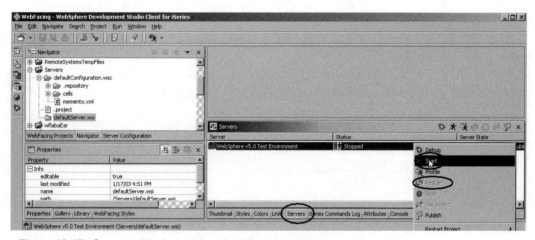

Figure 12.17: Servers view in workbench with pop-up menu

In the Servers view,

- Right-click the server you are using.

- Select **Start** or **Restart** from the pop-up menu (whichever is enabled).

After the server starts, switch to the Navigator view or the WebFacing Projects view:

- Right-click the **wflabxx** project.

- Select **Run on Server** from the pop-up menu.

Now the application will display and run as it should. You have repaired the problem.

Note: When you create a Web project with the same name as the one that you deleted, you might encounter the Repair Server Configuration dialog again. Click the **OK** push button on the dialog and the project should be created without any problems.

Analysis

You have completed the exercise Deleting WebFacing Projects. Here is what you did:

- You created and deleted a WebFacing project.

- You tried to run the still-existing application that shared the EAR file and you encountered run-time problems.

- You learned that creating and deleting a project with a shared EAR file requires additional clean-up to synchronize the WAS test environment with the Web projects.

- You performed the necessary repairs to synchronize the WAS environment with the project infrastructure for development.

You are ready to move on. Next you will use Page Designer to enhance the index.html page created by the WebFacing Tool.

Enhancing index.html using Web tools

This chapter is a diversion from the core of the WebFacing Tool. In this exercise, you use Web tools, also from Development Studio Client, to update the index.html file. This file, created by the WebFacing Tool, is the starting point for your WebFaced application. You will use Page Designer and other, related tools in the workbench to enhance the index.html page.

The index.html page is very plain. In this exercise, you will add color and pictures to the page to make it more interesting and more appropriate as a Web page. At the same time, you will have a chance to use some of the other Development Studio Client tools. This chapter is separated into Version 4.0 and Version 5.0 exercises because the Page Designer interface has been changed dramatically between the two versions of Development Studio Client.

Goal of the exercise

The goal of this exercise is to use Web tools to enhance the index.html Web page. You will use Page Designer and other, related tools to perform these tasks, and then test the modified page.

At the end of this exercise, you should be able to

- Use Page Designer components to create a more attractive browser interface

- Add a style sheet to the page

- Add a heading that moves

- Add a graphic from the sample gallery

- Create a logo with a Web design tool

- Test the new index.html page

Scenario

You have created a WebFaced application, but the starting page is rather plain. You want to enhance the look of the index.html page to give it a more professional appearance.

The Development Studio Client workbench contains several tools you can use to design and enhance Web pages. Inside the workbench, you also have access to sample pictures, icons, animations, and so on. You will use some of these tools and samples to make the page more attractive.

If you are working with Development Studio Client Version 5.0, then continue here. If you are working with Version 4.0, skip ahead to Working with Development Studio Client Version 4.0 on page 251.

Working with Development Studio Client Version 5.0

You are going to link index.html to a cascading style sheet. The style sheet used in this exercise is a sample included in the workbench. The first step, however, is to locate the index.html file and open it in Page Designer.

Opening Page Designer

Page Designer is comparable to SDA for 5250 panels or a GUI builder for GUI windows, but, as its name indicates, it helps with designing Web pages. As in SDA or CODE Designer, instead of typing source statements in an editor, Page Designer creates the source for you from your design choices. Here, the generated source consists of HTML tags instead of DDS statements.

To open Page Designer, in the Development Studio Client workbench,

- Open the WebFacing perspective.

You should now have the WebFacing project view in your workbench environment, as shown in Figure 13.1.

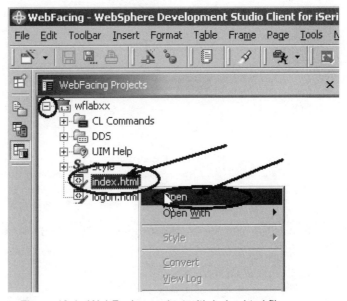

Figure 13.1: WebFacing project with index.html file

- Expand the **wflabxx** project.

- Right-click the **index.html** icon.

- Select **Open** from the pop-up menu.

Page Designer appears in the upper right pane of the workbench and displays the index.html page as the WebFacing Tool created it (Figure 13.2).

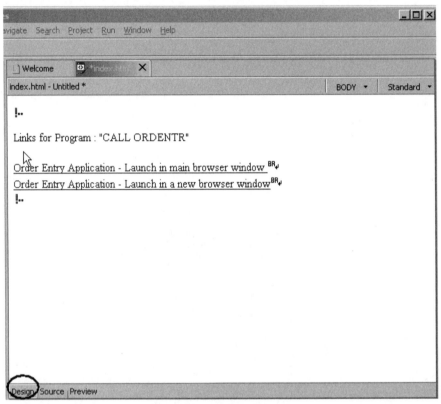

Figure 13.2: Page Designer displaying the design page

Make sure that you are on the design page in Page Designer:

■ Click the **Design** tab.

Working with Page Properties

First you need to move the links down on the page:

- Click just above the first tag, which shows as an exclamation mark (see Figure 13.3).

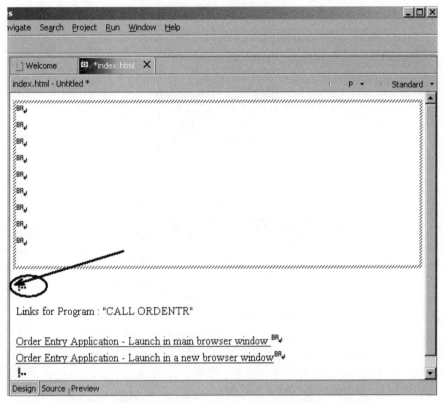

Figure 13.3: Adding some space in the upper half of the index.html page

- Press the **Enter** key a number of times, as shown in Figure 13.3.

To change the page properties,

- Right-click the background of the index.html page in Page Designer.

■ Select the **Page Properties** option from the pop-up menu, as shown in Figure 13.4.

Figure 1.4: Page Properties on pop-up menu in Page Designer

The Page Properties dialog opens, as shown in Figure 13.5.

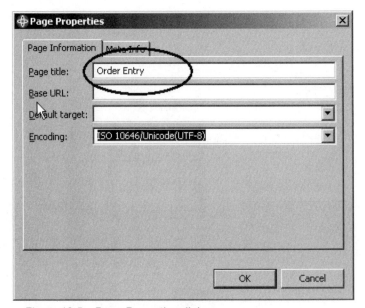

Figure 13.5: Page Properties dialog

- Change the **Page title** field to **Order Entry.**

- Click the **OK** push button on the Page Properties dialog.

When this page displays in a browser, the title in the Window title bar will be Order Entry.

Linking a cascading style sheet to the Web page

Now you will add a style to your index.html page. You can use a style employed by your company, or you can use one of the sample style sheets provided with Development Studio Client.

In the lower left pane of the workbench,

- Click the **Gallery** tab, if the Gallery view is not already active.

- Scroll to the bottom of the Gallery view, until you can see the Style Sheet icon.

- Click the **Style Sheet** icon to select it.

- Click the **Thumbnail** tab on the right bottom pane in the workbench.

You should see thumbnail icons of all the available styles, as shown in Figure 13.6.

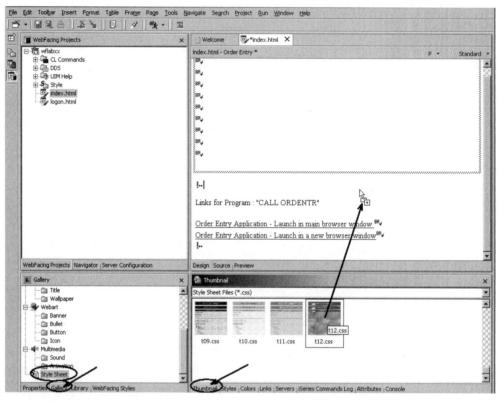

Figure 13.6: Page Designer, linking a style to the Web page

In the thumbnail view,

- Scroll to the bottom of the view until you see style sheet t12.css in the list (or select another style sheet that you like best).

- Click the thumbnail picture of **t12.css** with your left mouse button.

- Keep the left mouse button down and drag the mouse cursor to the Page Designer window. The cursor will change from the circular shape shown in the margin to the shape shown immediately below it. When the latter cursor shape appears in the Page Designer window, let go of the left mouse button.

After a short while, the style sheet properties are applied and the colors in the page change to the style sheet definitions, as shown in Figure 13.7.

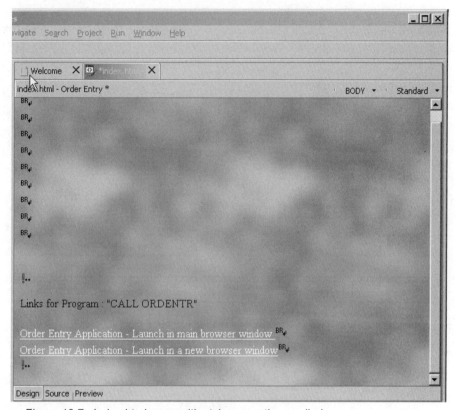

Figure 13.7: Index.html page with style properties applied

Designing and adding a logo

Now that you have specified the overall Web page look, I want you to use the WebArt Designer to create a logo for the page.

To start the WebArt Designer,

- Select the **Tools** menu option in the workbench.

■ Select **WebArt Designer** from the pull-down menu, as shown in Figure 13.8.

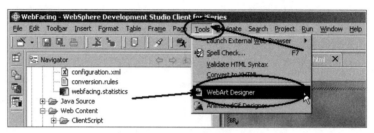

Figure 13.8: Tools menu with WebArt Designer

The WebArt Designer displays, as shown in Figure 13.9.

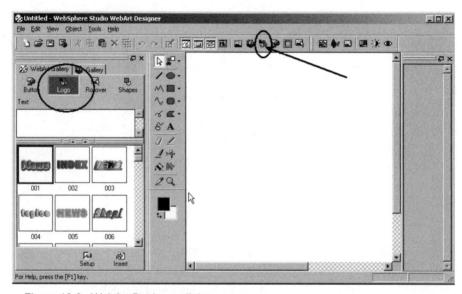

Figure 13.9: WebArt Designer dialog

The WebArt designer shows the template gallery on the left, where you will find sample logos, buttons, rollovers, images, and more. The white area in middle of the dialog is the canvas that you use to create and change objects. In this exercise, I want you to create a logo from scratch. (You can also select one from the template gallery as the basis for your own logo.)

- Click the **Create Logo** button above the canvas, as shown by the arrow in Figure 13.9, or use the **Object → Create Logo** menu option.

This invokes the Logo Wizard dialog. In this dialog, shown in Figure 13.10,

- Enter **your company name** along with **wflabxx** in the Text entry field.

- Select **Font name** Comic Sans MS.

- Select **Font size** 46.

■ Select the **Center** radio button in the Alignment group box.

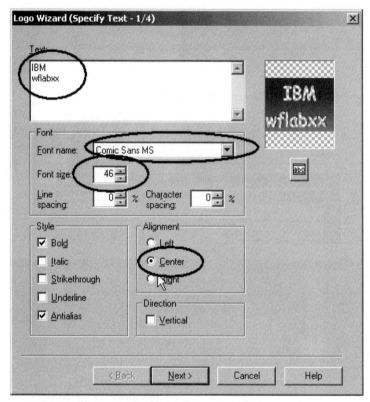

Figure 13.10: Logo Wizard *dialog*

Note the creation of a sample logo in the upper right corner.

■ Click the **Next** push button to go to the next page of the wizard.

The Select Color page displays, as shown in Figure 13.11.

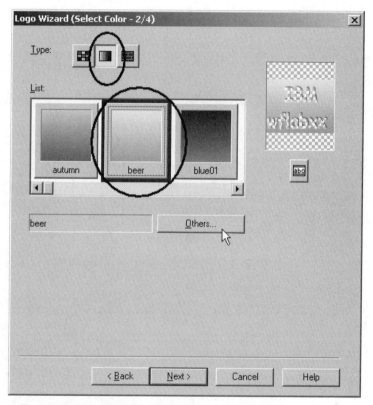

Figure 13.11: Logo Wizard with Select Color *page*

- Click the **gradation Type** push button (the middle of the three Type push buttons).

Note: The other push buttons select color types solid and textured.

- Select **beer** from the colors available, or any color you like best. You can scroll through the list to find a gradation you like.

Note: You can create your own color gradation by pressing the **Others** push button on this dialog.

■ Press the **Next** push button to go to the next page.

The Select Outline page appears as shown in Figure 13.12.

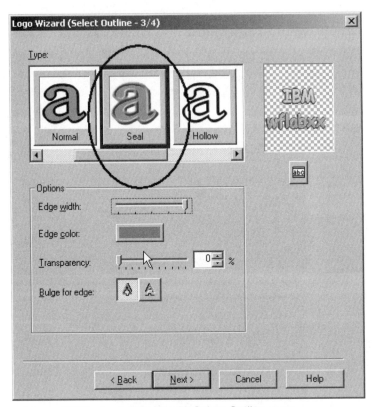

Figure 13.12: Logo Wizard with Select Outline *page*

■ Select the **Seal** outline from the list, or any outline you like best.

■ Press the **Next** push button.

The Select Text Effect page of the Logo Wizard displays, as shown in Figure 13.13.

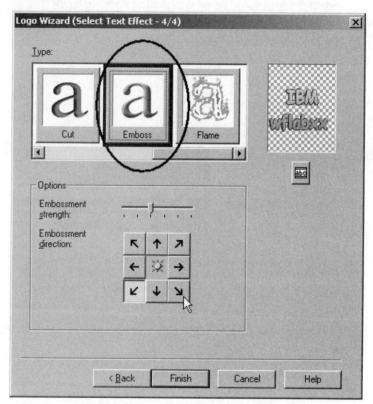

Figure 13.13: Logo Wizard with Select Text *Effect page*

- Select the **Emboss** text effect, or one that you like best.

- Click the **Finish** push button.

You will return to the WebArt Designer window, as shown in Figure 13.14.

Figure 13.14: WebArt Designer with new logo object

Resize the logo object on the canvas:

■ Click the logo object to select it.

■ Move the cursor to the rectangle at the right bottom corner of the canvas. (Watch the cursor change shape.)

■ Drag the rectangle up and to the left so the object becomes smaller, as shown in Figure 13.14.

Now you need to save this object. First, you need to save it as a WebArt object so that you can work with it later in WebArt Designer. Afterward, you will save it in another format for use with your Web page.

■ Select the **File** option on the WebArt Designer menu bar.

- Select **Save Object** from the pull-down menu.

The Save Object dialog appears, as shown in Figure 13.15.

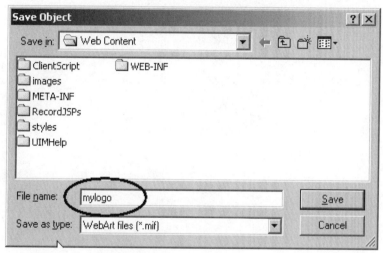

Figure 13.15: WebArt Designer save dialog

- Enter **mylogo** in the **File name** entry field.

- Click the **Save** push button.

Now you need to save the object in a format that can be displayed on a Web page.

- Select the **File** menu option from the WebArt Designer menu bar again.

- Select option **Save wizard for web** from the pull-down menu.

The Save Wizard dialog displays, as shown in Figure 13.16.

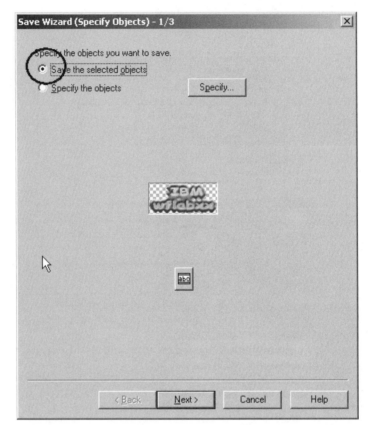

Figure 13.16: Save Wizard with Specify Objects *page*

- Select the **Save the selected object** radio button.

- Click the **Next** push button.

The Select File Format page (Figure 13.17) displays.

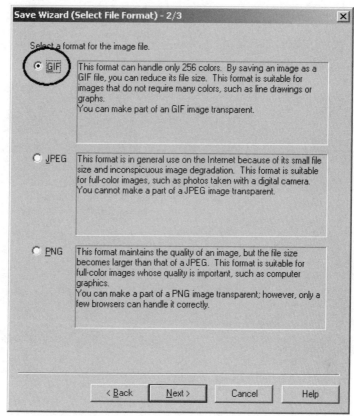

Figure 13.17: Save Wizard with Select File Format *page*

■ Select the **GIF** radio button.

■ Click the **Next** push button.

On the GIF Format page that appears (Figure 13.18),

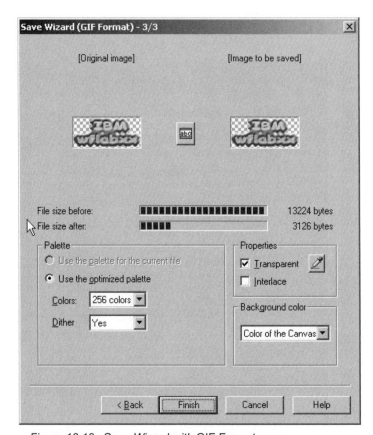

Figure 13.18: Save Wizard with GIF Format page

■ Click the **Finish** push button.

On the Save As dialog that displays (Figure 13.19),

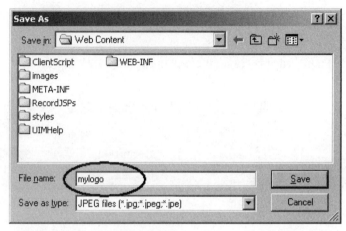

Figure 13.19: Save As dialog

■ Your WebFacing project is located in the workbench workspace, so you need to specify where the workspace is located on your workstation. Make sure the dialog points to the Web Content directory. If you used the default workspace location, the file structure will be the same structure as shown in Figure 13.20:

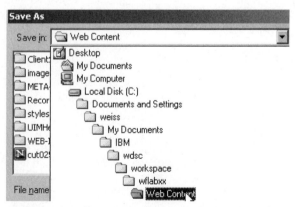

Figure 13.20: Directory structure showing default workspace location

- Enter **mylogo** in the **File name** entry field.

- Click the **Save** push button.

If a message box like the one in Figure 13.21 displays,

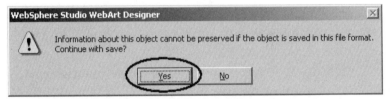

Figure 13.21: Message dialog when saving object as GIF file format

- Click the **Yes** push button.

If the GIF Attribute Settings dialog looks like Figure 13.22,

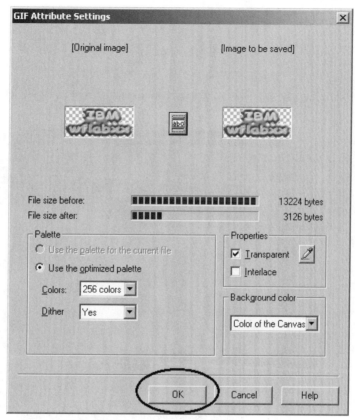

Figure 13.22: GIF Attribute Settings *dialog*

■ Click the **OK** push button.

Close WebArt Designer:

■ Select the **File** option from the menu bar.

■ Select the **Exit** option from the pull-down menu.

You return to the WebFacing perspective, displaying the WebFacing Projects view.

Switch to the Navigator view and find your logo:

■ Click the **Navigator** tab.

- Expand the **wflabxx** project.

- Expand the **Web Content** folder.

The mylogo.gif file appears in the list as shown in Figure 13.23.

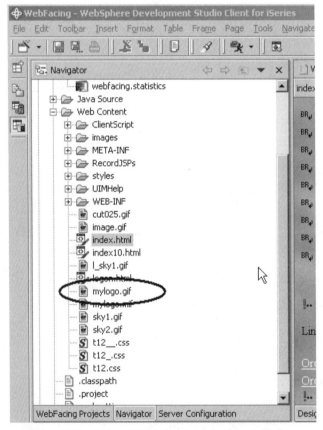

Figure 13.23: View of Web Content directory with mylogo.gif.

If it does not appear, you might need to refresh the list:

- Right-click the **Web Content** folder.

- Select the **Refresh** option from the pop-up menu.

Hopefully the file now appears in the Web Content folder. If it does not, go to Windows Explorer and search for mylogo.gif on your hard drive, then move it to the Web Content folder in the Development Studio Client workspace. If you did not use the default location, as shown in Figure 13.20, do a search for the workspace and the wflabxx directory. Move the mylogo.gif file into the Web Content subdirectory under the wflabxx directory.

Drag the logo to your Web page, which is still open in Page Designer. (If Page Designer is closed, double-click index.html to open the tool.)

In the Navigator view,

- Select the **mylogo.gif** file.

- Keep the left mouse button pressed.

- Drag the file to the upper left corner in the Page Designer window.

- Let the mouse button go.

You have just placed the logo on the design page, as shown in Figure 13.24.

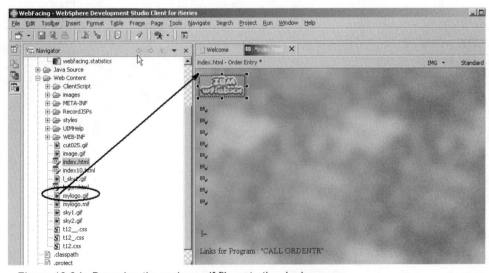

Figure 13.24: Dragging the mylogo.gif file onto the design page

Adding a Heading 1 tag to the page

In this section, you will insert a large heading below the logo:

■ Position the cursor just below the logo at the first BR tag.

■ Select **Insert** from the workbench menu bar.

■ Select **Paragraph** from the pop-up menu.

■ Select **Heading 1** from the submenu, as shown in Figure 13.25.

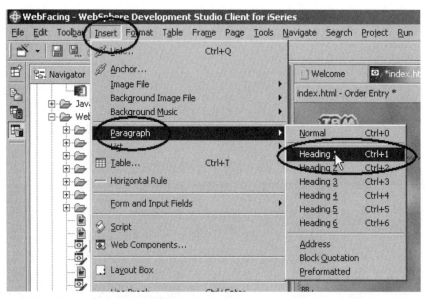

Figure 13.25: Selecting to insert a Heading 1 tag

A frame appears where you can enter text:

- Enter **your company name Order Entry Application**, as shown in Figure 13.26.

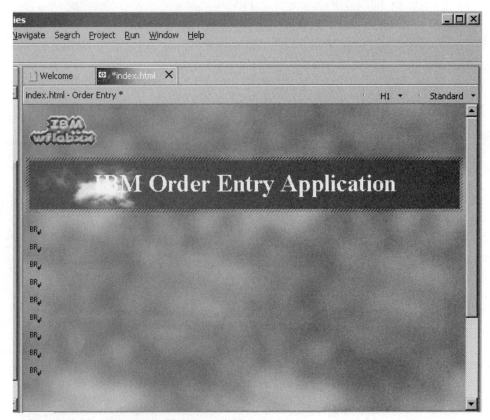

Figure 13.26: Web page with logo and title

Now you will insert one of the sample pictures included with Development Studio Client.

Adding a picture to the page

At the bottom left of the workbench,

- Select the **Gallery** tab.

- Expand the **Image** folder.

■ Select the **Illustration** folder.

On the dialog pane beside the Gallery view,

■ Select one of the sample illustrations in Figure 13.27; in this example I use cut025.gif.

■ Drag the picture onto the design window below the heading.

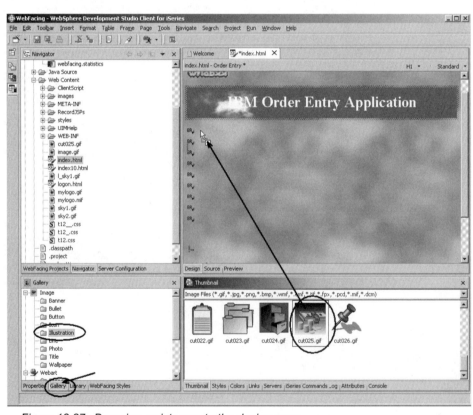

Figure 13.27: Dragging a picture onto the design page

The design window now contains a picture, as shown in Figure 13.28.

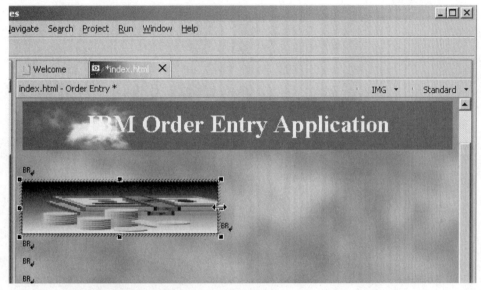

Figure 13.28: Design window with picture added

You are almost finished. You just need to add some moving text to the page.

Adding moving text to the page

- Position the cursor in the design window underneath the picture.

- Select **Insert** from the workbench menu bar.

- Select **Paragraph** from the pull-down menu.

- Select **Heading 3** from the submenu.

Your design window will look similar to Figure 13.29.

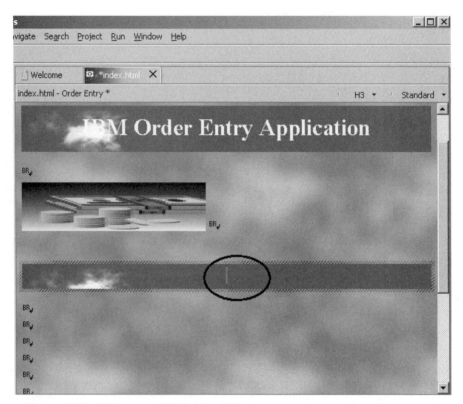

Figure 13.29: Web page with Heading 3 frame

Leave the cursor positioned inside the Heading 3 frame.

- Select **Insert** from the workbench menu bar.

- Select **Others** from the pull-down menu.

■ Select **Marquee** from the submenu, as shown in Figure 13.30.

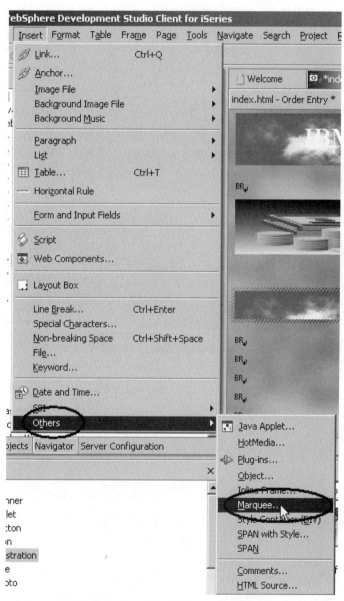

Figure 13.30: Selection of the Marquee *option*

The Insert Marquee dialog displays as shown in Figure 13.31.

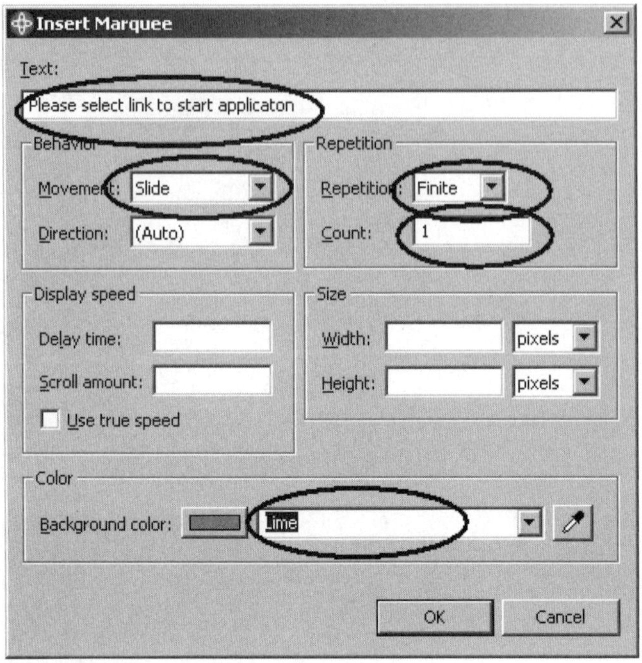

Figure 13.31: Insert Marquee *dialog*

- Enter the following in the Text entry field: **Please select link to start application**.

- Select **Slide** in the Movement combination box.

- Select **Finite** in the Repetition combination box.

- Select **1** in the Count combination box.

Those two last selections just specify that the text is not to slide indefinitely. If you think your user would prefer some more movement on the page, feel free to change these settings.

- Select **Lime** in the Background color combination box.

- Click the **OK** push button.

The design page should look like Figure 13.32.

Figure 13.32: Design page with Header 3 text

To save some space, remove some of the line break tags:

- Position the cursor on the **BR** tag.

■ Press the **Delete** key until the links appear on your page as shown in Figure 13.33.

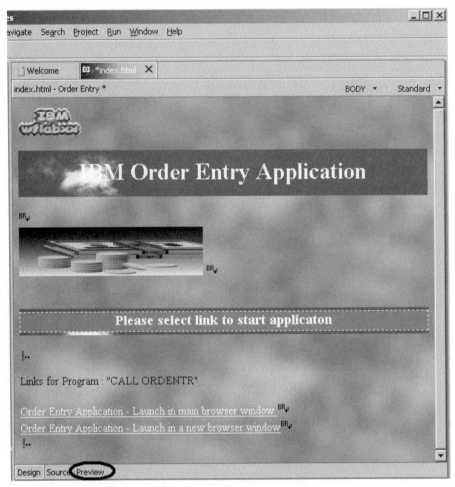

Figure 13.33: Page Designer design page with completed page

To see the page as it would appear in a browser,

■ Click the **Preview** tab at the bottom of the design page.

You will notice that your Heading 3 text is sliding (see Figure 13.34).

Figure 13.34: Web page shown in browser, with text moving

Changing the text color in Page Designer

You might notice that the text color and the background interfere with each other a little bit. One easy way of changing this is to apply another color to certain areas of the text. To complete that task, go back to the design page:

■ Click the **Design** tab.

■ Select the text (IBM in Figure 13.35) you want to change by swiping the area with the mouse cursor.

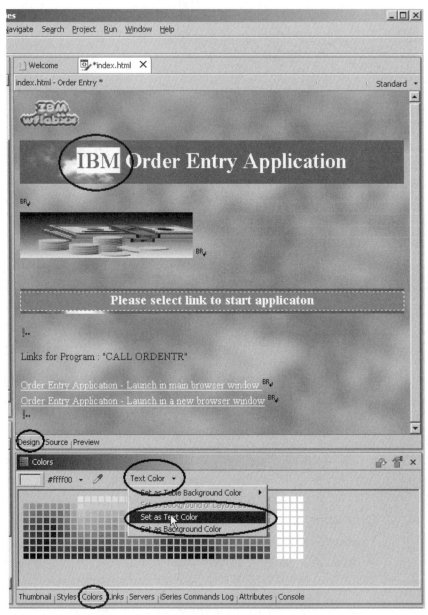

Figure 13.35: Selecting color choice for selected text area

On the bottom dialog underneath the Page Designer window,

- Select the **Colors** tab.

- Select a color with your mouse cursor.

- Select the **Text Color** option from the Colors dialog.

- Select the **Set as Text Color** option from the pull-down menu.

Except for a bit of clean-up, you are finished; now the selected text will display with the color you chose.

Cleaning up the page

One more thing you need to do is remove the default text added by the WebFacing Tool, as shown in Figure 13.36.

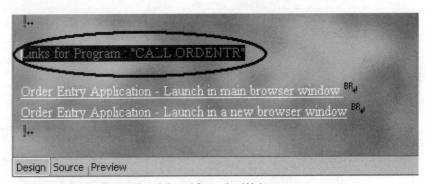

Figure 13.36: Text to be deleted from the Web page

- Select the text.

- Press the **Delete** key.

- Select the **Preview** tab to view your completed page; it should look like Figure 13.37.

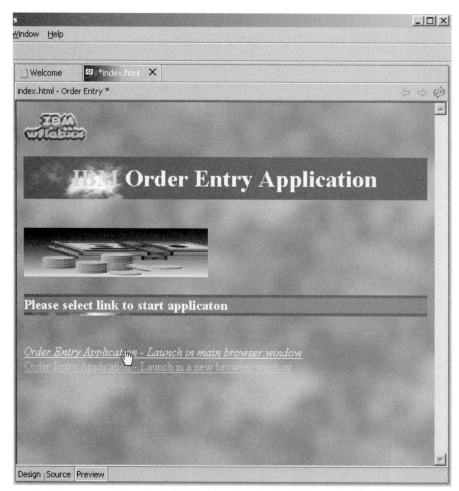

Figure 13.37: Completed Web page in Preview window

- Save the index.html file.

- Exit Page Designer.

In the Navigator view or WebFacing Projects view,

- Right-click your **wflabxx** project.

- Select **Run on Server** from the pop-up menu.

Your newly designed index.html page will open, and you can run your application.

Move forward to Analysis (page 288). (In the next section I describe the same scenario, except as it applies to the Version 4.0 user interface.)

Working with Development Studio Client Version 4.0

You are going to link index.html to a cascading style sheet. The style sheet used in this application is a sample included in the workbench. You will change the heading of the page, add your own logo, and then add some moving text. The first step, however, is to locate the index.html file and open it in Page Designer.

You need to open the Web perspective to find the right dialogs for the task. You then need to copy and paste the index.html file that you work with. This is necessary because Page Designer will remove one line of source from the file (because it assumes that the line is incorrect). Unfortunately, WebFacing needs this line, so after you finish with Page Designer, you will copy this line from your backup copy and add it to the updated index.html. If you do not do this, the links on this page will not work anymore.

After making the backup copy, you are ready to use the index.html file with Page Designer.

Switching to the Navigator view

In the Development Studio Client workbench, open the Web perspective:

- Select the **Perspective** option on the workbench menu.

- Select the **Open** option on the pull-down menu.

■ Select the **Other** option from the submenu, as shown in Figure 13.38.

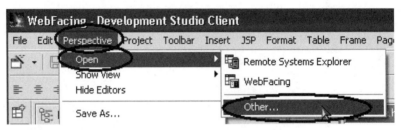

Figure 13.38: Opening the Web perspective

On the Select Perspective dialog, as shown in Figure 13.39,

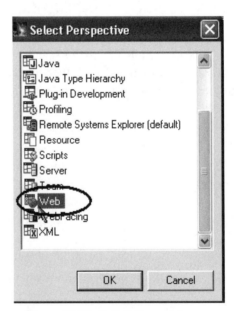

Figure 13.39: Select Perspective dialog

■ Select **Web** from the list of available perspectives.

■ Click the **OK** push button.

You should now have the Web perspective open in your workbench with the Navigator view open. You will use this view to locate and then work with the index.html file.

- Expand the **wflabxx** project.

- Expand the **webApplication** folder.

- Locate the index.html file in this folder.

As mentioned before, you are making a backup copy of this file:

- Right-click the **index.html** icon.

- Select **Copy** from the pop-up menu, as shown in Figure 13.40.

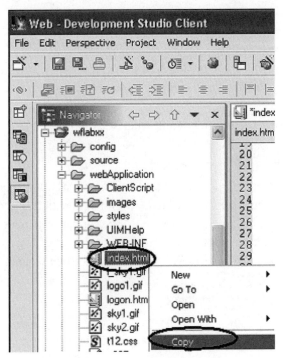

Figure 13.40: Selecting the Copy *action*

The Folder Selection dialog displays (Figure 13.41).

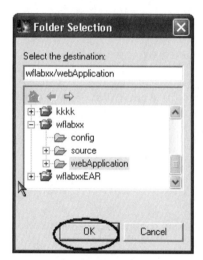

Figure 13.41: Folder Selection dialog

■ Click the **OK** button on the **Folder Selection** dialog.

A file with the name Copy of index.html will be created. You will use this file later to copy a line and add it to the original file.

The next step is to examine the index.html page and change it using Page Designer.

Starting Page Designer

Page Designer is comparable to SDA for 5250 panels or GUI windows for GUI pages, but, as its name indicates, it helps with designing Web pages. As in SDA or CODE Designer, you need not type source statements in an editor, because Page Designer creates the source for you from your design choices. Here, the generated source consists of HTML tags instead of DDS statements.

To open Page Designer,

■ Double-click the **index.html** file.

Page Designer opens on the right side of the workbench.

This is where you can enhance the Web page. You are ready to use Page Designer. You will notice three tabs at the bottom of the Page Designer work area (see Figure 13.42). These tabs allow you to switch between different views.

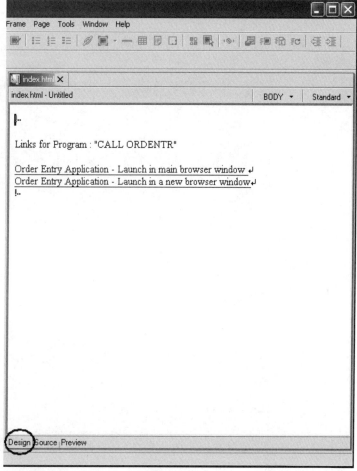

Figure 13.42: Page Designer with three tabs, one of them the Design tab

These views are

- The normal Design view

- An HTML Source editor view

- A Preview view, which shows the page in its current state in a browser window

Make sure you are on the design page by

- Clicking the **Design** tab, as shown in Figure 13.43.

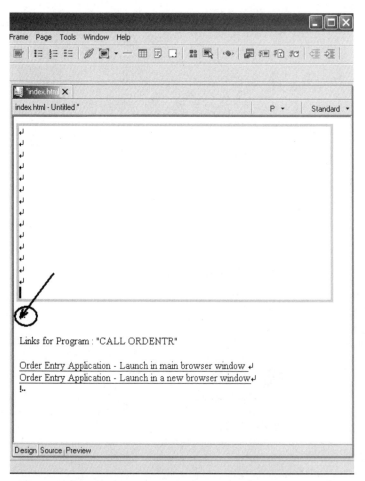

Figure 13.43: Adding blank space to the Web page

Working with Page Properties

- Move the labels down by clicking before the first tag, which displays as an exclamation mark.

- Press the **Return** key a number of times.

- Right-click the background of the design work area.

- Select **Page Properties** from the pop-up menu.

The Attributes dialog (Figure 13.44) opens.

- Change the text in the Page title field to **Order Entry**.

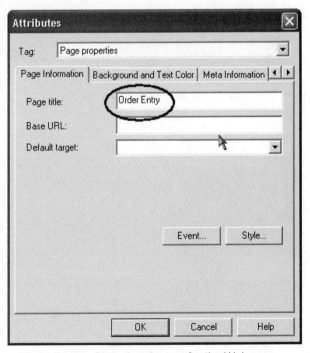

Figure 13.44: Changing the text for the Web page

- Click the **OK** push button to close the Attributes dialog box.

The page now has a title. Now you will give this page more color, by adding a background and specifying attribute definitions for text and links. This is accomplished by linking this page to a style sheet.

Linking a cascading style sheet to the Web page

Now you will add a style sheet to the Web page. You can use a style sheet employed by your company or you can use one of the sample style sheets provided with Development Studio Client.

In the lower right pane in the workbench,

- Click the **Thumbnail** tab.

At the left bottom pane in the workbench,

- Click the **Gallery** tab.

- Scroll to the bottom of the Gallery view until you can see the Style Sheet icon.

- Click the **Style Sheet** icon to select it.

You should see thumbnail icons of all the styles available as shown in Figure 13.45.

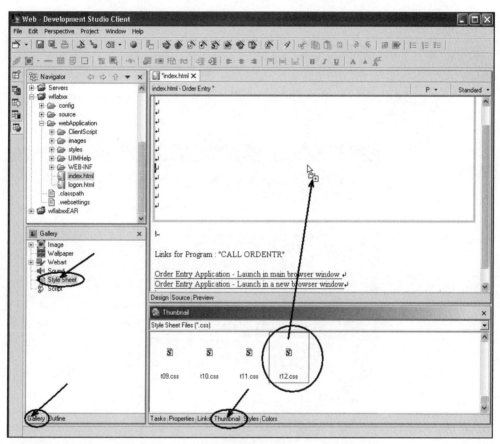

Figure 13.45: Linking a style to the Web page

In the thumbnail view,

- Scroll to the bottom of the view until you see style sheet t12.css in the list (or select another style sheet that you like best).

- Click the thumbnail picture of **t12.css** with your left mouse button.

- Keep the left mouse button down and drag the mouse cursor to the Page Designer window. The cursor will change from the circular shape shown in the margin to the shape shown immediately below it. When the latter cursor shape appears in the Page Designer window, let go of the left mouse button.

After a short while, the style sheet properties are applied and the colors in the page change to the style sheet definitions, as shown in Figure 13.46.

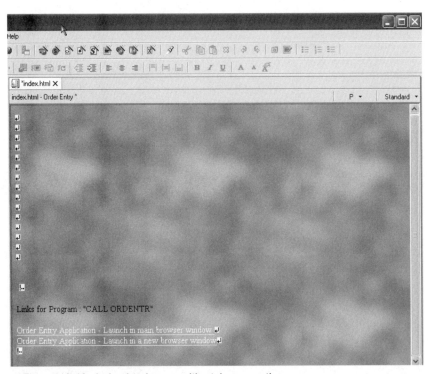

Figure 13.46: index.html page with style properties

Adding a logo to the page using the Logo Wizard

Now you will add a Logo using the Logo Wizard, provided with Development Studio Client.

- Click the first line break tag in the upper left corner of the design page, to position the cursor at the target location for the logo.

- Select **Insert → Logo** from the workbench main menu bar (Figure 13.47).

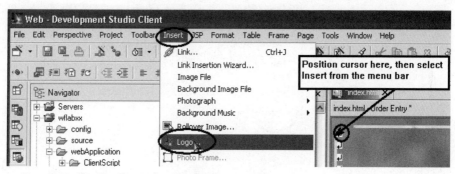

Figure 13.47: Starting Logo Wizard from Insert menu

The Create Logo dialog opens.

In the Text field on top of the wizard page,

- Type **your company name** (in my sample, IBM), as shown in Figure 13.48.

- Type **wflabxx**.

- Click the **Text Attributes** push button on the Create Logo page.

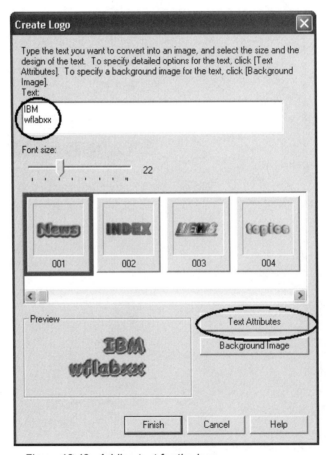

Figure 13.48: Adding text for the logo

The first of four text attribute pages appears (Figure 13.49).

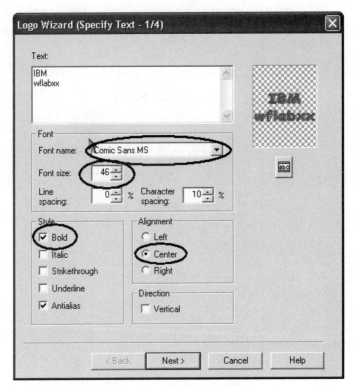

Figure 13.49: Logo Wizard Specify Text page

- Select **Comic Sans MS** in the Font name combination box.

- Select **46** in the Font size combination box.

- Select the **Bold** check box.

- Select the **Center** radio button.

- Click the **Next** push button.

The Select Color page displays (Figure 13.50).

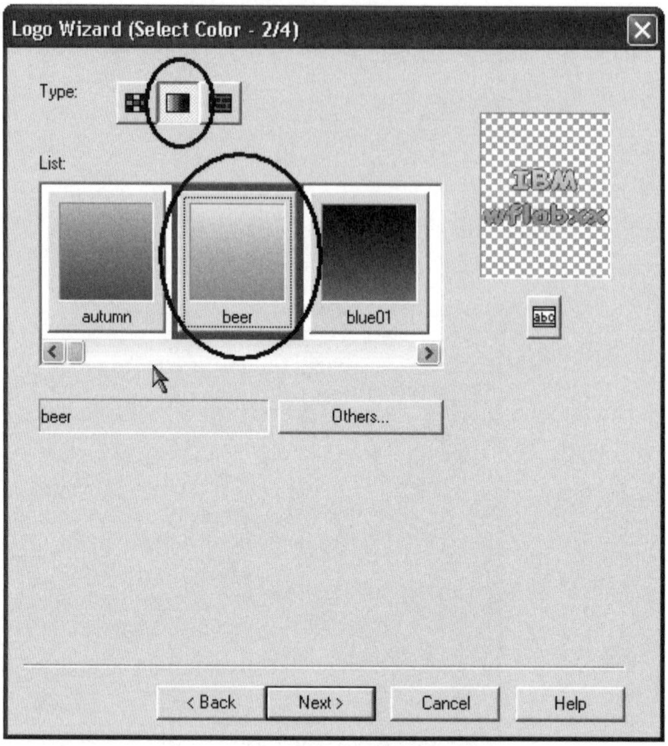

Figure 13.50: Logo Wizard Select Color page

- For Type select **gradation** by clicking its push button (the middle of the three Type push buttons).

- Click the color **beer** push button. (Maybe I am influenced by my German background, but I think beer is a really nice color combination. The liquid stuff is not bad either.)

- Click the **Next** push button.

The Select Outline page appears, as shown in Figure 13.51:

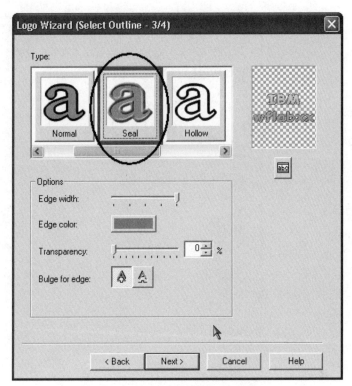

Figure 13.51: Logo Wizard Select Outline *page*

■ Click the **Seal** push button from the Type list.

■ Click the **Next** push button.

The Select Text Effect page appears, as shown in Figure 13.52.

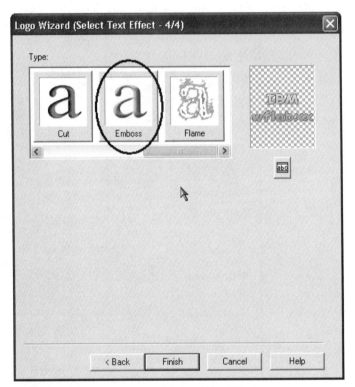

Figure 13.52: Logo Wizard Select Text Effect page

- Click the **Emboss Type** push button.

- Click the **Finish** push button.

You are back in the Create Logo page. If you like, you might want to select an attractive background for your logo by using the **Background Image** push button. I will let you discover this feature on your own.

On the Create Logo page,

- Click the **Finish** push button (Figure 13.53).

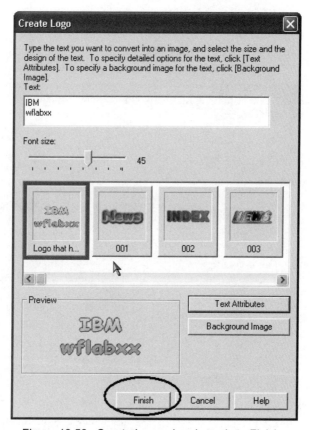

Figure 13.53: Create Logo wizard, ready to Finish

Back in Page Designer, the logo will appear. It will be a bit big, so I want you to resize it:

- Click the logo.

- Locate the little square on its right bottom corner.

- Move the cursor on top of it so that the cursor changes shape to two arrows.

- Click the rectangle.

- Drag the rectangle toward the upper left corner to shrink it.

Figure 13.54 gives you an indication of how small it should be, but it does not matter if it is not exactly the way I sized it in the picture. As long as you like your logo and its size, you are doing just fine.

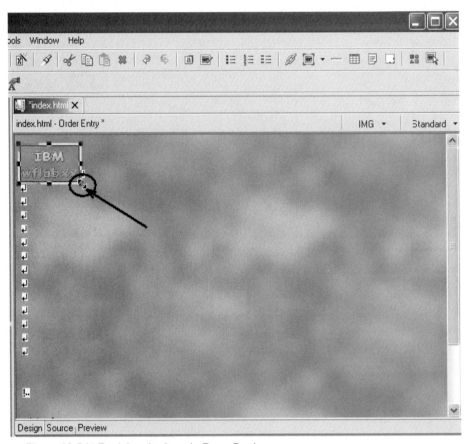

Figure 13.54: Resizing the logo in Page Designer

You are finished with the logo design, but some more work needs to be done.

Adding a Heading 1 tag to the page

Now I want you to insert an attractive heading below the logo:

- Position the cursor just below the logo at the first line break tag as shown in Figure 13.55.

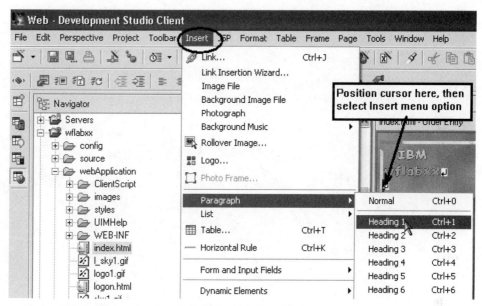

Figure 13.55: Menu structure to insert a Heading 1 tag

- Select **Insert** from the workbench menu bar.

- Select **Paragraph** from the pop-up menu

- Select **Heading 1** from the submenu.

A frame appears where you can enter text:

■ Enter **your company name Order Entry Application**, as shown in
Figure 13.56.

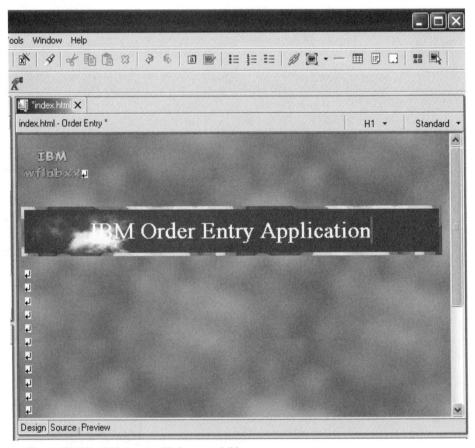

Figure 13.56: Web page with logo and title

Now I want you to further enhance this page by inserting one of the sample pictures
that come with Development Studio Client.

Adding a picture to the page

In the workbench underneath the Navigator view,

■ Select the **Gallery** tab.

■ Expand the **Image** folder.

■ Select the **Illustration** folder.

On the dialog pane beside the Gallery view,

■ Click the **Thumbnail** tab to show the selection of illustrations available.

■ Select one of the sample illustrations, as shown in Figure 13.57. (I use file u005cut.gif.)

■ Drag that picture onto the design window to a position below the heading.

Figure 13.57: Dragging a picture onto the design page

The design window now contains a picture, as shown in Figure 13.58.

Figure 13.58: Design window with picture added

You might want to resize the picture to fill more of the page.

You are almost finished. You just need to add some moving text to the page.

Adding moving text to the page

■ Position the cursor in the design window underneath the picture.

■ Select **Insert** from the workbench menu bar.

■ Select **Paragraph** from the pull-down menu.

■ Select **Heading 3** from the submenu.

A Heading 3 frame is created on the design page, as shown in Figure 13.59.

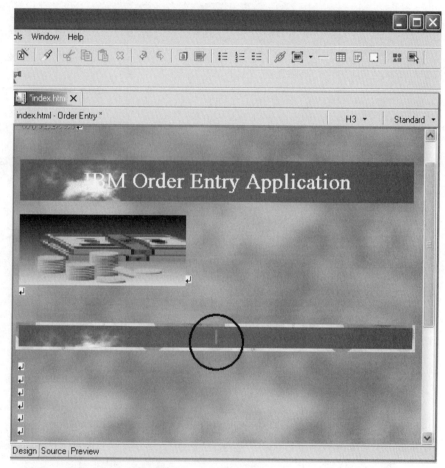

Figure 13.59: Web page with Heading 3 frame

Leave the cursor positioned inside the Heading 3 frame.

■ Select **Insert** from the workbench menu bar.

■ Select **Others** from the pull-down menu.

■ Select **Marquee** from the submenu, as shown in Figure 13.60.

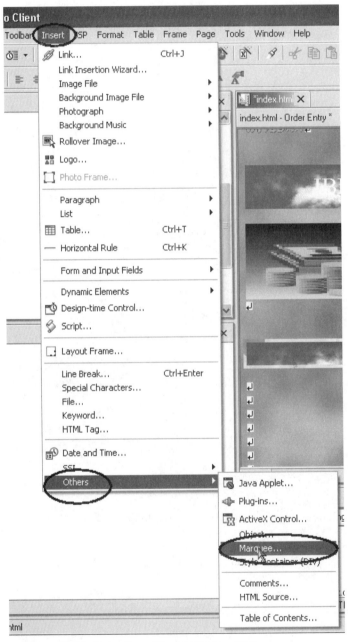

Figure 13.60: Selection of the Marquee *option*

The Attributes dialog displays, as shown in Figure 13.61.

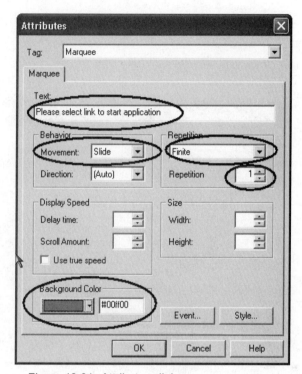

Figure 13.61: Attributes *dialog*

- Enter the following in the Text entry field: **Please select link to start application**.

- Select **Slide** in the Movement combination box.

- Select **Finite** in the Repetition combination box.

- Select **1** in the Repetition combination box.

Those two last selections just specify that the text is not to slide indefinitely. If you think your user would prefer some more movement on the page, feel free to change these settings.

■ Select a green color in the Background Color combination box.

■ Click the **OK** push button.

The design page should look like Figure 13.62.

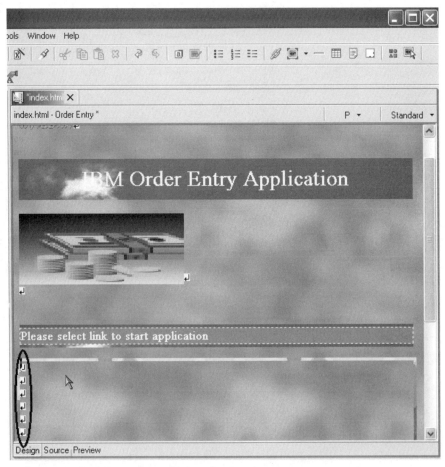

Figure 13.62: Design page with Header 3 text

To save some space, remove some of the line break tags:

- Position the cursor on the **line break tags**, as shown in Figure 13.25.

- Press the **Delete** key until the links appear on your page as shown in Figure 13.63.

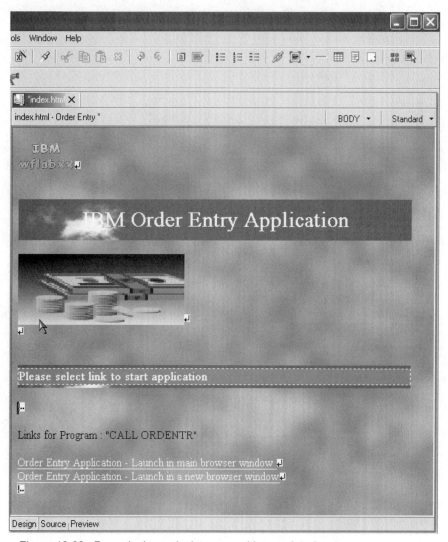

Figure 13.63: Page designer design page with completed page

To see the page as it would appear in a browser,

- Click the **Preview** tab at the bottom of the design page.

You will notice that your Heading 3 text is sliding (see Figure 13.64).

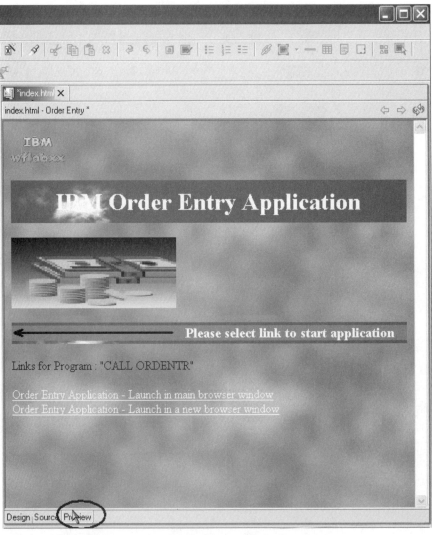

Figure 13.64: Web page shown in browser, with text moving

Changing the text color in Page Designer

You might notice that the text color in the Heading 1 area and the background color interfere a little bit with each other. One easy way to change this problem is to apply another color to certain areas of the text. To complete that task, go back to the design page:

- Click the **Design** tab.

- Select the text (*IBM* in Figure 13.65) you want to change by swiping the area with the mouse cursor.

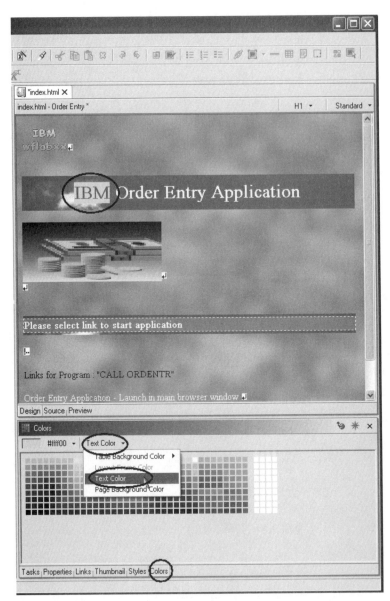

Figure 13.65: Selecting color for selected text area

On the bottom dialog underneath the Page Designer window,

- Select the **Colors** tab.

- Select a color with your mouse cursor from the color palette.

- Select the **Text Color** option from the Colors dialog menu bar.

- Select the **Text Color** option from the pull-down menu.

Except for a bit of clean-up, you are finished; now the selected text displays with the color you selected.

Cleaning up the page

One more thing you need to do is remove the default text added by the WebFacing Tool, as shown in Figure 13.66.

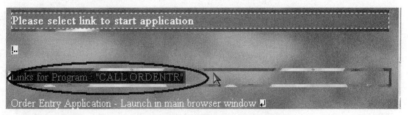

Figure 13.66: Text to be deleted from Web page

- Select the text.

- Press the **Delete** key.

■ Select the **Preview** tab to view your completed page; it should look like Figure 13.67.

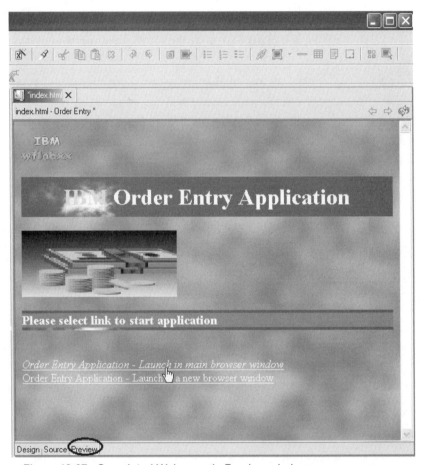

Figure 13.67: Completed Web page in Preview window

■ Save the index.html file.

You are almost ready to run the application again. As I mentioned in the beginning of this section, Page Designer deletes one line from the HTML source, which it assumes is incorrect, even though it is actually needed on the page. Version 5.0 of Page Designer fixed this problem, but I will show you how to fix it for Version 4.0.

In the Navigator view, you need to open Page Designer with the backup copy of the index.html file:

■ Double-click the **Copy of index.html** file (Figure 13.68).

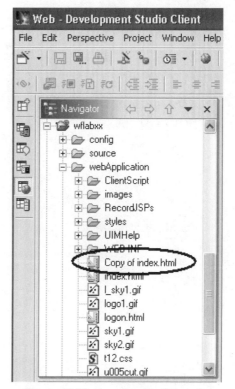

Figure 13.68: Loading file Copy of index.html

Another Page Designer session opens for the Copy of index.html file. In this new Page Designer session,

■ Click the **Source** tab.

In the source editor, as shown in Figure 13.69,

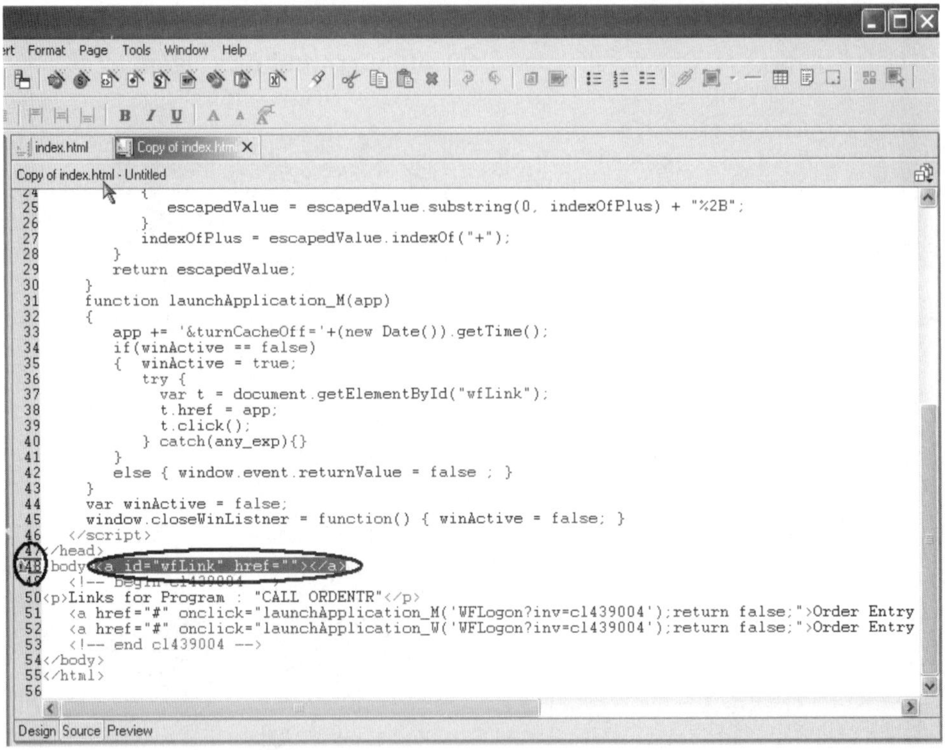

Figure 13.69: Editor with source of Copy of index.html

- Scroll down to near the bottom.

Around line 47 you will see a line with a warning icon:

- Select the **<a id=?wfLink? href=? ?> </a>** string, beside the body tag, as shown in Figure 13.32.

- Right-click the selected text.

- Select **Copy** from the pop-up menu.

Page Designer should still be open with the index.html file. If not, you need to open it:

■ Click the **Page Designer window bar** of the open index.html file, to give it focus.

■ Click the **Source** tab, to switch to the source editor window.

In the source editor window of the index.html file,

■ Locate the line with the <body> tag.

■ Position the cursor behind the <body> tag, as indicated by the arrow in Figure 13.33.

■ Add a blank character behind the <body> tag.

■ Right-click after the added blank character.

■ Select **Paste** from the pop-up menu.

The string from the Copy of index.html file is now inside the index.html file, as shown in Figure 13.70.

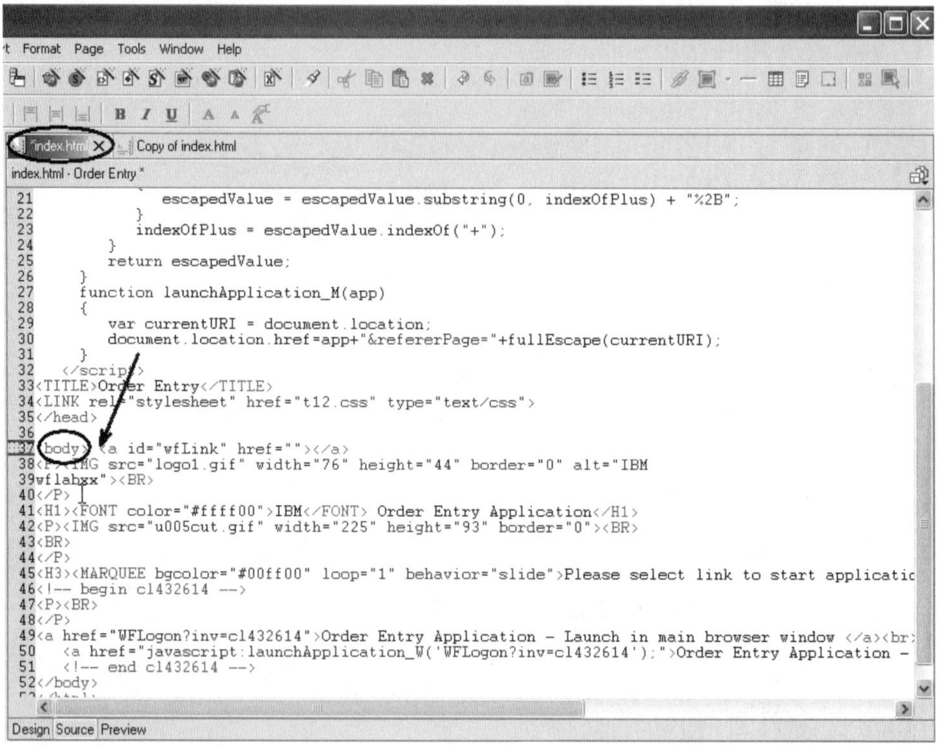

Figure 13.70: Page Designer with index.html file and copied string

■ Close the Copy of index.html file in Page Designer.

■ Save the index.html file.

■ Close the index.html file in Page Designer.

Switch to the WebFacing perspective:

■ Click its icon on the side toolbar of the workbench, as shown in Figure 13.71

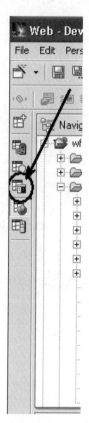

Figure 13.71: Workbench side toolbar with open perspectives

In the Navigator view or WebFacing Projects view,

■ Right-click the **wflabxx** project.

■ Select **Run on Server** from the pop-up menu.

Your newly designed index.html page displays, and you can run your application.

Analysis

You have completed the exercise Enhancing index.html Using Web Tools. You learned how to design a Web page using Page Designer in Development Studio Client. Here is what you did:

- You created a heading.

You added an image.

- You created and modified a logo.

- You added a marquee to the Web page.

After this sidestep into Web tools, you now return to WebFacing. The next two exercises cover tracing and debugging.

You are ready to move on to the next exercise: Tracing the WebFacing Run Time.

Tracing the WebFacing run time

When running your WebFaced application, you may at times want to know more about what is occurring in your WebFacing environment. You can perform certain actions called tracing and debugging, to learn more about how your application is running. These features, however, are somewhat hidden, so this exercise and the next will show you how they work.

The goal of the exercise

The goal of this exercise is to make you aware of tracing capabilities in the WebFacing run time. You will set the tracing levels to a higher value than the default and switch from a lean nontrace run time to one in which tracing is enabled.

At the end of this exercise, you should be able to

- Locate the Tracing Read Me file

- Locate the WebFacing run time that allows tracing

- Rename the WebFacing run times to enable tracing

- Set the tracing flags to a higher level so that the WebFacing run time gives you useful tracing information

- Locate the trace log file

Scenario

You are running the WebFaced application, but at times the application behaves differently than it does in the 5250 environment. You want to investigate what is causing this behavior. The default WebFacing run time was compiled without tracing enabled in order to improve performance. To allow tracing, you need to switch to a different run time, which is also part of the WebFacing Tool. You also need to raise the tracing level from the low default value.

After you perform these changes and restart the application server, you can run the WebFaced application again and the tracing data will be stored in a log. You will be able to read through this log and try to understand what is causing the different behavior of the WebFaced application, or you can discuss the log output with an IBM representative to determine the cause of the problem.

Tracing a WebFaced application

As discussed before, you want to investigate the reasons why your WebFaced application behaves differently than the 5250 application.

Locating the tracing files

- Start Development Studio Client and go to the WebFacing perspective.

Before you start this exercise, make sure the application server in the test environment is stopped.

To stop the server,

- Click the **Server** tab in the note book at the bottom right workbench pane.

If the application server is in Started status,

- Right click the application server entry.

- Select the **Stop** option from the pop-up menu, as shown in Figure 14.1.

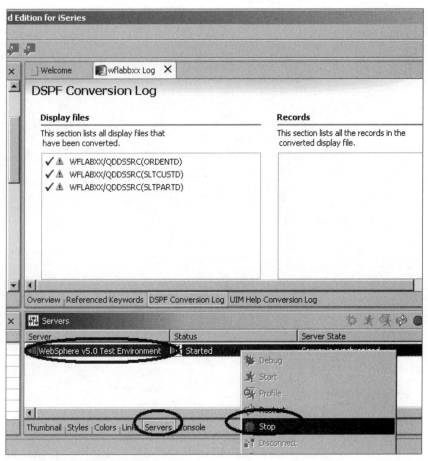

Figure 14.1: Stopping the server

Now use the Navigator view in the left upper pane of the workbench. If the Navigator view is not visible,

- Click the **Navigator** tab at the bottom of the WebFacing Projects view.

- Expand the **wflabxx** project.

- Expand folder **Web Content**.

- Expand folder **WEB-INF**.

■ Expand folder **lib**, as shown in Figure 14.2.

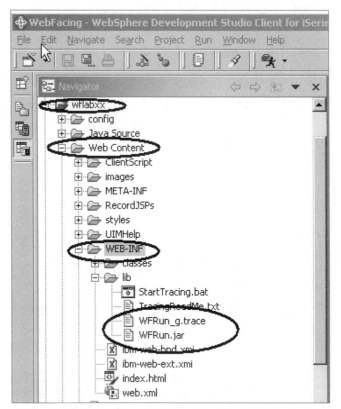

Figure 14.2: Location of WFRun files shown in Navigator view

In the lib folder, you will find the WFRun.jar file. This is the WebFacing run time used to support your WebFaced user interface. There is also a WFRun_g.trace file. This is the same WebFacing run time but compiled with tracing enabled.

You need to disable the current run time by renaming it so that it becomes a dummy file, and then rename the tracing run time to WFRun.jar.

Tip: A file called TracingReadMe.txt is also inside this folder. I strongly suggest that you read through this file to find more in-depth information about tracing in the WebFacing environment.

- Right-click the **WFRun.jar** file icon.

- Select **Rename** from the pop-up menu.

- The cursor will be at the file name; rename the file **WFRun.jat**.

- Press the **Enter** key.

If you receive a message dialog as shown in Figure 14.3,

- Click the **Yes** push button.

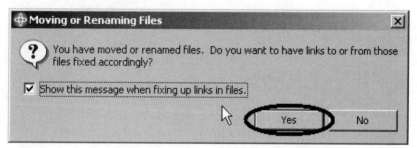

Figure 14.3:   Message that appears during rename of the WFRun.jar file

After the rename operation is completed,

- Right-click the **WFRun_g.trace** file icon.

- Select **Rename** from the pop-up menu.

■ The cursor will be at the file name; rename the file **WFRun.jar**. Your screen should look like Figure 14.4.

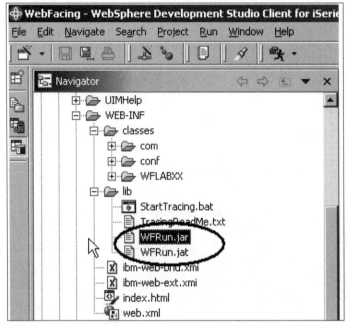

Figure 14.4: WFRun files renamed

If the rename was successful,

■ Go to Changing Trace Flags (page 296).

If the rename does not work and an error displays,

■ Right-click **WFRun_g.trace**.

■ Select the **Rebuild Project** option from the pop-up menu.

After the rebuild is complete:

■ Right-click the **WEB-INF** folder icon.

■ Select the **Refresh** option from the pop-up menu.

Tip: If you continue to encounter problems deleting the WFRun.jar file, I suggest that you shut down Development Studio Client and restart it; this will unlock all files.

Check the list in folder lib again. Three situations might occur:

1. You might have the following three files in the list:
   - WFRun_g.trace
   - WFRun.jar
   - WFRun.jat

   This could happen if WFRun.jar was locked when you tried to edit the name.
   - Delete WFRun.jar.
   - Rename WFRun_g.trace to WFRun.jar as described in the previous section.

2. You might have the following two files:
   - WFRun_g.trace
   - WFRun.jar

   This could also happen because of locked files. Begin the renaming task again. Go back up to the heading Locating the Tracing Files (page 296).

3. You may have the following two files:
   - WFRun.jar
   - WFRun.jat

   If so, you are in good shape and may proceed to the next section.

Changing trace flags

Now that you have enabled the new WebFacing run time, you need to increase the flag values that indicate the level of tracing you desire.

In the Navigator view (Figure 14.5),

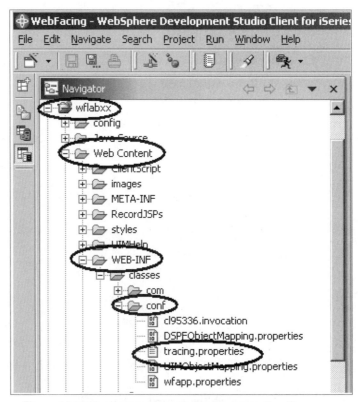

Figure 14.5: Navigator view with tracing.properties file

- Expand the **wflabxx** project icon.

- Expand the **Web Content** folder.

- Expand the **Web-INF** folder.

- Expand the **classes** folder.

- Expand the **conf** folder.

- In the **conf** folder, locate the tracing.properties file.

- Double-click **tracing.properties** to open the file in a text editor.

In the text editor, look for the lines containing the tracing flag settings. They are circled in Figure 14.6:

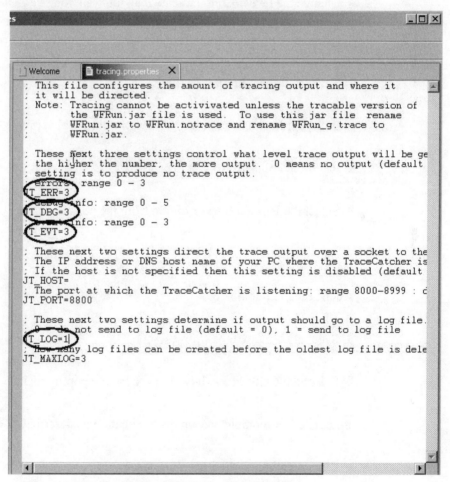

Figure 14.6: Editor window with changed tracing flags

- Change the **JT_ERR** level to **3**.

- Change the **JT_DBG** level to **3**.

- Change the **JT_EVT** level to **3**.

Find the JT_LOG flag.

- Change the **level** to **1**, to indicate that you want to use a LOG file to record the trace data. You could also feed the trace data to the DOS console. The Trace Readme file contains details about how to set up the DOS console.

- Save the tracing.properties file.

Now run the application again. In the Navigator or WebFacing Projects view,

- Right-click the **wflabxx** project.

- Select the **Run on Server** option from the pop-up menu.

If you encounter publishing errors,

- Click the **Navigator** tab.

- Right click the **wflabxx** project icon.

- Select the **Rebuild Project** option from the pop-up menu.

After the rebuild is completed, run the application as described above.

- Click on a link in the index.html page.

Because tracing is enabled, the application will run more slowly.

■ Go through a scenario to add one order:

   ◆ Select a customer.
   ◆ Select one part.
   ◆ Confirm the order.
   ◆ Exit the application.

Go to the Navigator view and look at the log file:

■ Right-click the **wflabxx** icon.

■ Select the **Refresh** option from the pop-up menu.

■ Expand the **wflabxx** project.

■ Expand the **Web Content** folder.

■ Expand the **WEB-INF** folder.

■ Expand the **trace** folder.

You should find a log file similar to the one shown in Figure 14.7.

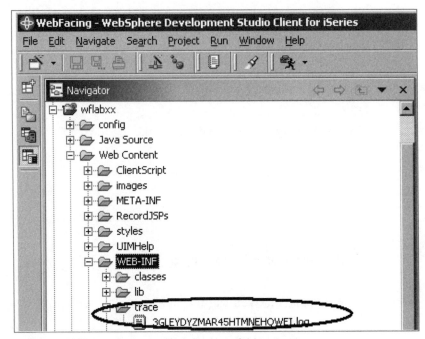

Figure 14.7: Log file in the Web Projects folder structure

To view the log file,

■ Double-click the **.log** file in the trace folder.

This opens an editor window with the content of the .log file. As you can see in Figure 14.8, there are many details captured in the log at this tracing level. For example, you can see the values the entry fields contain as they are passed to the program.

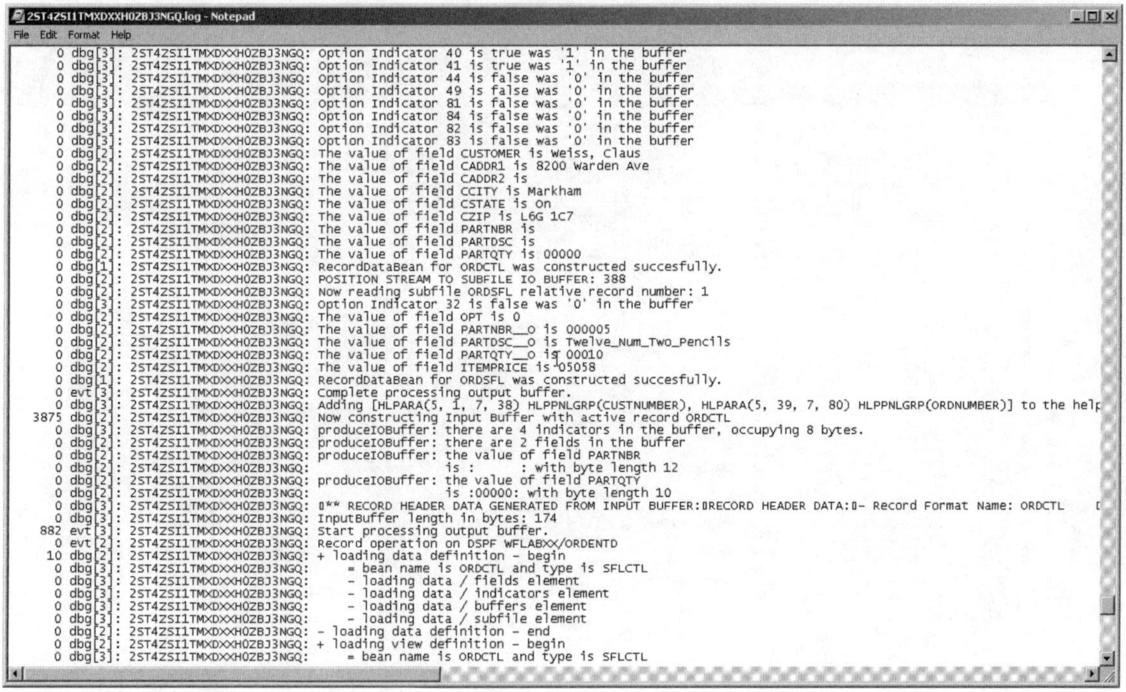


```
   0 dbg[3]: 2ST4ZSI1TMXDXXH0ZBJ3NGQ: Option Indicator 40 is true was '1' in the buffer
   0 dbg[3]: 2ST4ZSI1TMXDXXH0ZBJ3NGQ: Option Indicator 41 is true was '1' in the buffer
   0 dbg[3]: 2ST4ZSI1TMXDXXH0ZBJ3NGQ: Option Indicator 44 is false was '0' in the buffer
   0 dbg[3]: 2ST4ZSI1TMXDXXH0ZBJ3NGQ: Option Indicator 49 is false was '0' in the buffer
   0 dbg[3]: 2ST4ZSI1TMXDXXH0ZBJ3NGQ: Option Indicator 81 is false was '0' in the buffer
   0 dbg[3]: 2ST4ZSI1TMXDXXH0ZBJ3NGQ: Option Indicator 84 is false was '0' in the buffer
   0 dbg[3]: 2ST4ZSI1TMXDXXH0ZBJ3NGQ: Option Indicator 82 is false was '0' in the buffer
   0 dbg[3]: 2ST4ZSI1TMXDXXH0ZBJ3NGQ: Option Indicator 83 is false was '0' in the buffer
   0 dbg[2]: 2ST4ZSI1TMXDXXH0ZBJ3NGQ: The value of field CUSTOMER is Weiss, Claus
   0 dbg[2]: 2ST4ZSI1TMXDXXH0ZBJ3NGQ: The value of field CADDR1 is 8200 Warden Ave
   0 dbg[2]: 2ST4ZSI1TMXDXXH0ZBJ3NGQ: The value of field CADDR2 is
   0 dbg[2]: 2ST4ZSI1TMXDXXH0ZBJ3NGQ: The value of field CCITY is Markham
   0 dbg[2]: 2ST4ZSI1TMXDXXH0ZBJ3NGQ: The value of field CSTATE is On
   0 dbg[2]: 2ST4ZSI1TMXDXXH0ZBJ3NGQ: The value of field CZIP is L6G 1C7
   0 dbg[2]: 2ST4ZSI1TMXDXXH0ZBJ3NGQ: The value of field PARTNBR is
   0 dbg[2]: 2ST4ZSI1TMXDXXH0ZBJ3NGQ: The value of field PARTDSC is
   0 dbg[2]: 2ST4ZSI1TMXDXXH0ZBJ3NGQ: The value of field PARTQTY is 00000
   0 dbg[1]: 2ST4ZSI1TMXDXXH0ZBJ3NGQ: RecordDataBean for ORDCTL was constructed succesfully.
   0 dbg[2]: 2ST4ZSI1TMXDXXH0ZBJ3NGQ: POSITION STREAM TO SUBFILE IO BUFFER: 388
   0 dbg[2]: 2ST4ZSI1TMXDXXH0ZBJ3NGQ: Now reading subfile ORDSFL relative record number: 1
   0 dbg[3]: 2ST4ZSI1TMXDXXH0ZBJ3NGQ: Option Indicator 32 is false was '0' in the buffer
   0 dbg[2]: 2ST4ZSI1TMXDXXH0ZBJ3NGQ: The value of field OPT is 0
   0 dbg[2]: 2ST4ZSI1TMXDXXH0ZBJ3NGQ: The value of field PARTNBR__O is 000005
   0 dbg[2]: 2ST4ZSI1TMXDXXH0ZBJ3NGQ: The value of field PARTDSC__O is Twelve_Num_Two_Pencils
   0 dbg[2]: 2ST4ZSI1TMXDXXH0ZBJ3NGQ: The value of field PARTQTY__O is 00010
   0 dbg[2]: 2ST4ZSI1TMXDXXH0ZBJ3NGQ: The value of field ITEMPRICE is 05058
   0 dbg[1]: 2ST4ZSI1TMXDXXH0ZBJ3NGQ: RecordDataBean for ORDSFL was constructed succesfully.
   0 evt[3]: 2ST4ZSI1TMXDXXH0ZBJ3NGQ: Complete processing output buffer.
   0 dbg[3]: 2ST4ZSI1TMXDXXH0ZBJ3NGQ: Adding [HLPARA(5, 1, 7, 38) HLPPNLGRP(CUSTNUMBER), HLPARA(5, 39, 7, 80) HLPPNLGRP(ORDNUMBER)] to the help
3875 dbg[2]: 2ST4ZSI1TMXDXXH0ZBJ3NGQ: Now constructing Input Buffer with active record ORDCTL
   0 dbg[3]: 2ST4ZSI1TMXDXXH0ZBJ3NGQ: produceIOBuffer: there are 4 indicators in the buffer, occupying 8 bytes.
   0 dbg[2]: 2ST4ZSI1TMXDXXH0ZBJ3NGQ: produceIOBuffer: there are 2 fields in the buffer
   0 dbg[2]: 2ST4ZSI1TMXDXXH0ZBJ3NGQ: produceIOBuffer: the value of field PARTNBR
   0 dbg[2]: 2ST4ZSI1TMXDXXH0ZBJ3NGQ:                  is :         : with byte length 12
   0 dbg[2]: 2ST4ZSI1TMXDXXH0ZBJ3NGQ: produceIOBuffer: the value of field PARTQTY
   0 dbg[2]: 2ST4ZSI1TMXDXXH0ZBJ3NGQ:                  is :00000: with byte length 10
   0 dbg[3]: 2ST4ZSI1TMXDXXH0ZBJ3NGQ: ▯** RECORD HEADER DATA GENERATED FROM INPUT BUFFER:▯RECORD HEADER DATA:▯- Record Format Name: ORDCTL    ▯
   0 dbg[3]: 2ST4ZSI1TMXDXXH0ZBJ3NGQ: InputBuffer length in bytes: 174
 882 evt[3]: 2ST4ZSI1TMXDXXH0ZBJ3NGQ: Start processing output buffer.
   0 evt[2]: 2ST4ZSI1TMXDXXH0ZBJ3NGQ: Record operation on DSPF WFLABXX/ORDENTD
  10 dbg[2]: 2ST4ZSI1TMXDXXH0ZBJ3NGQ: + loading data definition - begin
   0 dbg[3]: 2ST4ZSI1TMXDXXH0ZBJ3NGQ:     = bean name is ORDCTL and type is SFLCTL
   0 dbg[3]: 2ST4ZSI1TMXDXXH0ZBJ3NGQ:     - loading data / fields element
   0 dbg[3]: 2ST4ZSI1TMXDXXH0ZBJ3NGQ:     - loading data / indicators element
   0 dbg[3]: 2ST4ZSI1TMXDXXH0ZBJ3NGQ:     - loading data / buffers element
   0 dbg[3]: 2ST4ZSI1TMXDXXH0ZBJ3NGQ:     - loading data / subfile element
   0 dbg[2]: 2ST4ZSI1TMXDXXH0ZBJ3NGQ: - loading data definition - end
   0 dbg[2]: 2ST4ZSI1TMXDXXH0ZBJ3NGQ: + loading view definition - begin
   0 dbg[3]: 2ST4ZSI1TMXDXXH0ZBJ3NGQ:     = bean name is ORDCTL and type is SFLCTL
```

Figure 14.8: .log file in editor window

You might have noticed that the WAS console also displays the following level of detail. You do not need to access the log file; you could just look at the console output and work with that information, shown in Figure 14.9.

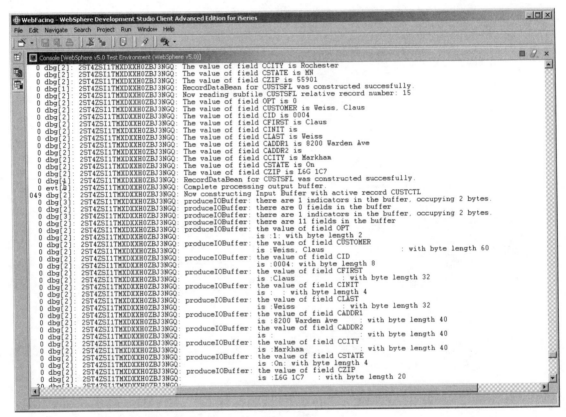

Figure 14.9: WAS console with detailed trace information

During normal operations, the tracing run time does not need to be enabled, but if problems occur in your environment or in the WebFacing run time, the trace information can give valuable feedback to determine the source of the problem.

Switching back to the default run time

Now that you know how to set up tracing capabilities in the WebFacing Tool, you can go back and work with the regular WebFacing run time.

First, stop the application server as described near the beginning of this chapter.

Then in the Navigator view,

- Expand the **wflabxx** project.

- Expand the **Web Content** folder

- Expand the **WEB-INF** folder

- Expand the **lib** folder.

- Rename the **WFRun.jar** file back to **WFRun_g.tracing**.

- Rename the **WFRun.jat** file back to **WFRun.jar**.

If you receive error messages during the renaming of these files,

- Right click any file in the project.

- Select the **Rebuild Project** option from the pop-up menu.

- Try the rename again.

After successfully renaming these two files,

- Expand the **classes** folder and then the **conf** folder.

- Edit the **tracing.properties** files.

- Change all tracing settings back to **0**.

- Save the file.

Your WebFacing project will return to nontracing mode.

Analysis

You have completed the exercise Tracing the WebFacing Run Time. Here is what you did:

- You located the WebFacing run time .jar file in the Web Projects folder structure.

- You renamed the file to disable it and then put a trace-enabled run time in its place.

- You changed the tracing properties file to indicate a higher tracing level.

- You ran the application and checked the run-time log file.

- You re-enabled the nontracing run time.

You are ready to move on to the next exercise, Debugging the Server Program.

Debugging the server program

In theory, the server program that operates your WebFaced user interface should provide the results you expect. However, you might need to debug this program to investigate how it runs the application and why the WebFacing run-time environment does not exactly mimic 5250 behavior and results. In doing so, you will discover what values are returned from the workstation file, which indicators are on or off, and which path in your program is executed.

You could use a green-screen debugger to debug the program in the server job, but the Development Studio Client workbench comes with a built-in debugger more suited to your workstation environment.

The Version 5.0 and Version 4.0 debuggers for Development Studio Client are quite different, so I have split this exercise into two parts for the two versions. The Version 5.0 debugger is easier to use because it is fully integrated into the Eclipse workbench. Version 4.0 users, however, do not worry. The debugger you will use works as well; it just needs to be launched as a separate tool.

I also added a section on how to use Service Entry Points for Development Studio Client Version 5.0.1 users, who are connected to an iSeries server with OS/400 V5R2.

The goal of this exercise

The goal of this exercise is to set up the debugging environment for server jobs on the iSeries host. This knowledge will help you for programs invoked not only by the WebFacing environment, but by any environment on an iSeries server.

At the end of the exercise, you should be able to

- Locate and identify the job started by the WebFacing environment

- Start the debugger

- Point the debugger to the program you want to debug

- Start the debug server on the iSeries host (for Version 4.0 users)

- Set breakpoints in the program source

- Monitor variables in your program

- Step through your program statements

- Step into called programs

- Step over called programs

Scenario

Imagine that when testing your modernized application, you decide you want to change how the server program drives your user interface. Suddenly, you discover that the program does not work the way you want.

You need to know what is happening in your program, but you do not know how to find this information. Debugging might be the magic word for a programmer, but you do not know how to tell the debugger that you want to examine the server program in a server job started by the WebFacing environment. This is difficult because the program is not interactive, and you cannot start it from the debugger or from a command line. The job where the program runs is created on the fly, as a server job on your iSeries host. You need a way to point the debugger to the program in a certain job.

In this exercise, you use the debugger to examine the server program, but you will also start to understand how you can use this debugger for your other interactive and batch programs as well. If you have already used the built-in integrated iSeries debugger, this should be very familiar for you. However, the instructions on how to locate the job where your WebFaced application runs will be new.

Setting up the integrated debugger with service entry points

If you are using Development Studio Client Version 5.0 and OS/400 V5R2, you can use Service Entry Points to debug the WebFaced RPG program. If you are using an earlier version of OS/400 or Development Studio Client Version 4.0, skip to the next topic: Your WebFaced Application's Job Environment. The only difference between these two ways of setting up the debug environment is that the Service Entry Point automatically starts the debugger in any job for a given program and user ID, whereas the manual way of starting the debugger is to point to a program in a certain job.

With a Service Entry Point, you are setting up the debugger to identify a breakpoint in a specific program. This will cause the debugger to take control if the program reaches this breakpoint, allowing you to debug from that point on. You also have to specify a user profile as part of the Service Entry Point setup, so that the debugger is invoked only if the program is started by this user. The Service Entry Point has the advantage that you can set up a breakpoint for a debug session before you actually start the program and have the job information where the program runs. This is a very useful feature in a non-interactive program environment where jobs are created on the fly as requests come in.

To run the integrated iSeries debugger in Development Studio Client Version 5.0, make sure that you have the latest PTFs for OS/400 V5R2. Check the WDSc Web site. As I am writing this section, the following PTFs are required for the ingrated iSeries debugger to work:

- MF30131 5722999

- SI07641 5722SS1

- SI07934 5722SS1

- SI08512 5722SS1

- SI08017 5722SS1

- SI08015 5722SS1

- SI08017 5722SS1

You will also need the Development Studio Client with fix pack 5.0.1 applied to run the integrated debugger.

Setting a service entry point

In order to set a Service Entry Point, you need the debugger started and you need to have the source of the program that you want to debug accessible in the source view of the debug perspective. Here I want you to start the debugger for the ORDENTR program. The easiest way to do this is to switch to the Remote System Explorer (RSE) perspective and use it to start the debug session.

If the RSE perspective is still open in the background,

- Click the **RSE** icon on the sidebar of the workbench (Figure 15.1).

Figure 15.1: RSE icon on sidebar

Otherwise,

- Click the **Open perspective** icon.

- Select **Remote System Explorer** from the pop-up menu as shown in Figure 15.2.

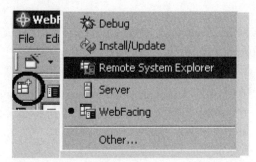

Figure 15.2: Select perspective icon with menu

In the RSE perspective,

- Expand your **iSeries** connection. This is the same iSeries connection you used to run the WebFaced application.

- Expand the **iSeries Objects** node.

- Expand the **Library list** node.

If you are not currently connected, this will connect you to the iSeries. Since you want to debug an interactive program to set the Service Entry Point, you need to start a 5250 emulation and sign on to the iSeries server.

On the command line in the emulation session, use the Start Remote System Explorer Server (STRRSESVR) command as shown in Figure 15.3.

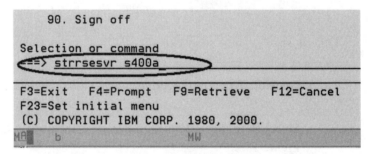

```
    90. Sign off

Selection or command
 ==> strrsesvr s400a

F3=Exit   F4=Prompt   F9=Retrieve   F12=Cancel
F23=Set initial menu
(C) COPYRIGHT IBM CORP. 1980, 2000.
MA  b                    MW
```

Figure 15.3: Command to start an interactive RSE session

- Key in *STRRSESRV CONNECTION*, where *CONNECTION* is the name of the connection you are using in the RSE.

Your 5250 session will be busy and display a message that the RSE communications server is running; just leave it that way and go back to the RSE perspective in the workbench.

Now you can start the ORDENTR program for debugging.

In the library list (Figure 15.4),

- Expand the **wflabxx** node.

- Locate the **ORDENTR** program.

To start the debug session,

- Right-click the **ORDENTR** program in the tree view.

- Select **Debug As** from the pop-up menu.

- Select **Interactive** from the submenu.

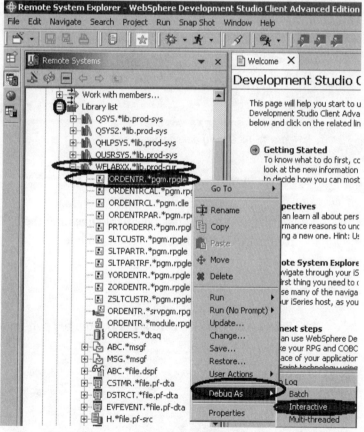

Figure 15.4: RSE perspective with pop-up menus for debugging

The debug perspective displays with the source view in the middle left area of the workbench. Figure 15.5 shows the source view only.

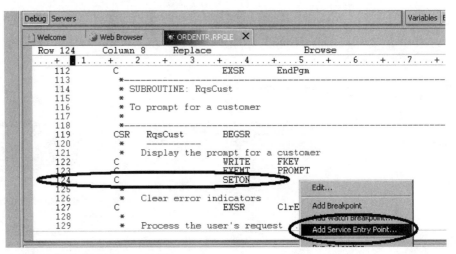

Figure 15.5: Debug perspective

In this source view,

- Scroll down to the first executable line after the EXFMT operation for record format PROMPT in the program, on line 124.

- Right-click this line.

- Select **Add Service Entry Point** from the pop-up menu.

The Add Service Entry Point dialog appears as shown in Figure 15.6.

Figure 15.6: Add Service Entry Point dialog

The required information is already filled in. You have a chance to change the user ID if the current one is not the one you use to invoke the WebFaced application.

■ Click the **OK** push button.

Now this Service Entry Point is registered, and when the user invokes this program, the debugger will be started and the program will be stopped at the Service Entry Point.

Run your application:

■ Open the WebFacing perspective, if it is not open already.

■ Right-click your **wflabxx** project.

■ Select **Run on Server** from the pop-up menu.

The index.html file displays in the browser.

■ Select the link that starts your WebFaced application.

■ Press **command key 4** to prompt for the customer selection list.

Now the execution in this program is at line 124 and the debugger takes control. The debug perspective has focus; the source view for program ORDENTR is shown, and the program is stopped at the Service Entry Point. What you saved yourself by using the Service Entry Point is the need to start the ORDENTR program up front to identify a job before being able to start a normal debug session. Service Entry Points will make your life a lot easier when debugging any of your regular batch programs; they are very useful not only for WebFaced applications.

For instructions on debugging your program you can now skip to the heading Working with the Debug Perspective (page 320). The debugging is the same whether you use Service Entry Points or a regular startup of a debug session; only the invocation steps are different. You will notice in the screen shot under that heading that the normal debug session stops in the actual beginning of the program, whereas your program stopped at the Service Entry Point.

Your WebFaced application's job environment

To debug your server program without using Service Entry Points, you need to tell the debugger the whereabouts of the iSeries job in which the program is running. To create the job, you first need to start your WebFaced application. The fact that Web-Facing job names start with QQF will help you pinpoint the correct job.

Starting your WebFaced application

To begin debugging the sample Order Entry application, you need to start it:

- Open the **WebFacing perspective**, if it is not open already.

- Right-click your **wflabxx** project.

- Select **Run on Server** from the pop-up menu.

The index.html file displays in the browser.

- Select the link that starts your WebFaced application.

The job is created, your program starts, and the first application page displays. Now you are ready to attach the debugger to the job you just started.

Locating the job the WebFaced application is running in

To find the job that the WebFaced application is using, you need to switch to the Remote System Explorer (RSE) perspective.

Working with the Remote System Explorer to identify the job

If the RSE perspective is still open in the background,

■ Click the **RSE** icon on the sidebar of the workbench as shown in Figure 15.7.

Figure 15.7: RSE icon on sidebar

Otherwise,

■ Click the **Open perspective** icon.

■ Select **Remote System Explorer** from the pop-up menu as shown in Figure 15.8.

Figure 15.8: Select perspective icon with menu

In the RSE perspective (see Figure 15.9),

■ Expand your **iSeries connection**. This is the same iSeries connection you use to run the WebFaced application.

■ Expand the **iSeries Jobs** node.

■ Expand the **Your active jobs** node.

■ Locate the job that starts with QQF.

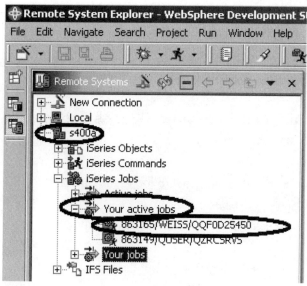

Figure 15.9: RSE perspective with iSeries jobs

Tip: If there is more than one QQF job listed under your user ID, there may be jobs still running that you did not close properly, or somebody else may be using your user ID. For example, perhaps you closed the browser without pressing F3, and the program did not end. Select the job with the highest number (this is the one that you started last), or end all your QQF jobs with the proper iSeries command, start your WebFaced application again, and refresh this job list.

As mentioned before, the debugger you use in Development Studio Client Version 5.0 is different from the one that you would use in Version 4.0. Therefore, this exercise is split into two sections for the two versions. Only complete the section that applies to the version you are using. Skip to the heading Using the Distributed Debugger in Development Studio Client Version 4.0 (page 327).

Using the integrated iSeries debugger in Development Studio Client Version 5.0

The integrated iSeries debugger has its own debug perspective. This perspective will open when the debugger is started.

Starting the integrated iSeries debugger

To start the debug session,

- Right-click the QQF job in the tree view.

- Select **Debug As** from the pop-up menu.

- Select **iSeries job** from the submenu.

A message appears as shown in Figure 15.10.

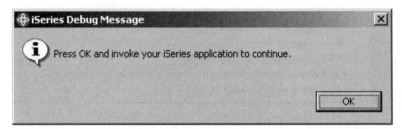

Figure 15.10: Debug message

- Press the **OK** push button in the message dialog.

The debug perspective displays, as shown in Figure 15.11.

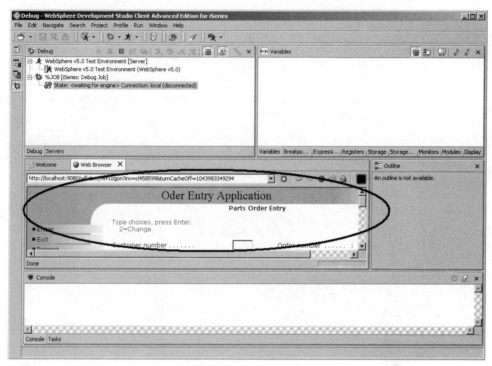

Figure 15.11: Debug perspective

To activate the debug session, use the browser window:

■ Press **command key 4** in the **Order Entry Application** page.

Working with the Debug perspective

Tip: If you had a production library instead of the wflabxx test library, you would need to enable the Update Production Files debug option. You can do this for individual debug sessions in the debug Launch Configurations dialog, or you can use the workbench Preferences option under the Window menu option. In the Preferences dialog select the Debug node and then the iSeries debug node. In the corresponding preferences page check the Update production files check box.

The debug session for the active ORDENTR program starts, and you see three different views as shown in Figure 15.12:

1. The source view, containing the program source being debugged.

2. The monitor view, with more information about the program. The active view here is the expression monitor, where you can see the content of your program variables.

3. The Call stack.

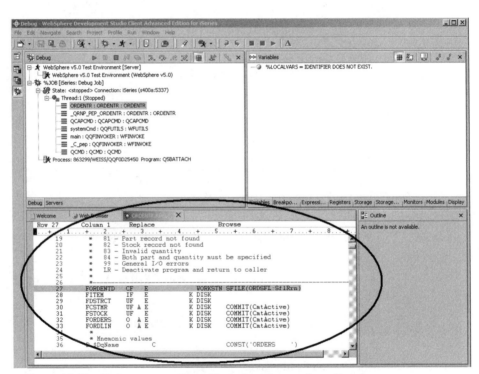

Figure 15.12: Debug perspective with source view and monitor view

To work with the program,

- Scroll down in the source view to line 130, as shown in Figure 15.13.

- Select the **line number**.

- Right-click the **line number** to set a breakpoint.

- Select the **Add Breakpoint** option from the pop-up menu.

Tip: You can also double-click in the prefix area to set a breakpoint.

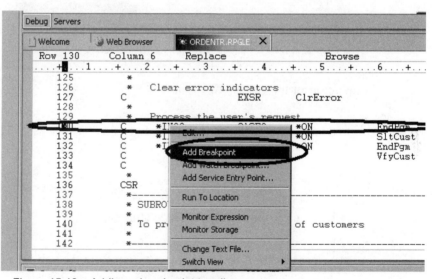

Figure 15.13: Adding a breakpoint to a line

You will notice a small blue icon on the left side of the line, indicating that a break-point is set for this line, as shown in Figure 15.14.

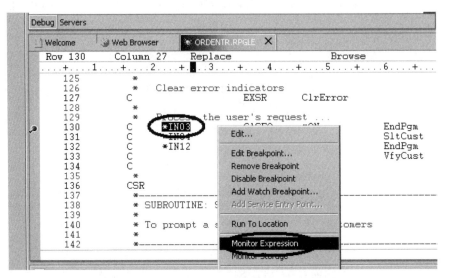

Figure 15.14: Selecting a variable to be added to the monitor

To monitor for the content of variable *IN03,

- Double-click indicator ***IN03** in line 130.

The indicator name is highlighted.

- Right-click the highlighted indicator name.

- Select the **Monitor Expression** option from the pop-up menu.

Now the variable *IN03 displays in the Monitors view, as shown in Figure 15.15.

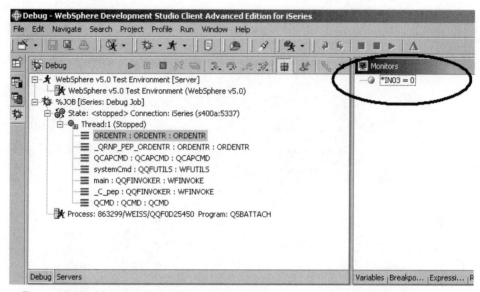

*Figure 15.15: Monitors view with variable *IN03*

Now add *IN04 to the monitor as well, following the same steps as before.

You are ready to run the application:

■ Press the **Resume** button to run your program, as shown in Figure 15.16.

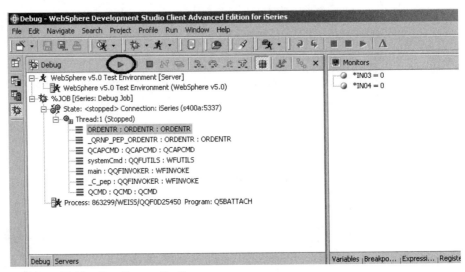

Figure 15.16: Run the application

The execution will stop on line 130, and you will see line 130 highlighted, as shown in Figure 15.17.

```
Welcome      ORDENTR.RPGLE   X    Web Browser
Row 130        Column 1      Replace              Browse
...+....1....+....2....+....3....+....4....+....5....+....6....+....7....+....8..
    125        *
    126        *     Clear error indicators
    127        C                      EXSR       ClrError
    128        *
    129        *     Process the user's request ...
    130        C         *IN03        CASEQ      *ON        EndPgm
    131        C         *IN04        CASEQ      *ON        SltCust
    132        C         *IN12        CASEQ      *ON        EndPgm
    133        C                      CAS                   VfyCust
    134        C                      ENDCS
    135        *
    136        CSR                    ENDSR
    137        *------------------------------------------------------
    138        *  SUBROUTINE: SltCust
    139        *
    140        *  To prompt a selection list of customers
    141        *
    142        *------------------------------------------------------
```

Figure 15.17: Debug window with current line highlighted

Now you can step through the program.

- Click the **Step Into** push button on the debug toolbar, as shown in Figure 15.18.

Figure 15.18: Step Into button on debug toolbar

You are on the line that conditions *IN04.

- Check the value of *IN04.

Tip: You can change the value of variables by going to the Monitors view and double-clicking the variable. This will allow you to edit the value.

- Step further through the program.

You will come to a statement that calls program SLTCUSTR.

Stepping into a called program

Now you can decide whether you want to debug the called program or just let the pro-gram run. If you are not interested in debugging the called program, you would select **Step Over** or **F6**; that would call the program without debugging it. If you need to debug the programs in the call hierarchy, you would select **Step Into**. I want to show you how to debug programs in the call hierarchy, so select **Step Into** on this statement.

You will notice that the program source for the called program, in this case SLT-CUSTR, is now loaded into the debugger source view, as shown in Figure 15.19.

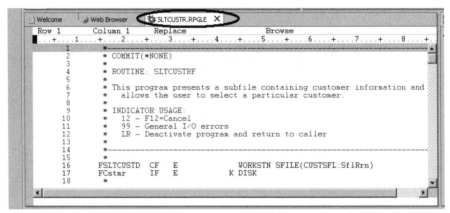

Figure 15.19: Source of program SLTCUSTR shown in debugger window

You can now step through this program and complete the following tasks:

■ Set breakpoints.

■ Monitor for variables.

Ending the debug session

I leave it up to you to work more with the debugger. When you are finished, complete the debug session:

■ Click the **Run** push button on the debugger toolbar.

■ Go back to the browser window in the workbench.

■ End your application by pressing **F3**.

■ Check the debug view for any nonterminated sessions, and use the **Terminate and Remove** option on the pop-up menu of any active debug sessions.

Close the debugger perspective:

- Right-click its icon on the workbench sidebar.

- Select **Close** from the pop-up menu.

You have completed the debugging exercise in Development Studio Client Version 5.0 and can now skip to the "Analysis" heading.

Using the Distributed Debugger in Development Studio Client Version 4.0

The Distributed Debugger is shipped with Version 4.0 of Development Studio Client, but it is not fully integrated into the Studio workbench. The debugger features are very similar to the Version 5.0 features, except the user interface is a bit different and the debugger is launched as a separate tool, outside the workbench.

Starting the IBM Distributed Debugger

To start the debug session,

- Right-click the QQF job in the tree view.

- Select the **Debug** option from the pop-up menu.

A Debugger Logon dialog opens, as shown in Figure 15.20.

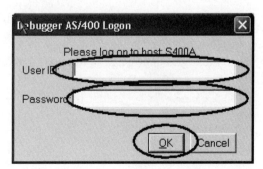

Figure 15.20: Debugger Logon dialog

- Type in your **User ID**.

- Type in your **Password**.

- Click the **OK** push button.

An error message might display, as shown in Figure 15.21.

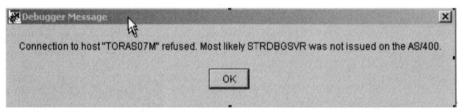

Figure 15.21: Error message that comes up if the debug server is not started

To fix the problem,

- Switch to the **Remote Systems Explorer** perspective in the workbench.

In the command window of the RSE perspective,

- Run the **Start Debug Server** command, STRDBGSVR, on your iSeries host, or go to an emulation window and run the command there. There are no parameters required for this command.

- Click the **OK** push button on the message dialog.

You will see the logon dialog again, but now it should be connected to the debug server.

The Distributed Debugger Attach dialog appears, as shown in Figure 15.22.

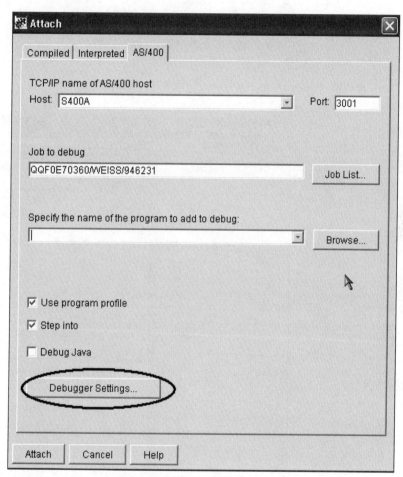

Figure 15.22: AS/400 page in Attach dialog

The input fields in the Attach dialog are already filled with the correct values. You do not need to specify a program name because the first active program in the job will be put in debug mode.

I will show how to enable the debug option Update Production Files, in case you are working with a production library instead of the wflabxx test library:

- Click the **Debugger Settings** push button.

A dialog appears as shown in Figure 15.23.

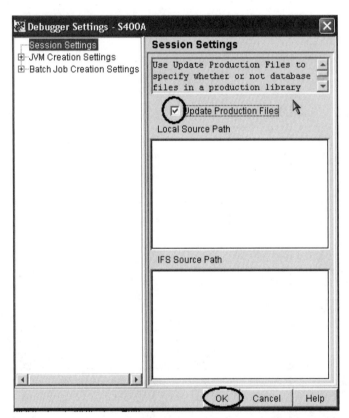

Figure 15.23: Debugger Settings *dialog to enable the Update Production Files option*

- Select the **Update Production Files** check box.

- Click the **OK** push button.

Back in the Attach dialog,

- Click the **Attach** push button.

A message box displays, telling you to start your program, as shown in Figure 15.24.

Figure 15.24: Message to start your program

Since your program is already started,

- Click the **OK** push button in the message box.

Tip: If the message box does not show up, it might be hidden. Check the task-bar for an icon showing D. Click the icon to bring the message to the foreground.

A progress bar as shown in Figure 15.25 will display.

Figure 15.25: Progress bar

Now the debugger is ready to connect to your program, but the program has to be active for the debugger to take control:

- Go back to the workbench.

The browser window with the first application page should be visible.

- Click the **browser window** to give it focus.

- Press **command key 4** to see the customer list.

The Distributed Debugger window opens with your program source loaded, as shown in Figure 15.26.

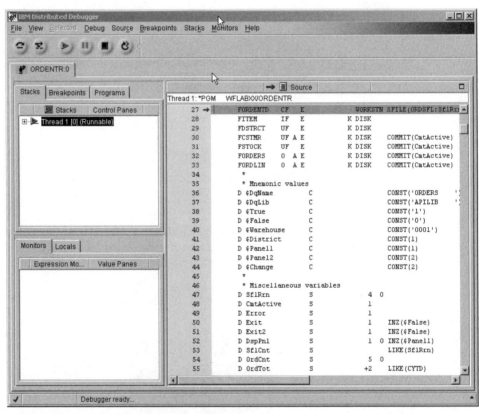

Figure 15.26: Distributed Debugger with source

Scroll down in the source pane to line 124.

- Select the **line number**.

- Double-click the **line number** to set a breakpoint.

- Double-click indicator ***IN03** in line 130.

The indicator name will be highlighted.

- Right-click the highlighted indicator name.

- Select **Add to Program Monitor** from the pop-up menu, as shown in Figure 15.27.

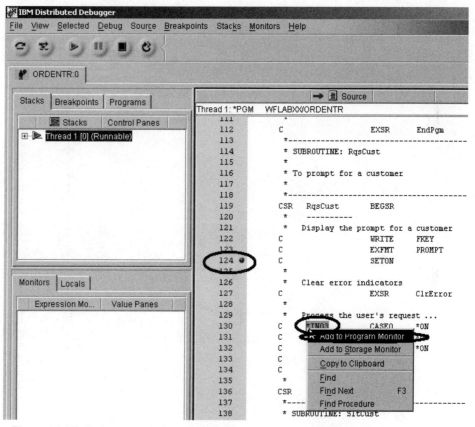

Figure 15.27: Debugger window with breakpoint and pop-up menu

The variable content will display in the Monitors pane, as shown in Figure 15.28.

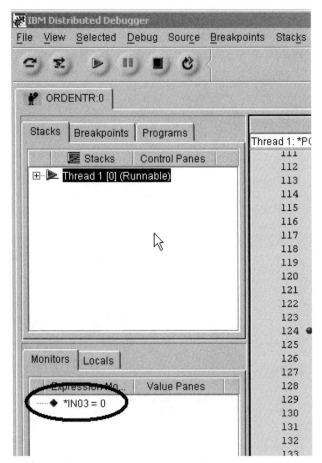

Figure 15.28: Debugger window with Monitors pane

■ Do the same for *IN04.

To activate the program,

- Press the **Run** push button in the debugger toolbar, as shown in Figure 15.29.

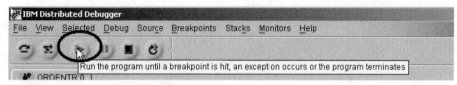

Figure 15.29: Debugger Run push button in toolbar

The program will stop at the breakpoint.

Now you can step through the program.

- Press **F7** on your keyboard.

Tip: You can also use the Step Debug tool button or you can select the Debug menu option in the Debugger window. Then select the Step Debug option from the pull-down menu, as shown in Figure 15.30.

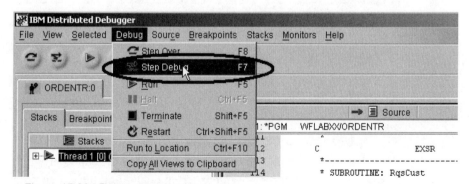

Figure 15.30: Debug menu options

■ Check the value of your indicators; the value for IND04 should be 1.

■ Step through your program until you come to the line that conditions *IN04 (see Figure 15.31).

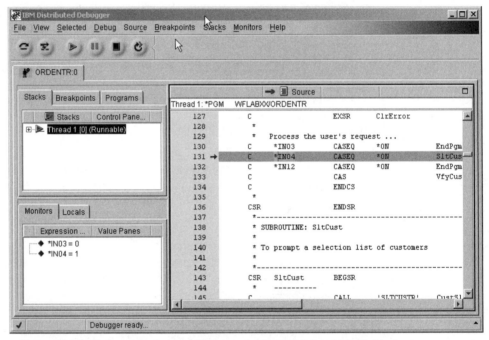

Figure 15.31: Debugger window with current active statement highlighted

■ Step further through the program.

You will come to a statement that calls program SLTCUSTR.

Stepping into a called program

Now you can decide whether you want to debug the called program or just let the pro-gram run. If you are not interested in debugging the called program, you would select **Step Over** or **F8**. That would call the program without debugging it and stop at the next line after the call. If you need to debug the programs in the call hierarchy, you would select **Step Debug**. I want to show you how to debug programs in the call hierarchy, so select **Step Debug** on this statement.

You will notice that the program's source, in this case SLTCUSTR, is now loaded into the debugger source view, as shown in Figure 15.32.

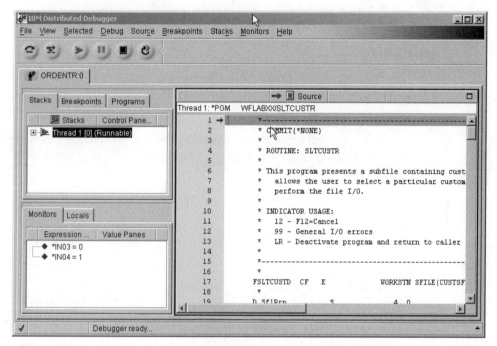

Figure 15.32: Source of program SLTCUSTR shown in debugger window

You can now step through this program by completing the following tasks:

- Set breakpoints.

- Monitor for variables.

- Work with the call stack.

Ending the debug session

I leave it up to you to work with the debugger. When you are finished, complete the debug session:

- Click the **Run** push button on the debugger toolbar.

- Go back to the browser window in the workbench.

- End your application by pressing **F3**.

- Close the debugger window.

Analysis

You have completed the exercise Debugging the Server Program. Here is what you accomplished:

- You started the WebFaced application and pointed the debugger to the job where the ORDENTR program was started.

- You set breakpoints in the program.

- You selected variables to monitor.

- You ran the program to a breakpoint.

- You stepped through the program.

- You stepped into another program at a call statement.

- You looked at the debug source view of this called program.

- You terminated the program.

- You ended the debug session.

You are ready to work with the next exercise, Using the WebFacing Environment API.

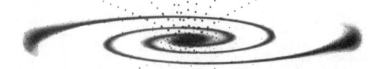

Using the WebFacing environment API

When running your application, you might want to know whether it is using the original 5250 user interface or the WebFaced browser user interface. There is an Application Program Interface (API) available on OS/400 that you can use to determine which user interface is active. This exercise shows you how to use this API in an RPG environment, but you can also use it for a different ILE language such as COBOL or CL.

The goal of the exercise

The goal of this exercise is to make you aware of how to use the WebFacing API in your own environment. You will use the API to change the field content for the user interface yet ensure that the change is applied only when you invoke the application through the WebFacing server. You perform this task in the Remote System Explorer perspective, creating and changing the RPG program so that you can learn more about how to work in the Development Studio Client programming environment.

At the end of this exercise, you should be able to

- Start the Remote System Explorer (RSE) perspective

- Use the library list filter

- Locate the RPG source member in the RSE tree view

- Change the RPG source member using the built-in LPEX editor

- Create a program from the altered source member

- Deal with compile errors

- Use the WebFacing environment API

- Use the Web setting for Program-defined HTML

Scenario

You have WebFaced your application, but you want to add specific features that are not available in the original 5250 format. In your environment, you need to run this application with a 5250 and WebFaced user interface simultaneously. However, you do not want to maintain two separate applications for the two types of interfaces. You therefore need the capability to determine, in the logic of your program, whether it is driving the 5250 user interface or a WebFaced user interface. The WebFacing Environment API gives you this capability. It is installed on the iSeries host with the WebFacing PTF, and it is implemented in the QQFENV service program.

In this exercise, you create a module and then create a program where you bind the QQFENV service program. You will change the ORDENTR program to use the WebFacing environment API. Specifically, you want to highlight the customer locations such that if they are located in the city of Markham, their name displays in a large heading 2 font size. First, you need to change the display file to increase the length of the Customer name field so that you can accommodate the additional HTML tags needed for this change. Then you will change the RPG logic to determine whether the application uses a 5250 or a browser-based user interface. If it uses a browser-based user interface, you add logic to the program to include the H2 HTML tags around the data.

Changing the display file

Before you change the RPG source member, I want you to change the way the customer name displays in the ORDENTD member of the ORDCTL record format.

Since you will do most of this exercise in the RSE perspective, switch to the RSE now. The RSE should be open and its icon visible on the left taskbar of the workbench, as in Figure 16.1.

Figure 16.1: Switching to RSE by using its icon from the taskbar

■ Click the icon and switch to the **RSE** perspective.

In the Remote Systems view (Figure 16.2),

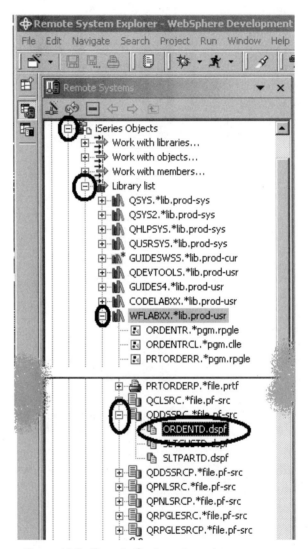

Figure 16.2: Remote Systems tree view

- Expand the connection you have been using for the WebFacing project.

- Expand the **iSeries Objects** node.

- Expand the **Library list** node.

- Expand the **wflabxx** library.

- Expand the **QDDSSRC** source file.

- Right-click the **ORDENTD** member.

- Select the **Open with** option from the pop-up menu.

- Select the **CODE Designer** option from the submenu.

CODE Designer appears after a moment.

- Select the **SCREEN1** tab to work with the Screen1 group.

- Use the arrow as indicated in Figure 16.3 to switch to the **ORDCTL** record format.

Figure 16.3: CODE designer with ORDENTD member loaded

Now that the ORDCTL record format has focus, you can work with the record format's fields to add 10 characters to the length of the **Customer name** field, which contains the customer name. With these additional 10 characters in the field, you can add HTML tags to highlight it for certain conditions in the WebFaced environment.

To extend the Customer name field,

- Position the mouse cursor at the end of the field and watch the cursor change into two arrowheads, as shown in Figure 16.4.

- Click the left mouse button and drag the cursor to the right.

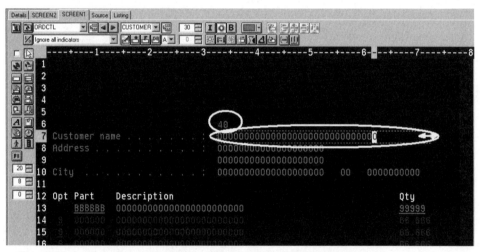

Figure 16.4: Customer name field extended to 40-character length

A number appears on top of the field, indicating the current field length.

- Move the mouse to the right until the field length is 40.

- Release the mouse button.

Now you need to change the Web setting for this field so that you can include HTML tags that are resolved at run time.

- Select the **Web Settings** tab underneath the design window, as shown in Figure 16.5.

- Select **Program defined HTML** from the list of available Web settings for this field.

- Check the **Use field value as HTML** check box.

- Save the member.

- Exit CODE Designer.

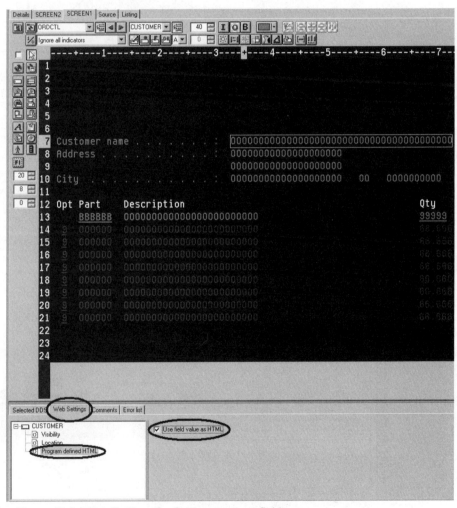

Figure 16.5: Web Settings for Customer name *field*

Back in the Remote Systems view (Figure 16.6),

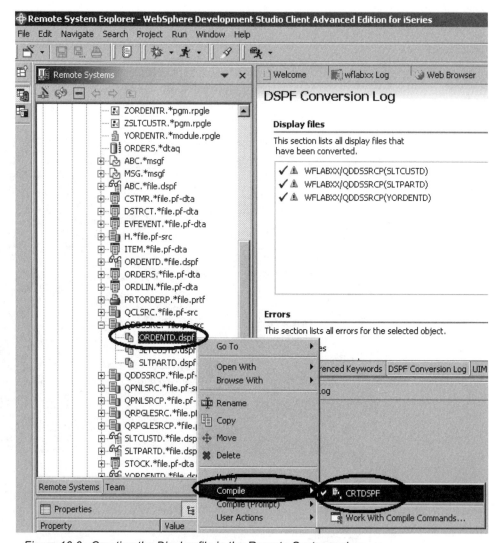

Figure 16.6: Creating the Display file in the Remote Systems view

■ Right-click the **ORDENTD** member.

■ Select the **Compile** option from the pop-up menu.

■ Select the **CRTDSPF** option from the submenu.

> **Tip:** If you want to create the Display file using the RSE job instead of sending it to a batch job queue, use the **Preferences** option under the Windows menu option in the workbench. Select **Remote Systems → iSeries → Command Execution** and then deselect the Compile in batch check box.

The Display file is created, and now you can change the RPG program to accommodate the required changes.

Using the WebFacing environment API

In this section, you want to enhance the WebFaced user interface without impacting the 5250 user interface. To do this, you have to add logic to your RPG program to help you determine whether the program is invoked from a browser or a 5250 terminal.

How the WebFacing environment API works

First, let's investigate how the WebFacing environment implements the API. It is provided as a service program, for which you have to invoke the QqfEnvironment procedure. This procedure returns a 1 if the application is running in the WebFaced environment, and it returns a 0 if it is running in a 5250 environment. The return data type is an integer.

Here is an example of how to use the WebFacing environment API in an RPG program:

```
D* The Prototype for the procedure
DWebFaced         PR            10I 0 Extproc('QqfEnvironment')
C* Invoke the procedure and use the return value in a condition
C                 If          WebFaced = 1
C*  Code to be executed when WebFaced UI is used
C
C                 Else
C*  Code to be executed when 5250 UI is used
C
C                 EndIf
*
```

The D spec contains the Prototype, which defines the procedure name and the procedure interface. This procedure does not expect parameters; it only returns an integer value. The RPG name to execute this procedure is WebFaced.

The first C spec executes the procedure and uses the return value in the condition. If the return value is 1, then the program runs in the WebFacing environment; otherwise, it runs in the 5250 environment.

Now you will add the WebFacing environment API to the ORDENTR member.

Changing the ORDENTR member

In the Remote Systems tree view,

- Expand the **QRPGLESRC** source file in the wflabxx library.

- Double-click the **ORDENTR** member to invoke the LPEX editor.

After a moment, the editor window with the member loaded appears in the workbench.

- Scroll down to the end of the D specs, around line 90.

- Add a line by pressing the **Enter** key.

- In the new line, key in the prototype as shown in Figure 16.7.

- Add comments if you want.

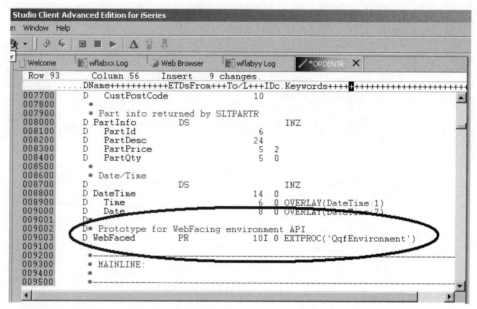

Figure 16.7: Editor with added prototype

Tip: The procedure name is case sensitive; you need to type it exactly as shown.

Now you have to add the logic that uses the QqfEnvironment procedure.

In the ORDENTR member (still in the editor), scroll down to line 192. After the line that formats the Customer name field, add the logic for the WebFacing condition as shown in Figure 16.8.

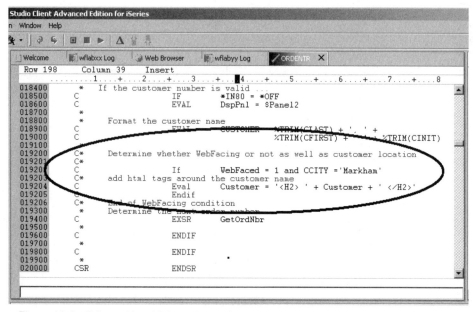

Figure 16.8: Editor with additional lines of logic

The first line invokes the procedure using the name WebFaced. The return value of WebFaced will be 1 if the application runs in a WebFacing environment. The "and" clause causes this condition to be true for customers from the city of Markham:

```
C*       Determine whether WebFacing or not, as well as customer location
C*
C                    If        WebFaced = 1 and CCITY ='Markham'
```

The next line adds H2 HTML tags to the Customer name field with the customer name embedded between the HTML tags:

```
C*      add HTML tags around the customer name
C                 Eval      Customer = '<H2> ' + Customer + ' </H2>'
C                 Endif
C*      End of WebFacing condition
*       Determine the next order number ...
```

This will work well in the browser, and the H2 tags will not display as output text, because in the Customer Web settings field you specified that you will supply the HTML yourself. The WebFacing conversion creates the correct code to take the values of the Customer name field and send them to the browser as part of the HTML data stream.

Before you close the file, do not forget to add the Endif operation code.

- Save the changes and exit the editor.

In the Remote Systems tree view,

- Right-click the **ORDENTR** member that you just changed.

- Select the **Compile** option from the pop-up menu, as shown in Figure 16.9.

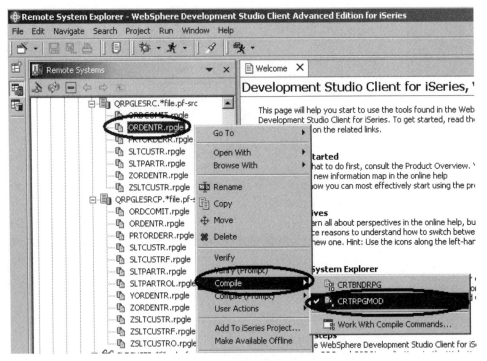

Figure 16.9: Creating a module from member ORDENTR

You need to bind the QQFENV Service Program, which contains the procedure QqfEnvironment, into the program you create. Therefore, you first need to create a module.

- Select the **CRTRPGMOD** option from the submenu.

The module is created. To work with the module now, in the Remote Systems tree view,

- Right-click the **wflabxx** library.

- Select the **Refresh** option from the pop-up menu.

Now the ORDENTR module shows up in the Remote Systems tree view, as shown in Figure 16.10.

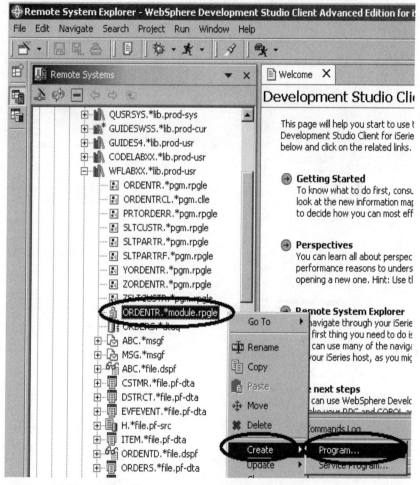

Figure 16.10: Remote Systems tree view with ORDENTR module

- Right-click the **ORDENTR** module.

- Select the **Create** option from the pop-up menu.

- Select the **Program** option from the submenu.

The Create Program (CRTPGM) dialog (Figure 16.11) opens.

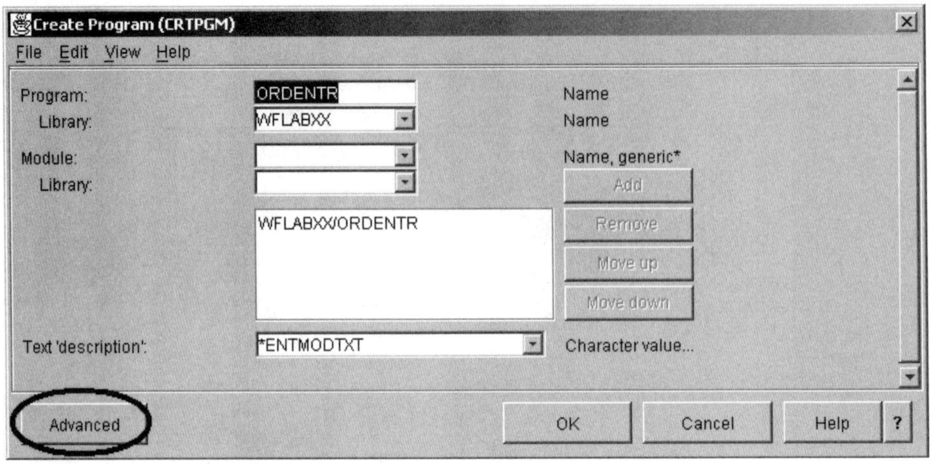

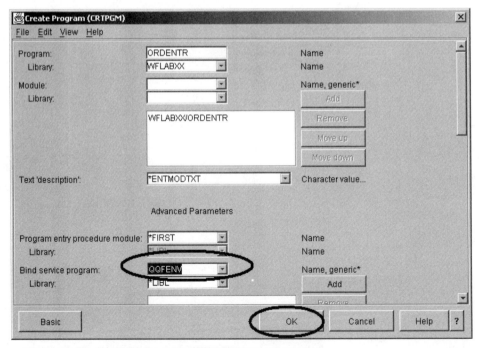

Figure 16.11: CRTPGM prompt with basic parameters

- Click the **Advanced** push button to show all possible parameters (Figure 16.12).

Figure 16.12: CRTPGM prompt with additional parameters

- Enter the Service Program name **QQFENV** in the Bind service program entry field.

- Click the **OK** push button to start program creation.

Check the iSeries Commands Log for the completion message (Figure 16.13).

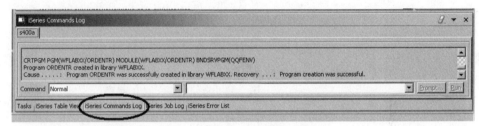

Figure 16.13: Completion message for CRTPGM command

If the program is created, you are ready to go back to the WebFacing perspective and finish up this task. Otherwise, find out what went wrong by checking the messages and the job log.

Tip: The Remote Systems tree view also allows you to work with the iSeries job and look at the job logs.

Converting the ORDENTD member

You have altered the ORDENTD display file source to change the length of the Customer name field and apply the program-supplied HTML Web setting. Now you need to reconvert the member.

Switch to the WebFacing perspective:

- Click the WebFacing perspective icon on the workbench taskbar, as shown in Figure 16.14.

Figure 16.14: WebFacing perspective icon on the workbench taskbar

In the WebFacing perspective,

- Expand the **wflabxx** project.

- Expand the **DDS** icon.

- Right-click the **ORDENTD** member.

- Select the **Convert** option from the pop-up menu.

After the conversion completes successfully, you can run the application.

Running the Web application

Now you can see the new feature of your application in action.

- Right-click the **wflabxx** project icon.

- Select **Run on Server** from the pop-up menu.

- Run the application.

■ Click **Prompt**.

■ Select **Weiss, Claus** from the list to obtain the screen shown in Figure 16.15.

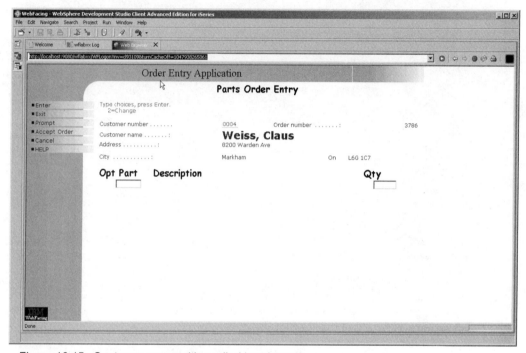

Figure 16.15: Customer name with applied header style

You will notice that the customer name is displayed in a large bold font since the style for heading 2 is defined that way.

■ Now press **command key 6** to accept the order, so that you can select a different customer.

■ Press **command key 4** to select a customer.

■ Select **Farr, George** from the list of customers. Your screen should look similar to Figure 16.16.

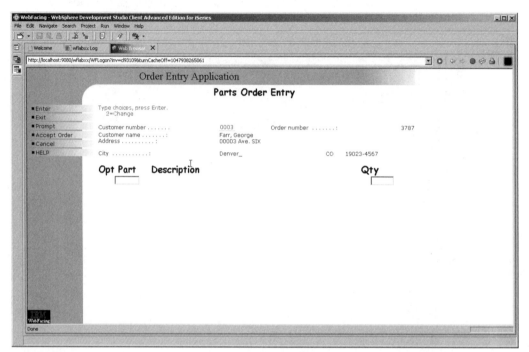

Figure 16.16: Customer name displayed with normal font because customer location is not Markham

Since George is based in Denver according to this database, this customer name is displayed in regular font.

You might want to test the 5250 user interface to make sure that it still works.

Analysis

You have completed the exercise Using the WebFacing Environment API. Here is what you accomplished:

- You changed the Customer name field length to accommodate extra data so that you can add HTML tags to the output data.

- You changed the Web settings for the Customer name field, so that the data of this field is used as part of the HTML data stream.

- You changed the RPG program to use the WebFacing Environment API and add HTML tags to the output under certain conditions.

- You created a module and a program, and then bound the QQFENV Service Program to this program.

- You reconverted the ORDENTD member so that your changes applied in the WebFacing environment.

- You tested your changes to verify that they appeared in the browser-based user interface.

You are ready to move on to the next exercise: More Tips for Web Settings.

More tips for Web settings

In a previous chapter, I showed you how to use Web settings to enhance your Web user interface. In this chapter, I will introduce the Web setting not covered before and I'll walk you through some examples to show you how to use these features in your own environment.

First of all, let me give you a summary of all Web settings available. Table 17.1 shows the different Web settings available and the corresponding DDS objects available in display files. You can see that there are many we have not worked with yet.

Table 17.1: WebSettings and Corresponding Display File Objects.

Web Setting	DDS Object
Command key labels Command key order Display size Insert into script	Record formats Subfile control record formats
Visibility Location HTML, program defined HTML user defined HTML insert	Constants Input fields Output fields
Options for values	Input fields with VALUES keyword
Create graphic Create hyperlink	Output fields
Send to browser as a hidden input element	Hidden fields

The goal of these exercises

The WebFacing Tool contains many more capabilities to enhance the user interface. This chapter provides exercises that you might want to go through selectively as you feel you need these capabilities.

I will start by showing you how to add your own HTML to the HTML generated by the WebFacing Tool. There are three different ways to add HTML with Web settings: you can (1) specify that HTML tags be inserted before, inside, or after the WebFacing generated HTML; (2) specify that you will provide the HTML from the RPG or COBOL program at run time; or (3) decide to tell the WebFacing tool not to generate HTML for a field and instead supply your own HTML.

I will show you how to add a pop-up calendar to your WebFaced user interface, and I will also show you where you can find more interesting controls to help you get the most out of WebFacing.

Web settings are also available on a record format level, to deal with command key labels and the command key order for individual record formats. In addition, you can add your own JavaScript to be run when the record format is displayed. If you work with secondary display size, you have the Display size Web Setting that you use to select the size for the WebFacing conversion.

I also address the problem of column heading alignment on subfiles, since you might encounter problems if your column headings are made up of a string that uses blanks to align the column heading with the subfile columns themselves.

I also explore how to add certain features to a WebFacing project template so that they are added automatically to all new WebFacing projects that you create.

Scenario

You have accomplished the basic WebFacing tasks, but now you want to add some more features to your Web application. Here are some tips and examples on how you can accomplish these tasks.

Let's look at the individual Web settings to give you an idea about whether you might want to use these in your own shop.

Adding HTML tags to the page

As I mentioned before, you can use three different Web settings to add your own HTML for adapting the application to your environment and hiding the green-screen heritage in your Web user interface.

Inserting HTML

You can insert additional HTML code before, inside, and after the DDS 5250 control that is generated by the WebFacing Tool. A popular use of this capability is to add a button behind a field for use of an extra function not available in the 5250 panel. Adding something extra to the generated Web page, however, can sometimes cause problems, especially if your original 5250 panel is very crowded. In that case, there is no space to place these additional controls into the table grid the WebFacing Tool creates, and the addition completely misaligns the resulting Web page.

You can use the insert html Web setting to place a graphic on your Web page without using extra space. The graphic in the sample that I use here displays behind the customer number field and provides an additional capability when the user clicks on this graphic. This Web setting also gives you a chance to write some JavaScript. I will guide you through three different scenarios to show you how to use this capability.

Adding a graphic with a link to the page

First you will add a graphic after the Customer number input field; clicking on this graphic will simply send a request to a fixed URL.

- In the WebFacing Projects view of the WebFacing perspective, find the DDS directory. Select the ORDENTD source member and start CODE Designer.

■ Select the **SCREEN2** group tab, as shown in Figure 17.1.

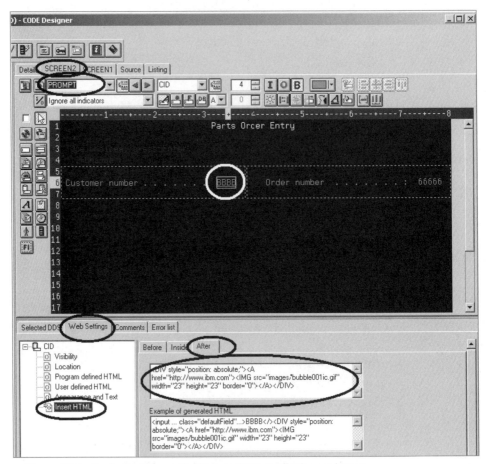

Figure 17.1: Code Designer with Web settings to display an image

■ Select the **PROMPT** record format in this group.

■ Select the **Customer number** (CID) field in the design pane.

■ Select the **Web Settings** tab below the design pane.

- Select the **Insert HTML** node from the Web Settings list.

- Select the **After** tab in the notebook for the Insert HTML Web setting.

Add the following HTML into the entry field on the After page:

```
<DIV "style=position: absolute;"><A href="http://www.ibm.com"><IMG
src="images/bubble001ic.gif" width="23" height="23" border="0"></A></DIV>
```

You can copy and paste this code from file sample_graphic_web_page.txt on the CD that accompanies the book.

Tip: CODE Designer has a bug and sometimes doesn't accept the text in the Insert HTML entry fields. Click on the **Before** tab and the **After** tab to make sure the text is accepted by CODE Designer.

This will add the bubble001ic graphic after the customer number input field. When the user clicks the graphic, the browser will request the URL *www.ibm.com*.

- Save the member in CODE Designer.

- Convert the member in the WebFacing project.

You need to copy the bubble001ic.gif file to the WebFacing project directory structure in the workspace so it can be found during run time.

■ In the Navigator view, expand **wflabxx**, then **Web Content**, then **images**, as shown in Figure 17.2.

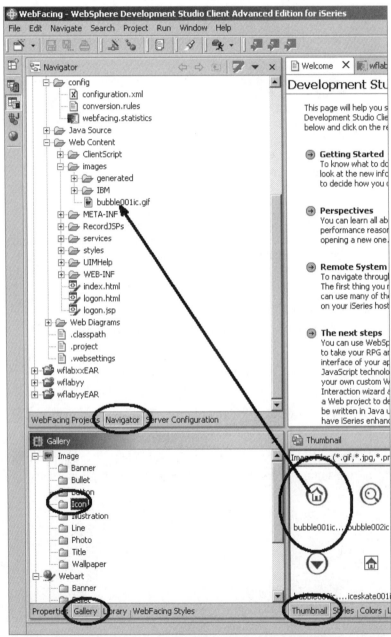

Figure 17.2: Adding the bubble001ic.gif file to the Web project images directory

- Select the **Gallery** tab in the pane below the Navigator view.

- Select the **Icon** directory in the Gallery tree view.

- Select the **Thumbnail** tab in the bottom right workbench pane.

- Drag the **bubble001.gif** from the Thumbnail page to the images directory in the wflabxx project.

Run the WebFaced application (Figure 17.3).

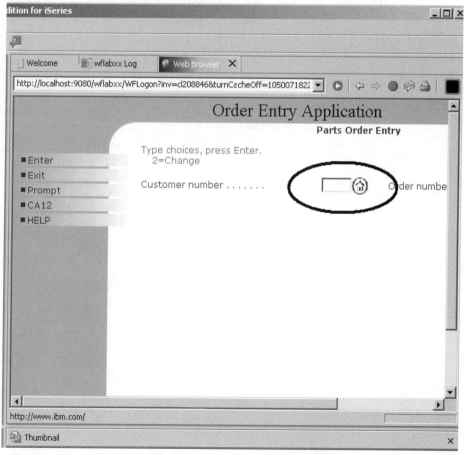

Figure 17.3: The Order Entry *page with an additional graphic beside the customer number entry field*

Clicking on the graphic will request the IBM home page (Figure 17.4).

Figure 17.4: Browser after clicking on bubble001ic graphic

This capability might come in handy. The next sample shows the same idea but now, instead of a link, you will invoke the submit command key.

Adding a graphic to invoke the Submit Command key to the program

Rather than just invoking a static Web page, a more useful feature might be to invoke the Customer list window when the user clicks the graphic beside the Customer number field. Here is a code sample to invoke CA04; this will send a request back to the program when the user clicks the graphic.

```
<DIV style= "position: absolute;"><A href=# onclick
="validateAndSubmit('CA04');"><IMG src="images/bubble001ic.gif"
width="23" height="23" border="0"></A></DIV>
```

This code uses the WebFacing JavaScript validateAndSubmit function. WebFacing JavaScript functions are stored in your WebFacing project under Web Content > ClientScript > webface.js. You can look at what kind of WebFacing JavaScript functions are available by double clicking the webface.js file and then using the editor to browse through the source. You can recognize JavaScript functions by the keyword "function" in front of their names.

Using the validateAndSubmit function, you can send a function key name as a parameter to the iSeries program based on an event in the browser. Here is a sample where you use the onclick event to trigger the action. Go ahead and try this out in the WebFacing Project view.

■ Open **CODE Designer** for the ORDENTD member (Figure 17.5).

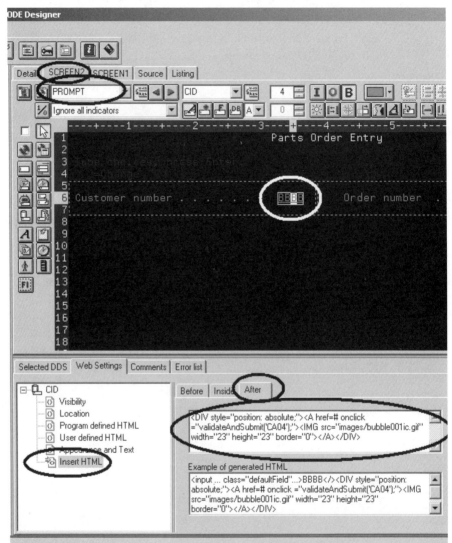

Figure 17.5: Adding HTML to submit request faking command key four

As in the previous example,

■ Bring up the **SCREEN2** group in the design pane.

■ Select the Customer number field.

- Select the **Web Settings** tab underneath the design pane.

- Select the **Insert HTML** node.

- Select the **After** tab.

- Add the HTML code sample from above into the entry field. You can copy and paste this sample from the sample_graphic.txt file in the CD accompanying the book.

- Position the cursor after the text and press the **Enter** key.

Tip: CODE Designer has a bug and sometimes doesn't accept the text in the Insert HTML entry fields. Click on the **Before** tab and the **After** tab to make sure the text is accepted by CODE Designer.

- Save the source member.

- Reconvert this member.

- Run the application.

Now on the first screen (Figure 17.6),

■ Click on the graphic behind the Customer number field.

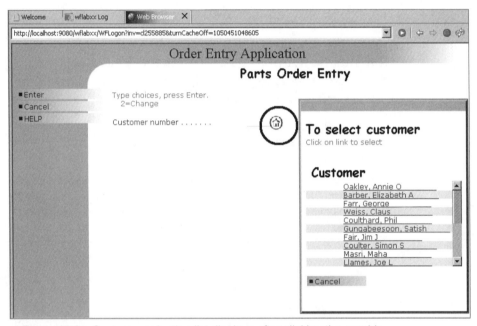

Figure 17.6: Customer selection list displays after clicking the graphic

This time the customer selection list pop-up window appears, the same behavior as if you clicked the Prompt push button, or pressed the F4 function key on your keyboard.

This implementation has one side effect, however. When you return to the Order Entry with a selected customer, you can still see the graphic on the Web page, as shown in Figure 17.7.

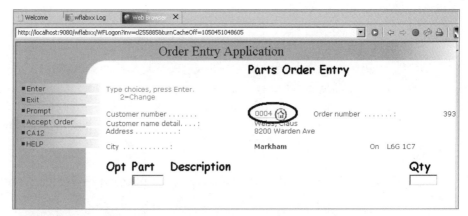

Figure 17.7: Order entry *page with graphic showing on output-only field*

The graphic should really not display, since you cannot select a customer on this page. I'll show you how to add JavaScript that sets the proper conditions for when the graphic displays. Here is the code:

```
<script type= "text/javascript">
var order_number = 0;
order_number = "<%=PROMPT.getFieldValueWithTransform("ORDNBR",
QUOTED_TRANSFORM)%>";
// if order number is not filled then display icon for customer prompting
if (order_number < 1  )
document.write(" <DIV style=\"position: absolute;\"><A href=# onclick
=\"validateAndSubmit('CA04');
\"><IMG src=\"images/bubble001ic.gif\" width=\"23\" height=\"23\" border
=\"0\"></A></DIV>");
</script>
```

If you have performed some JavaScript programming, then you already know what the code is doing. If you are new to JavaScript, here are some hints about what is going on.

First I identify that this piece of code is JavaScript so the browser knows how to interpret it (and that it is not plain HTML). In the second line, I define an order_number variable and initialize it to zero. JavaScript is loosely typed, so no type definition is needed. Because the order_number variable contains an order number after a customer has been selected, I get the value from the ORDNBR variable and copy it to the order_number variable (which I just defined).

The condition in line 4 just checks whether an order number has been assigned or not. If one is not assigned, the graphic displays. The statement inside the if structure is the same as I used in the previous example. The output from JavaScript is interpreted and rendered by the browser. Therefore, I use the write method to output the HTML I used previously to show the graphic. Also note that you need to use a special escape sequence in the HTML to display the quotation marks ("). The escape sequence \"will output a single". The /script just indicates that the JavaScript section ends here and regular HTML code resumes.

You can find the code sample on the CD in file sample_graphic_conditioned.txt.

To complete this exercise, switch to the WebFacing Projects view and open the ORDENTD member in CODE Designer. Then go through the same steps explained in the previous example, except this time, just delete the code that you added in the Web Settings page and insert the JavaScript for this example instead.

Again make sure CODE Designer recognizes the new text in this entry field.

- Save the member.

- Reconvert the DDS source.

- Run the application.

- Select a customer.

Now the graphic on the Order Entry screen with a selected customer is hidden, since the order entry number contains a value and the write method is not run, so that this HTML does not display in the browser (Figure 17.8).

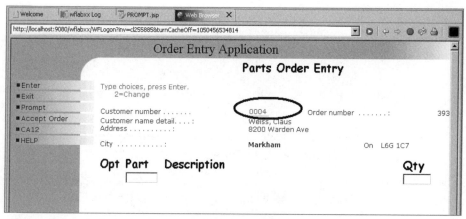

Figure 17.8: Order entry page, graphic is not visible

After this short side step into JavaScript, you might be ready for some more. In the next exercise, you can add a pop-up calendar to a date input field.

Adding a pop-up calendar

Pop-up calendars for Web pages are very popular, and it would be an ideal feature for some of your date fields on a WebFaced application. In this example, I am using a calendar downloaded for free from the Internet, under the following URL and navigation structure: *www.hotscripts.com/JAVASCRIPT/* → Script and Programs → Calendars.

You will find several pop-up calendars to download. I selected the JS calendar for this example. You will need to download this calendar if you want to follow the example in this exercise. Also note that the helper JavaScript file that I use is valid only for the JS calendar, but other calendars will work as well with their specific scripts.

I have added a different program, ORDENTRCAL, for this exercise. It contains an additional record format that requests the user to enter a date for the Order Entry application.

I suggest that you build a new WebFacing project called wflabcal. First, however, you need to switch to the Remote System Explorer perspective.

- Copy the **ORDENTDCAL** member from QDDSSRCP to QDDSSRC. ORDENTDCAL contains one more record format that is displayed when accepting an order; a delivery date must be specified in this record format. Remember that in the RSE you may use clipboard copy/paste to copy a source member from a source file into another one.

Now create the new WebFacing project and call it wflabcal.

- On the first page of the project wizard, specify to create a new EAR file for this project called **wflabcalEAR**.

- On the second wizard page, specify **J2EE level 1.3.**

- On the third page, select the following members from the QDDSSRC folder: **ORDENTDCAL**, **SLTCUSTD**, **SLTPARTD**.

- Skip the **UIM help panel** page.

- On the CL command page specify that you want to use the following command: **CALL ORDENTRCAL**.

- Specify to use your iSeries host user ID and password.

- Add this information to the list of **CL commands**.

- On the next page, select a style that you like.

- On the last page, select **create the project** and progress with conversion.

After a little while, the conversion completes, and you are ready to add the calendar. Before you do this, however, run the application and inspect the new panel.

To get to this page shown in Figure 17.9,

- Select a customer.

- Add a part to the order.

- Press **command key 6** to accept the order.

Figure 17.9: New page with delivery date input field

The new page displays.

Now you can add the calendar. You first need two JavaScript files and a cascading style sheet that you downloaded with the JS calendar. You also need some JavaScript helper functions; I extracted these out of the calendar examples and included them on the CD that is part of this book.

The JavaScript files are all copied into the Client Script \usr directory. From there they are automatically picked up by the WebFacing Tool and added to the WebFacing JSP files. Figure 17.10 is a sample of the directory structure and the files added.

Figure 17.10: Added files for the pop-up calendar

Remember that these files are specific to the JS calendar that I use; if you pick a different calendar, you need to copy different files.

The mycalendar.js file is on the CD that comes with this book. I just extracted the helper functions needed for this example from the very elaborate sample that comes with the JS calendar. The calendar.js and dcalendar-en.js are part of the JS calendar package. In fact, dcalendar-en is named calendar-en in the package, but it must be imported into the HTML stream for the browser after the calendar.js. Because the automatic import generator goes by alphabetic sequence, I gave this .js file a name that forces the import generation to occur after the calendar.js import; otherwise you would encounter a JavaScript error at run time.

The cascading style sheet, calendar-win2k-1.css, is also part of the JS calendar package. I copied it into the WebFacing project's styles directory.

I use a graphic beside the date field so that the user can click on the graphic and invoke the calendar. I chose one of the sample icons in the workbench gallery and copied that to the images directory in the WebFacing project.

You need to perform one last step before you add the calendar JavaScript to the Web settings for the Delivery date field: You need to add the cascading style sheet information for the calendar style sheet. You use the PageBuilder.jsp, inside the Chrome directory in your WebFacing project. In this JSP, you need to add the following tag:

```
<link rel="stylesheet" type="text/css" media="all" href="styles/calendar-
win2k-1.css" title="win2k-1" />
```

This information is also copied from the calendar examples. Figure 17.11 shows how it looks in the PageBuilder.jsp file. I added it underneath the link tag for the WebFacing style sheet.

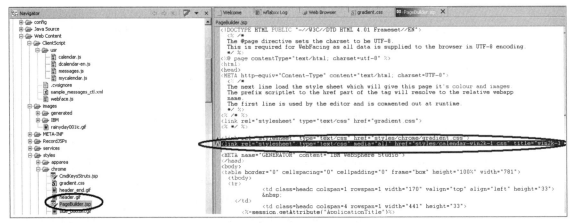

Figure 17.11: Cascading style sheet information in PageBuilder jsp

Now you need to invoke **CODE Designer** from the WebFacing Project view for the ORDENTDCAL member (Figure 17.12). In CODE Designer, you work with the SCREEN2 group, which for this scenario contains record formats PROMPTDATE and FKEY.

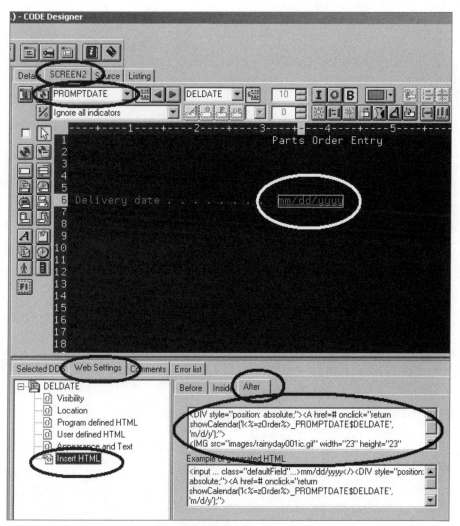

Figure 17.12: CODE Designer with Web settings to invoke pop-up calendar

- Select the **PROMPTDATE** record format in this group.

- In the Design pane, select entry field **DELDATE**.

- Click the **Web Settings** tab.

- Select the **Insert HTML** Web Settings node.

■ Select the **After** tab.

■ Enter the following code into the entry field for this Web setting. You can find this code in the invoke_calendar.txt file on the book's CD to copy and paste it.

```
<DIV style="position: absolute;"><A href=# onclick="return
showCalendar('1<%=zOrder%>_PROMPTDATE$DELDATE', 'm/d/y');">
<IMG src="images/rainyday001ic.gif" width="23" height="23"
border="0"></A></DIV>
```

The code will display an icon beside the delivery date field, the same way the graphic displays in the previous example. The calendar needs to get the ID for its associated control, which is the delivery date entry field DELDATE. The showCalendar function takes the ID and displays the calendar underneath the associated control. It also retrieves the current value from this control and moves the selected date value into this control when a date is selected. The entry field ID is ('1<%=zOrder%>_PROMPTDATE$DELDATE') for this entry field with the name DELDATE in the record format PROMPTDATE.

You can gather this information from the recordformat jsp when you need it for your own applications. Figure 17.13 shows a sample from the promptdate.jsp, which comes from the wflabcal project in the RecordJSPs directory.

```
<TD NOWRAP colspan=21 rowspan=1><span id='1<%=zOrder%>_PROMPTDATE$Unnamed1' class="wf_blue wf_field" onClick="setCursor(3, 2);"
</TR>
<TR id="1<%=zOrder%>r4" class="trStyle"><TD> </TD></TR>
<TR id="1<%=zOrder%>r5" class="trStyle"><TD> </TD></TR>
<TR id="1<%=zOrder%>r6" class="trStyle">
<% lastCol = 0; %>
<TD colspan=1> </TD>
<TD NOWRAP colspan=29 rowspan=1><span id='1<%=zOrder%>_PROMPTDATE$Unnamed2' class="wf_default wf_field" onClick="setCursor(6, 2)
<TD colspan=2> </TD>
<TD NOWRAP colspan=10 rowspan=1><INPUT <% if (isProtected) { %> readonly tabindex=< <% } %> id="1<%=zOrder%>_PROMPTDATE$DELDATE"
</TR>
<% /* %></TBODY></TABLE>
</BODY>
```

Figure 17.13: Sample of recordformat jsp and the IDs generated by WebFacing conversion

The second parameter for the showCalendar function is the date format. I selected m/d/y, but the calendar supports many more formats in case you need a different one.

■ Save the member.

- Reconvert the member.

- Run your application.

- Select a customer, order a part, and accept the order.

On the new delivery date page, you can try the new feature. First click the calendar icon: The calendar will appear with today's date; it picks up this value from the DELDATE entry field and initializes itself with that date. You can now pick a date from the calendar and it is automatically filled into the delivery date entry field, as shown in Figure 17.14.

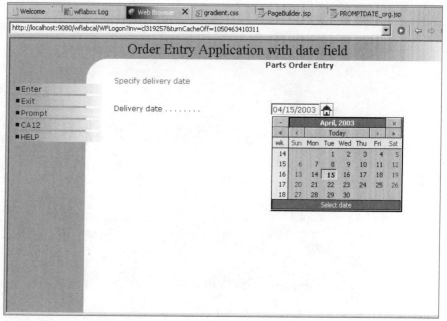

Figure 17.14: WebFaced application with added pop-up calendar

I hope that this excursion into JavaScript and downloadable JavaScript controls has encouraged you to apply these techniques to your own WebFaced applications.

User-defined HTML

In the previous chapter, I showed you how to use program-defined HTML by adding logic to your RPG program. You used the program defined HTML Web settings to indicate to the WebFacing conversion that you would provide HTML inside the field. This enabled the WebFacing conversion routine to generate the correct HTML and ensure that the actual HTML code does not display as data. Refer to Chapter 16 for the full example.

For user-defined HTML, you can add your own HTML to replace the HTML normally generated by the WebFacing Tool. I provide an example that shows you how to add the HTML strong attribute to the customer city information.

In the wflabxx WebFacing project, open the **ORDENTD** member with CODE Designer, as shown in Figure 17.15.

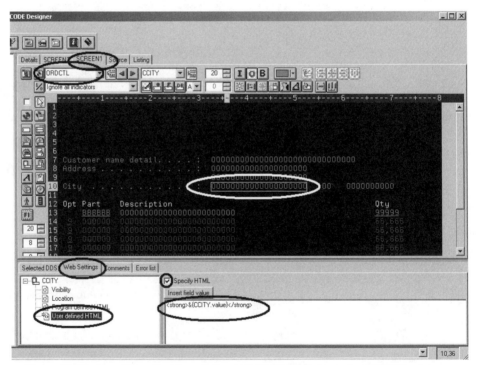

Figure 17.15: Specifying the User defined HTML *Web Settings in CODE Designer*

■ Select the group tab **SCREEN1**.

- Select the **ORDCTL** record format in this group.

- Select the **CCITY** field in the design pane.

- Select the **Web Settings** tab below the design pane.

- Select the **User defined HTML** node from the Web Settings list.

- Select the **Specify HTML** check box.

If the entry field does not contain the string &(CCITY).value),

- Click the **Insert field value** push button.

Before the string &(CCITY).value),

- Enter the HTML tag ****.

After the string &(CCITY).value),

- Enter the HTML end tag ****.

- Save the member in CODE Designer.

- Convert the **ORDENTD** member in the WebFacing project.

- Run the WebFaced Order Entry application.

- Start the order and select a customer. Your screen should be similar to Figure 17.16.

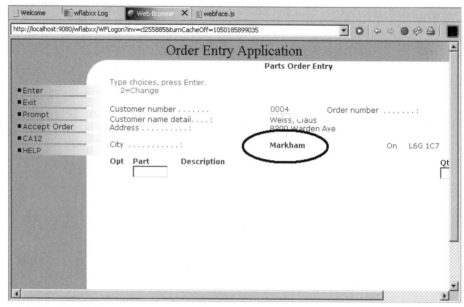

Figure 17.16: City text displays in bold font

With this option, you can ignore the HTML that is generated by default and take control over this part of the Web page.

Tip: When you use this option, the WebFacing HTML for this field is not generated, so you will have to supply all the necessary code. For example, if you use this Web setting for an input field, none of the HTML is generated to make this an input field. You need to supply the necessary HTML to make this an input field in addition to the other changes you want to make, or this field loses its input capabilities.

The advantage of Web setting capabilities is that you can add the HTML directly into your record formats, and none of it is lost when you reconvert. This saves you from having to add the HTML and JavaScript directly to the generated JSP every time you reconvert. The Web settings are captured in the DDS source as comments and are reapplied during WebFacing conversion.

Using the Appearance and Text Web setting

In this section, I want you to highlight the **Order number** field on the first screen. To accomplish this, you add your own style class, and then you can apply it to any other similar field in your WebFaced application. The WebFacing styles are located in the styles directory, inside the WebFacing project. You will use the Appearance and Text Web setting to indicate that this field belongs to the new style class.

Adding a new style class

In the WebFacing perspective switch to the Navigator view and expand the **wflabxx** WebFacing project. Inside the project expand the **Web Content** and the **styles** directories. In directory styles you will see subdirectory apparea, which contains the apparea.css file.

- Double-click the apparea.css file to open the style sheet editor.

Tip: If line numbers do not display in the editor, use the workbench preferences under the Windows menu option. Expand the **Web and XML files** node; expand the **CSS Files** node; select the **CSS Source** node; and select the **show line numbers** check box.

- In the editor, scroll to the bottom and add the new style class order_Number, as shown in Figure 17.17. File order_Number.txt on the book's CD contains this style class if you would rather copy/paste it in.

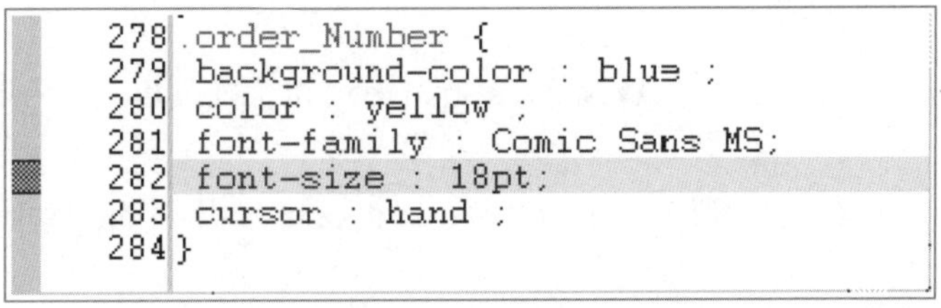

```
278 .order_Number {
279 background-color : blue ;
280 color : yellow ;
281 font-family : Comic Sans MS;
282 font-size : 18pt;
283 cursor : hand ;
284 }
```

Figure 17.17: Style sheet editor with new class order_number

Note: You need a period before the class name to indicate it is a class. Also, do not forget the semicolons at the of the lines.

Tip: You can always check how your object will appear in the browser by clicking the Preview area on the right side of the editor window.

- Save the **apparea.css** file.

- Close the editor.

You now need to invoke **CODE Designer** to apply the Web setting.

In the WebFacing Projects view, expand the **WebFacing project** and expand the **DDS folder**.

- Right-click the **ORDENTR** member.

- Select the **CODE Designer** option.

In CODE Designer,

- Select the **SCREEN2** group tab.

- Select the **Prompt** record format as the active record format.

- Select the Order number field **ORDNBR** in the design window.

- Select the **Web Settings** tab underneath the design window.

- Select the **Appearance and Text** node in the Web Settings list.

- Select the **Change style** class check box.

■ Enter **order_Number** in the style class entry field, as shown in Figure 17.18.

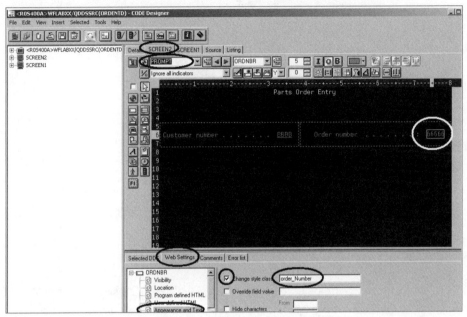

Figure 17.18: CODE designer with Appearance and Text Web Settings applied

■ Save the member.

■ Close **CODE Designer**.

In the WebFacing Projects view:

■ Convert the **ORDENTD** member.

■ Run the application.

■ Select a customer.

Your screen should look similar to Figure 17.19.

Figure 17.19: Order number formatted according to new style class definition

For any other field that you want to format similarly, you can just change its style class of this new class using Web settings.

Options for values

For entry fields associated with the Values DDS keyword, the WebFaced UI creates radio buttons by default. You have seen these used in the Order Entry application for subfile option fields.

To make these radio buttons more usable, the WebFacing Tool provides options for the Values Web setting.

You can use the main order screen to try it out.

In the wflabxx WebFacing project, open the **ORDENTD** member with CODE Designer.

- Select the **SCREEN1**group tab.

- Select the **ORDSFL** record format in this group.

- Select the **Option** field in the first row of the subfile list.

- Select the **Web Settings** tab below the Design pane.

■ Select the **Options for VALUES** node from the Web Settings list.

■ Select the **Options texts for VALUES keyword** radio button.

■ Select the **2=2** record from the list of valid values.

■ Enter **Change order detail** in the **New Label** entry field, as shown in Figure 17.20.

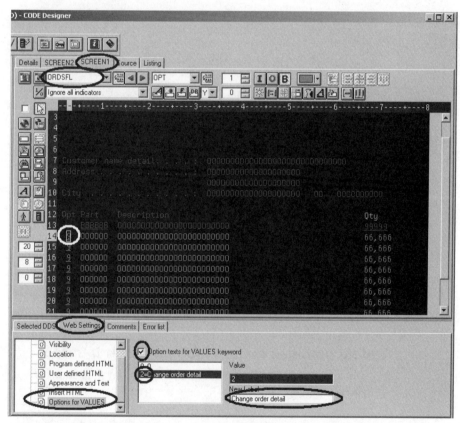

Figure 17.20: Specifying the 'Options for Values' Web settings in CODE designer

■ Save the member in CODE Designer.

■ Convert the member in the WebFacing project.

■ Run the application.

■ Add an order detail to the order.

■ Specify a customer, then select a part and specify the ordered quantity for this part.

Your screen should look similar to Figure 17.21.

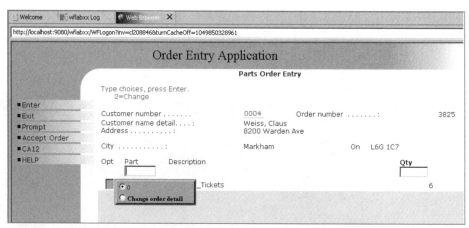

Figure 17.21: Radio button with text from Web settings

This adds the part to the order, and the radio button list displays when the cursor is moved on top of the option field. The Web settings text now replaces the number 2. To improve the appearance, you could also specify text for the 0 value.

Adding graphics to the WebFaced user interface

In this exercise, you add graphics to enhance your user interface. You have two choices for adding a graphic:

1. Display a static picture that you specify at design time.

2. Display a dynamic graphic and have your program supply the actual file name to display at run time.

Adding a static graphic to the user interface

Let's first use a static picture, since that method is pretty straightforward. In the customer list, for example, you might want to add a picture to animate the screen a bit more. You previously hid the text 1=Select. Now you want to display a picture instead. You can do this very easily by selecting a .gif file from one of the Windows installation directories.

- Select the **SLTCUSTD** member in the WebFacing project and open it with CODE Designer (Figure 17.22) to change the Web settings.

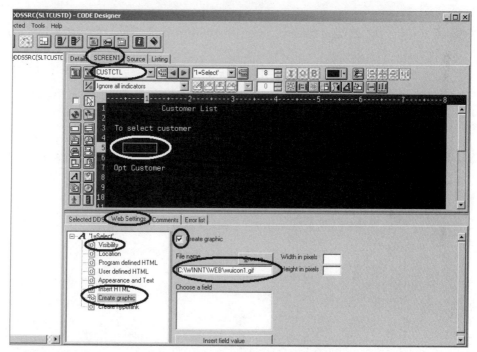

Figure 17.22: Code Designer with Web settings to display graphic

- Select the **SCREEN1**group tab.

- Select the **CUSTCTL** record format in this group.

- Select the **1 = Select** text.

- Select the **Web Settings** tab below the design pane.

- Select the **Visibility** node from the Web Settings list.

- Select the **Show field** radio button.

- Select the **Create Graphic** node from the Web Settings list.

- Select the **Create Graphic** check box.

- Browse for a picture file. In the sample I use C:\WINNT\WEB\wuicon1.gif.

- Save the picture file in CODE Designer.

- Convert the picture file in the WebFacing project.

The picture file is in fact copied into the WebFacing project environment so that it is available during run time in the application server.

- Run the WebFaced application.

The picture is displayed on the customer selection list window, as shown in Figure 17.23.

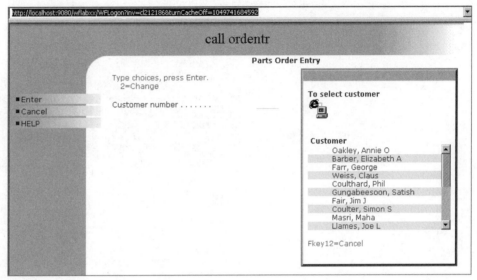

Figure 17.23: Customer list with graphic

Adding dynamic graphics to the user interface

Now you might want to add a dynamic picture and choose a file to display during run time. You can accomplish this for the parts subfile in the sample application. You will replace the part number in the parts list with a corresponding graphic. The graphic files names are the part numbers with the extension .gif; for example, the graphic for part number 000005 is stored in file 000005.gif.

■ Select the **SLTPARTD** member in the WebFacing project and open it with CODE Designer to change the Web settings (Figure 17.24).

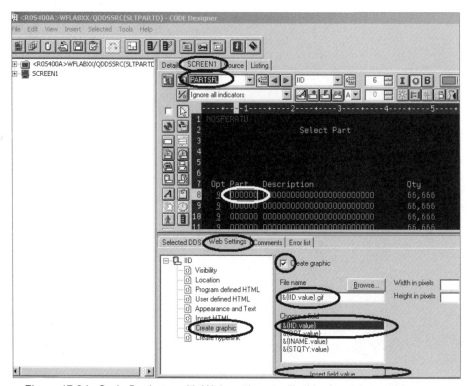

Figure 17.24: Code Designer with Web settings to display dynamic graphic

- Select the **SCREEN1** group tab.

- Select the **PARTSFL** record format in this group.

- Select the part field **IID** in the subfile.

- Select the **Web Settings** tab below the Design pane.

- Select the **Create Graphic** node from the Web Settings list.

- Select the **Create Graphic** check box.

All output fields in the record format are listed in the Choose a field list box.

■ Select the **&{IID.value}** field in this list box (IID is the name of the part number field).

Click the **Insert field value** push button. This will move the field name into the entry field File name. Since the part number is the name of the picture file, you just have to add the extension .gif to the File name and you are done.

The value that should be in the file name entry field is &{IID.value}.gif.

■ Save the member in CODE Designer.

■ Convert the member in the WebFacing project.

You need to copy the picture files to the WebFacing project directory structure in the workspace so that they can be found during run time. On the book's CD, the directory wf_book_pictures contains the picture files.

■ Use Windows Explorer to display the content of directory wf_book_pictures on the book's CD.

■ Select the **Edit** option from the Windows Explorer menu bar.

■ Select the **Select All** option from the pull-down menu.

■ Right-click one of the selected .gif files.

■ Select the **Copy** option from the pop-up menu.

■ In the workbench, in the Navigator view, expand the wflabxx project to **wflabxx → Web Content → images →generated**.

■ Right-click the **generated** directory.

■ Select the **Paste** option from the pop-up menu to paste the files into this directory.

■ Run the WebFaced application.

Your page should look like Figure 17.25.

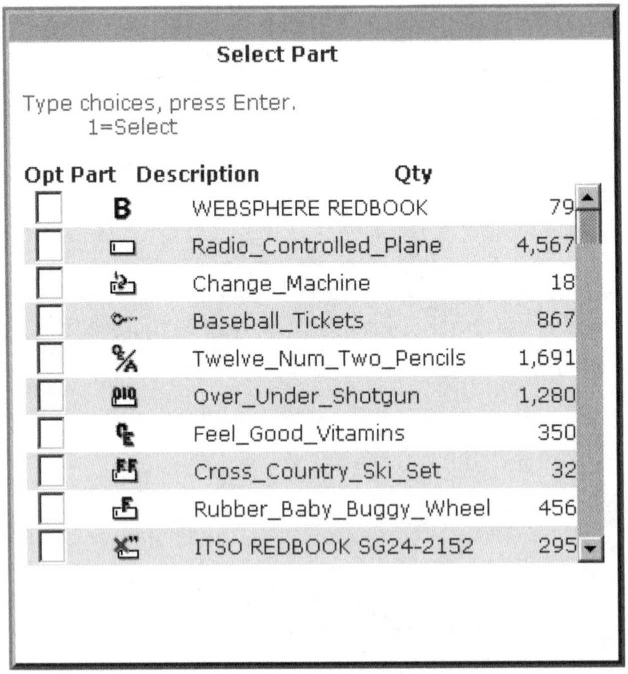

Figure 17.25: Part list with pictures instead of part numbers

If the picture files cannot be found, the page will look like Figure 17.26.

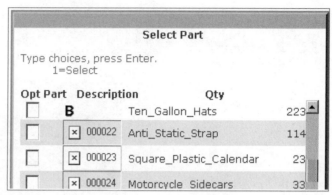

Figure 17.26: List with picture files not found

I hope you can use this feature to enhance your WebFaced applications.

More command key features

You have already had a chance in the previous chapters to work with command key properties. Now you can try changing command key labels.

Changing command key labels

Let's assume you want to change the label for a command key to make it more meaningful in the Web environment. However, you do not want to change it for the 5250 environment. Once again, Web settings come to the rescue for this requirement.

In the wflabxx project, from the WebFacing Projects view,

- Select the **ORDENTD DDS** source member and open it with CODE Designer.

In CODE Designer (Figure 17.27),

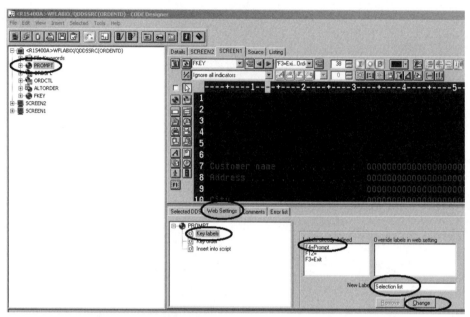

Figure 17.27: Relabeling a push button for the Web page

- Select the **Prompt** record format in the tree view.

- Select the **Web Settings** tab in the notebook at the bottom right of CODE Designer.

- Select **Key labels** from the tree view.

- Select the **F4=Prompt** in the Labels already defined list box.

- Enter **Selection list** in the New Label entry field.

- Click the **Change** push button at the bottom of this pane.

The Override labels in web setting list box should now contain your new label, as shown in Figure 17.28.

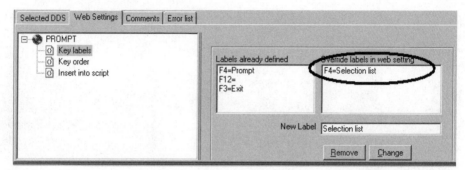

Figure 17.28: New label shown in Override labels in web setting list box

You are now finished with CODE Designer.

■ Close **CODE Designer** and save the changed member.

In the WebFacing perspective in the Projects view,

■ Convert the **ORDENTD** member.

■ Test the application.

You will see the changed push button label on the Web page, as shown in Figure 17.29.

Figure 17.29: Application page with new push button label

Note: You need to change only the command key description of the last record format written to the workstation file, because command key enablement is active only from the last record format.

Hiding command keys

If you want to disable a command key in the WebFaced environment, you can also use Web settings. Let's assume you want to disable command key 12 because it is redundant with the function of command key 3.

■ Open the **ORDENTD** member in CODE Designer (Figure 17.30).

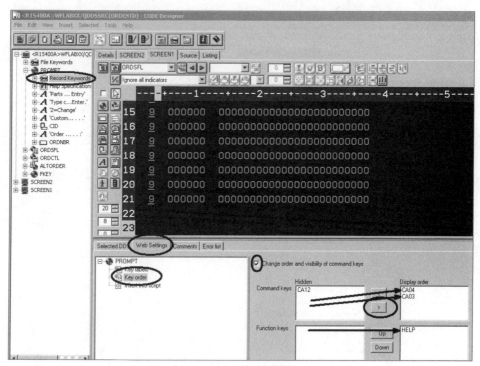

Figure 17.30: Hiding command keys using Web settings

■ Expand the **Prompt** record format.

■ Select **Record Keywords**.

■ Select the **Web Settings** tab.

■ Select **Key order**.

■ Check the **Change order and visibility of command keys** check box.

■ Select the **CA04** command key.

■ Move it to the **Display order** list box by pressing the → push button.

■ Select the **CA03** button.

■ Move it to the **Display order** list box by pressing the → push button.

■ Select the **HELP** function key.

■ Move it to the **Display order** list box by pressing the → push button.

■ Close **CODE Designer** and save the **ORDENTD** member.

■ Convert the member.

■ Test the application.

Your screen should look like Figure 17.31.

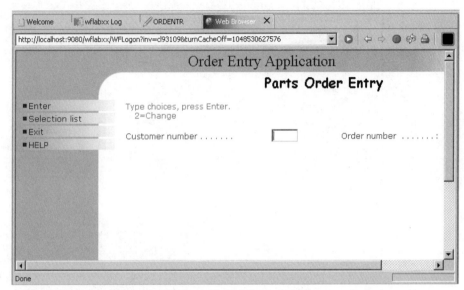

Figure 17.31: Application with Cancel push button hidden

Note: The command key is still active. If the user presses it, it will still function.

Changing command key order

If you want to change the order of how the push buttons are displayed on the Web page, you can use the same Web settings you use to hide the function keys. The instructions assume that you have used the instructions to hide command key from the previous section. Here we will move command key 4 after command key 3.

■ Open the **ORDENTD** member in CODE Designer (Figure 17.32).

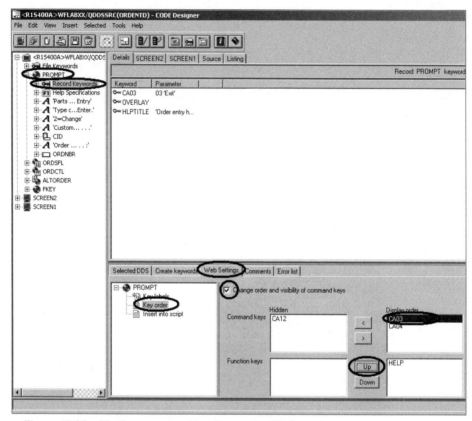

Figure 17.32: Moving command key 3 up using Web settings

- Expand the **Prompt** record format.

- Select **Record Keywords**.

- Select the **Web Settings** tab.

- Select **Key order**.

- Make sure the **Change order and visibility of command keys** check box is checked.

- Select the **CA03** command key in the Display order list box.

- Change the **Display order** by pressing the **Up** push button.

Now the command key 3 push button will display before the command key 4 push button.

- Close **CODE Designer** and save the **ORDENTD** member.

- Convert the member.

- Test the application.

Your screen should look like Figure 17.33.

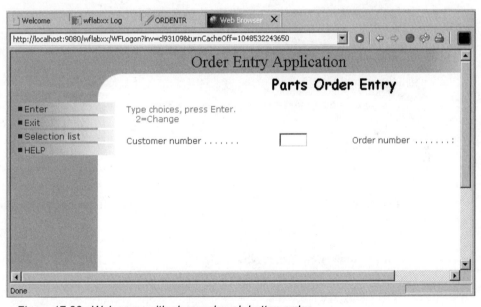

Figure 17.33: Web page with changed push button order

Aligning headings with columns

You might have noticed that the subfile headings in the WebFaced application do not align very well with the subfile columns themselves. See the misalignments in Figure 17.34.

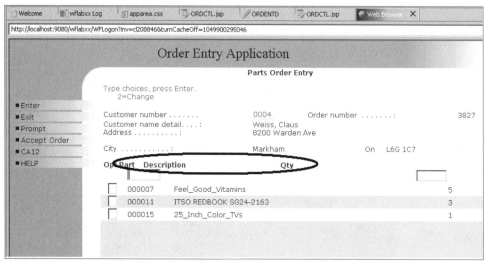

Figure 17.34: Subfile headings misaligned due to proportional font usage

The headings in the Order Entry Application are implemented in DDS as strings that depend on blank characters to occupy the same space as other characters. This works well in text-based user interfaces but does not work well in environments where you use proportional fonts. Here is an example of the difference between these font types:

Proportional font Times New Roman:

wwwwwww
iiiiiii

Nonproportional font `Courier New`:

wwwwwww
iiiiiii

You can see that an alignment based on counting spaces for a proportional font does not work, whereas using the same space for all characters works very well for a nonproportional font. In Development Studio Client Version 4 with Service Pack 4 applied and in Version 5, the alignment when using nonproportional fonts should work very well, although you might see minor problems when you have many one- and two-character input fields.

The easiest solution, then, is to use nonproportional fonts. The easiest way to do this is to edit the **appaera.css file** and change **wf_field** style class font attribute from Verdana to Courier New. This generally corrects the misalignment. On the other hand, nonproportional fonts make the user interface less attractive. A sample Web page with a nonproportional font and its effect on the heading alignment can be seen in Figure 17.35.

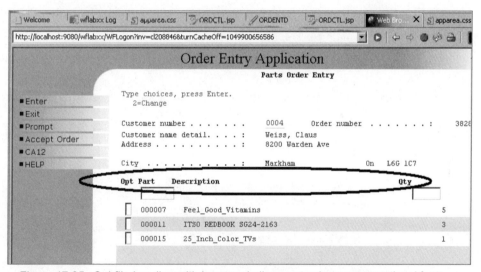

Figure 17.35: Subfile heading with improved alignment using nonproportional fonts

The best way to achieve heading alignment is to split the string that contains the sub-file column headings into single fields with fixed positions in the DDS source. With this method, WebFacing conversion aligns the headings correctly regardless of the font style.

Figure 17.36 shows you how to adjust the headings in the ORDCTL record format, using the LPEX editor.

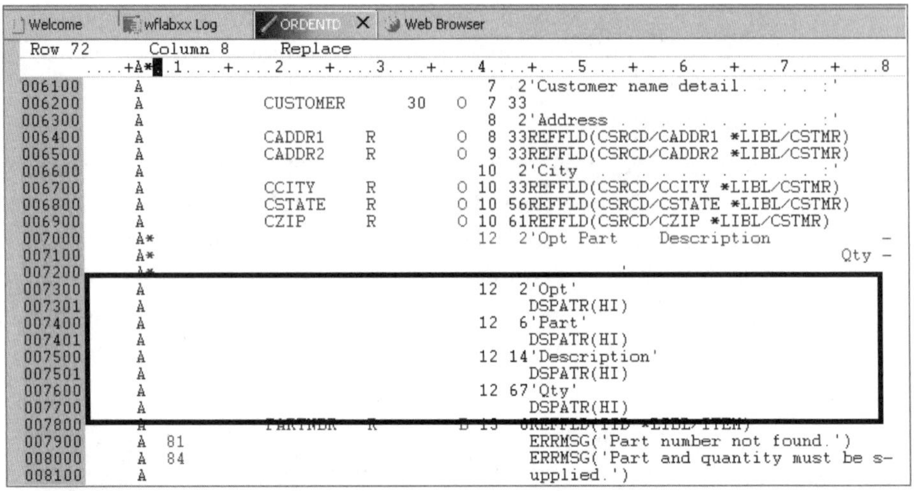

```
Welcome      wflabxx Log        ORDENTD  X   Web Browser
  Row  72        Column  8        Replace
....+A*.1....+....2....+....3....+....4....+....5....+....6....+....7....+....8
006100     A                                7   2'Customer name detail.....:'
006200     A              CUSTOMER    30   O   7 33
006300     A                                8   2'Address
006400     A              CADDR1    R       O   8 33REFFLD(CSRCD/CADDR1 *LIBL/CSTMR)
006500     A              CADDR2    R       O   9 33REFFLD(CSRCD/CADDR2 *LIBL/CSTMR)
006600     A                               10   2'City                           '
006700     A              CCITY     R       O  10 33REFFLD(CSRCD/CCITY *LIBL/CSTMR)
006800     A              CSTATE    R       O  10 56REFFLD(CSRCD/CSTATE *LIBL/CSTMR)
006900     A              CZIP      R       O  10 61REFFLD(CSRCD/CZIP *LIBL/CSTMR)
007000     A*                              12   2'Opt Part    Description        -
007100     A*                                                                Qty -
007200     A*
007300     A                               12   2'Opt'
007301     A                                      DSPATR(HI)
007400     A                               12   6'Part'
007401     A                                      DSPATR(HI)
007500     A                               12  14'Description'
007501     A                                      DSPATR(HI)
007600     A                               12  67'Qty'
007700     A                                      DSPATR(HI)
007800     A              PARTNBR   R       B  13  OREFFLD(ITB *LIBL/ITEM)
007900     A    81                                 ERRMSG('Part number not found.')
008000     A    84                                 ERRMSG('Part and quantity must be s-
008100     A                                       upplied.')
```

Figure 17.36: Editor with split heading strings positioned at specific column number

Now each heading is positioned exactly on top of the subfile columns.

Figure 17.37 shows the result of this change after saving and reconverting the member.

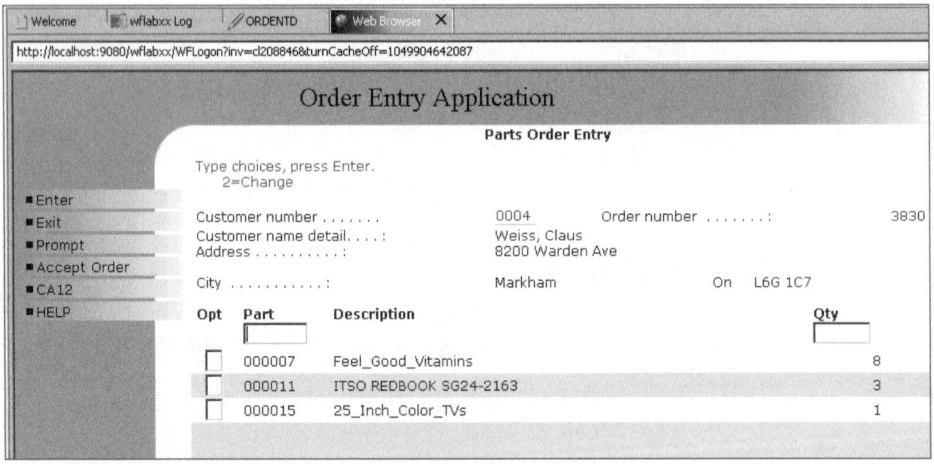

Figure 17.37: Heading alignment after splitting the headings string

Providing separate strings for heading and positioning them by column provides the most reliable alignment of headings and the corresponding subfile columns.

Right-aligning fields

If you need to right-align fields or headings, you can use the following HTML code. Put the tags around the fields and heading that you want to align to the right instead of the default left.

```
<DIV class="wf_rightJustify">
<INPUT ... >
</DIV>
```

The wf_rightJustify class is already included in apparea.css file.

To change the field alignment with Web settings, use the Insert HTML Web setting for the field. Add the first line from the code sample above in the Before page and the third line in the After page. Doing so will preserve your alignment choice even if you reconvert your source.

Changing the WebFacing project template

When you create a WebFacing project, the project template is copied from the product installation directory to the Development Studio Client workspace. If you have files you want to add to all WebFacing projects, you can in fact change the WebFacing template rather than copy files into each of the projects that you create. You might want to do this if you create a JavaScript function or if you have a graphic that you want available to all new WebFaced projects.

In the example here, I added a my.js JavaScript file and a wuicon1.gif graphic file to the template. I then created a WebFacing project in the workbench.

The directory structure for locating the template is as follows: *WDSC*\iseries\eclipse\plugins\com.ibm.etools.iseries.webfacing_5.0.0\ProjectTemplate\. WDSC is the default product directory. (If you chose a different name during installation just use it instead of WDSC.)

Inside the ProjectTemplate directory, you can see the directory structure of the WebFacing project. In there, you can add the file that should be added permanently to all new WebFacing projects. Figure 17.38 shows the my.js file added to the template directory.

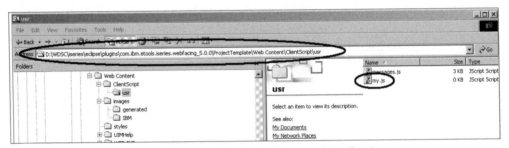

Figure 17.38: File my.js added to the ClientScript\usr template directory

---

Important: When installing a Service Pack for WDSC, the com.ibm.etools.iseries.webfacing_5.0.0 name will change to 5.x.y, depending on the Service Pack level you install. You then have to update the template in this new directory with your changes. The first Service Pack at general availability of the product will be 5.0.1. Since it is strongly suggested that you apply this Service Pack immediately after installing the product, I suggest you make any changes to the 5.0.1 template after updating the product to that level.

In Figure 17.39, you can see the WebFacing project structure created from a modified template.

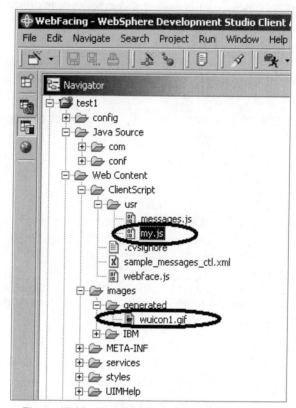

Figure 17.39: New WebFacing project created from modified template with additional files

The two files and the generated directory have been automatically added to the WebFacing project in the workbench.

Analysis

This chapter offered a variety of ways to enhance the WebFacing conversion results. Some of the Web settings give you excellent capability to override the default HTML generated by the WebFacing tool.

Adding graphics and allowing users to click these instead of using command keys offers an easy way to let the user interface appear more like a real Web application.

Here is what you did if you completed all the exercises:

- You added a graphic to click, one that links to a static Web page, using the Insert HTML Web settings.

- You added a graphic and used some JavaScript to simulate a command key being pressed when the graphic is clicked, using the Insert HTML Web settings.

- You added a pop-up calendar to support input for a date field, using the Insert HTML Web settings.

- You used your own HTML to emphasize the display of the city name using the User defined HTML Web settings.

- You added a new style class to emphasize the appearance of certain fields and used the Appearance and Text Web settings to implement this change.

- You enhanced the appearance of the radio buttons that are generated for entry fields with the VALUES keyword, using the Appearance and Text Web settings.

- You added a graphic to the user interface to enhance its appearance by using the Create Graphics Web settings.

- You changed the command key appearance by using the record format Web settings for command keys.

- You investigated alignment of fields and headings with subfile columns and you learned that using nonproportional fonts will prevent most alignment problems.

- You learned how split up subfile headings in the DDS source to align them correctly with subfile columns in the WebFaced user interface.

- You learned how to right-align fields when needed.

- You learned how to change the WebFacing project template to customize it for your individual needs.

You are ready to move on. The next chapter offers troubleshooting tips, so if you don't have any problems, you can skip it and go to Chapter 19 how to create your Web application on a remote Application server instead of running it in the WAS test environment of the Development Studio Client.

Troubleshooting tips

This chapter is not solely "hands-on"; rather, it is a summary of troubleshooting tips I have collected from frequently asked questions, the Development Studio Client Web site, and the WebFacing Redbook SG24-6901.

At some point, you will most likely be in a situation where something does not work as you might expect. Then it is up to you to investigate what is wrong. When working with a Web application, you have to deal with a couple of different environments and you will need to figure out which of these environments is causing the problem.

One thing that many people overlook is the job log on the iSeries host. If you are connected and a job is created, the job log is an excellent source of information for you when you want to investigate what is going wrong.

IBM has created a newsgroup in which WebSphere Development Studio Client customers can post questions. I suggest that you use this newsgroup to seek advice from fellow WebFacing users or IBM WebFacing developers and support folks:

News://news.software.websphere.studio400.

Another very valuable newsgroup for WebFacing information is run by MIDRANGE dot COM: *wdsci-l@midrange.com.*

If you think you are dealing with a bug in the WebFacing Tool, you might want to contact your IBM support organization and open a Problem Management Report (PMR). IBM will either work with you to determine the source of the problem and provide you with a fix if one is available already, or contact the IBM development group to correct the problem.

Here are some of the common problem situations that I and other customers have encountered when working in the WebFacing environment.

The WebFaced application does not start

When you click the link on the index.html page, the application does not start. The index.html page stays in the browser, no error message displays, and the application invocation seems to hang. This might be a problem with one of the following:

- The library list

- The invocation command you have specified in the WebFacing project

- The iSeries host setup itself
  - The use of limited capabilities user IDs
  - WebFacing PTF levels not in sync with the WebFacing runtime level

Check the application server console. If you do not see the Pagebuilder.jsp being invoked (see Figure 18.1), this is a good indication that the program on the iSeries host cannot be found.

Figure 18.1: WebSphere application server console without the Pagebuilder.jsp being invoked

Note: If you run an initial program at job startup to set up the library list, be aware that this program will not be run in the WebFacing environment. You will need to modify the job description to apply the correct library list or set up the environment to explicitly call a program during startup.

The first course of action is to check whether the command that you specified in the WebFacing project, in combination with the user ID that you used to log on for the WebFaced application, works in a 5250 environment.

Start a 5250 emulation session:

- Sign on with the same user ID and password that you used in the WebFacing project to run the WebFaced application.

- Enter the command that you specified in the WebFacing project exactly the same way on the 5250 command line.

If the application does not open in the 5250 environment, something is wrong with the library list or the command.

- Thoroughly check your application to get it running in the 5250 environment.

- With the same settings, start the WebFaced application.

If you need to change the user ID and password in the WebFacing project, use the WebFacing project Properties option in the WebFacing Perspective to change them.

If you need to change the invocation command, you have two options:

1. Use the WebFacing Project Wizard to delete the current entry and add a new, changed one.

2. Directly edit the file that contains the information.

To use the WebFacing Project Wizard (option 1):

- Switch to the WebFacing Project view.

- Expand the **WebFacing project**.

- Right-click the **CL commands** node.

- Select the **Add** option from the pop-up menu.

- The Specify CL commands wizard page displays.

- Select the **flawed invocation command** entry in the list and delete it.

- Specify a new **correct invocation command** and add it to the list.

- Click the **Finish** push button.

- Restart the WAS Test environment server to pick up the new invocation file content.

- Run your application.

To edit the file directly (option 2):

- Go to the Navigator view in the workbench.

- Look for the **.invocation** file in the WebFacing project structure under **Project → Web content → WEB-INF → classes → conf**.

- Edit the **.invocation** file to correct the command invocation.

- Save the file.

- Close the editor.

- Restart the WAS test environment server to pick up the new invocation file.

If the command in the 5250 environment worked fine and started the application without a problem, check the job log for the WebFacing job.

You can do this in the Remote System Explorer under the iSeries jobs node, or you can use a 5250 and issue a Work Active Job (WRKACTJOB) command.

- Look for a QQF job starting with the user ID you are using and then check the job log. Figure 18.2 shows the Remote System Explorer with a QQF job selected and the job log displayed.

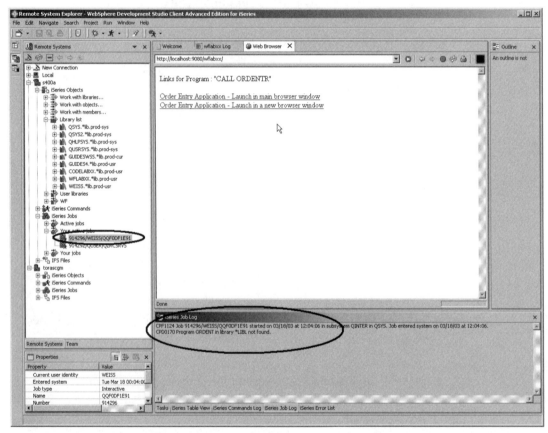

Figure 18.2: Using the RSE to display a job log

In Figure 18.2, the problem is an error in the command you are using to invoke the application.

If you cannot find a QQF job, that job might have ended:

- Use the Work Spool File (WRKSPLF) command for the User ID you used in the WebFaced application to check if there are any job logs from the terminated job that could give you more information.

Checking the WebFacing PTF level

Make sure you have the latest PTF level on your iSeries host. Check the WebSphere Development Studio Web page for WebFacing Tool information. If you have a mismatch, load and apply the PTFs, then **End** the WebFacing server and **Start** it again:

- In V5R1 or higher, use the End TCP/IP Server (ENDTCPSVR) *WEBFACING command, then the Start TCP/IP Server (STRTCPSVR) * WEBFACING command.

- In V4R5, use the End WebFacing Server (ENDWFSVR) command, then the Start WebFacing Server (STRWFSVR) command.

Run the WebFaced application again.

Problem with using limited-capabilities user IDS

Limited-capabilities user IDs will not work in a WebFacing environment. If you use the *YES or *PARTIAL parameter on the Limit capabilities (LMTCPB) parameter for a user ID, WebFacing will not work.

However, you can circumvent this problem. Set the initial program for these user IDs to OSYS/QQFINVOKER. This will cause the WebFacing run-time program to be invoked at logon time, which will enable these user IDs to run in a WebFaced application.

Note: After you change the user ID to this initial program, you cannot use it to sign on through a regular 5250 screen.

WebFacing server does not start

If you receive an application error after clicking the hyperlink to invoke the WebFaced application, check the error message just below it. The error message contains details about the cause of the error. One of the messages that I have frequently seen is that the WebFacing server is not started, as shown in Figure 18.3.

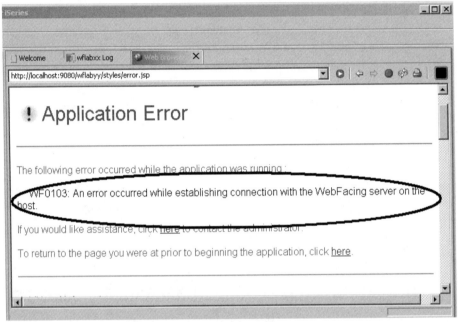

Figure 18.3: Browser with error message that WebFacing server is not started

In V5R1 or higher, use the Start TCP/IP server command to start the WebFacing server: STRTCPSVR *WEBFACING. In V4R5, use the Start WebFacing Server (STRWFSVR) command.

Note: Make sure that the iSeries system value QAUTVRT is higher than 0. Because the WebFacing server relies on Virtual Terminal jobs, you should check to make sure that this system value is set so that all WebFacing sessions are supported.

You will receive the same message if the iSeries server you have specified to connect to does not exist, so use the WebFacing project properties to make sure that the server name is correct.

Scroll a little further down to the additional information for the message, as shown in Figure 18.4.

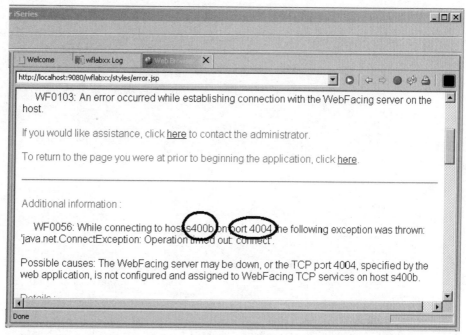

Figure 18.4: Additional error information shown in browser

This information will tell you which iSeries host the application attempted to access and which port number has been used to connect to the WebFacing server. Check that these values are correct. Port number 4004 is the default port that the WebFacing server uses.

You can use the Work with TCP/IP Network Status NETSTAT command and use parameter *CNN to check the connections and ports.

■ Make sure that port 4004 is listed on the Work with TCP/IP Connection Status list (Figure 18.5).

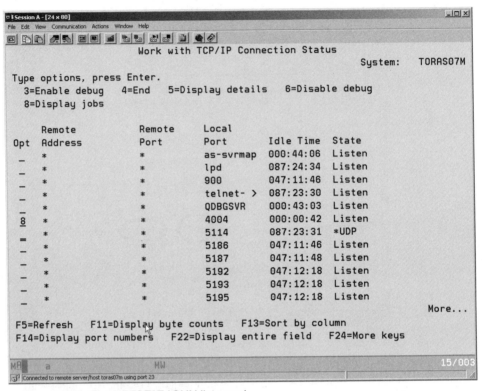

Figure 18.5: The NETSTAT *CNN list panel

■ Press **command key 14** on the list panel to show the port numbers.

■ Use **option 8** to check the jobs using this port (see Figure 18.6).

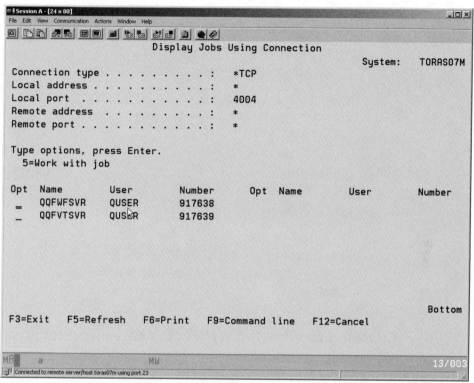

Figure 18.6: Display of jobs using port 4004

There should be two jobs listed, their names beginning with QQF. That means the WebFacing server is using port 4004.

If they are not QQF jobs,

- Check the port the WebFacing server is using by entering the Work with Service Table (WRKSRVTBLE) command.

- Look for an "as-WebFacing" service entry in the list. If there is none, then the port used is the default 4004 port. If there is an entry, use the display option to see what port is being used.

■ For more information on setting the WebFacing server port, check the WebFacing Help, under Tasks, the heading **Changing the port used by your WebFacing applications**.

Note: If the default port 4004 is not in use by some other service, there is no need to change the port number to something else.

If they are QQF jobs,

■ Check the job logs in both of them.

■ In case of any errors, check the PTF level. If your system has the current WebFacing PTFs applied, this is most likely a problem and should be reported to IBM support.

Checking whether the WebFacing server reacted to a request

You can easily check whether the WebFacing server on the iSeries host has been responding to a request by checking the idle time in the **Work with TCP Connections Status** list.

If the idle time is close to zero and you are the only user running WebFaced applications, then your last request has been received by the WebFacing server and the job logs should help you find the problem.

If the idle time is high, then the request did not make it to the WebFacing server. Check the iSeries server name you specified in the WebFacing project, and check the authentication. You can try removing the automatic authentication in the WebFacing project properties to force a sign-on dialog. If the sign-on dialog appears, you know that you reached the iSeries server and you can check the WebFacing server environment as described before.

Page cannot be displayed

The page cannot be displayed error (Figure 18.7) is most likely caused by an application server problem.

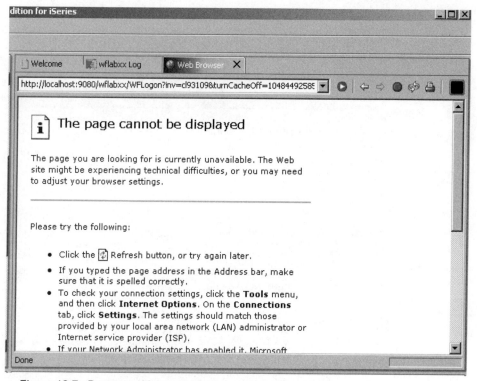

Figure 18.7: Browser with error page

When you receive a **The page cannot be displayed** error,

- Check whether the application server is started.

- If the application server is not started, start it.

- If it is already started, restart it.

The application server might be in a problem state, so restarting it will reset it. Close the browser and then try to run the application again.

Page cannot be found

When this error displays (Figure 18.8), the WebFacing project might be corrupted, or the WebFacing application has not been installed correctly, or the URL is incorrectly used.

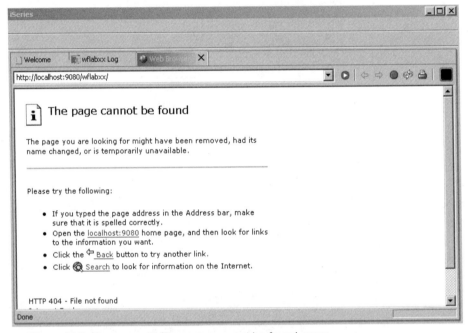

Figure 18.8: Browser with The page cannot be found *error*

Make sure that the index.html page exists in your WebFacing project:

■ Check in the Navigator view of the workbench in the following file structure: **Project → Web Content → index.html**.

If it is not there,

■ Rebuild the WebFacing project.

Also check the web.xml file, which contains the project information. If it is not created correctly, then you might see this error as well.

Check under **Project** → **Web content** → **WEB-INF** → **lib** → **web.xml** (Figure 18.9).

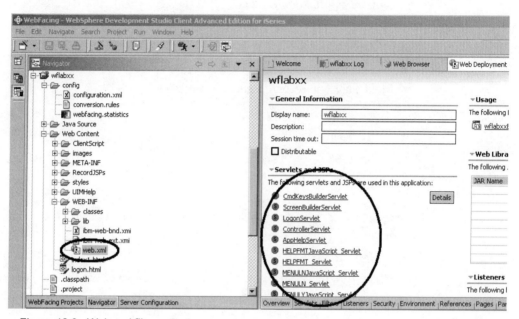

Figure 18.9: Web.xml file content

Double-click the **web.xml** file and check that it has WebFacing Servlets listed on the overview page as shown in Figure 18.9.

If they do not appear, then the project is corrupted. Try to rebuild the WebFacing project. If that does not result in a correct web.xml file, I suggest that you contact IBM support.

If the index.html file is there and the web.xml file looks correct, then the application might not be correctly installed.

When running in the test environment,

- Stop the application server.

- Publish the server.

- Make sure you receive a success message.

- Start the server again.

- Try to run the application.

If you are working with a remote application server on an iSeries host or any other platform outside your workstation,

- Make sure the application is installed correctly and use the application server console to verify that everything is installed correctly.

- Make sure the application is started.

- Restart the http server to make sure it picks up the application information.

- Restart the application server.

Invalid session

The Web environment is not based on persistent connections between the browser and the http server. When you run the WebFaced application and leave the browser for an extended period of time, the application will actually time out (see Figure 18.10).

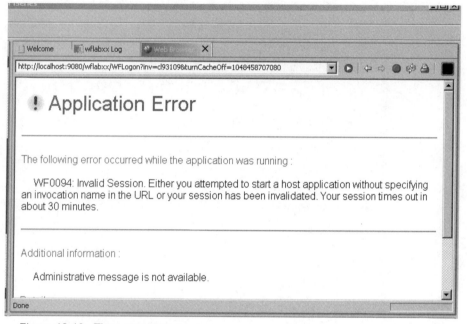

Figure 18.10: Time out error

In this environment, the server cannot detect whether a session has been interrupted permanently by problems with communications or by the workstation itself. To avoid having too many invalid sessions, the application server has a default session time out of 30 minutes. By default, a session will be invalidated after 30 minutes of idle time. If you try to use the session after 30 minutes of inactivity, you will see this error.

If this time interval of 30 minutes does not suit your environment, you can change the application server settings using the Administration console to change the time out values.

DDS and WebFacing are out of sync

If you change the display file DDS source member and recompile your program to work with the changed display file, you will also have to reconvert this DDS source member to create the corresponding JSPs and XML files in the WebFacing project. If you do not do this, you receive the error shown in Figure 18.11.

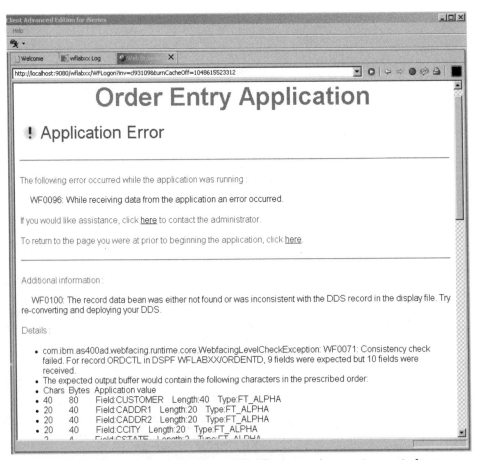

Figure 18.11: Error when application and WebFacing environment are out of sync

The example in Figure 18.11 shows a field being added to the record format.

- To fix this, reconvert the DDS member containing the changed record format.

Sometimes this error will also occur if the publishing failed to finish successfully.

- To fix this, stop the application server, republish the project, and start the application server again.

UTF-8 encoding error

If you are using J2EE level 1.2, then to be able to run on WAS Version 3.5 or Version 4.0, you need to set the UTF-8 encoding (that WebFacing uses to provide support for international character sets) in the application server.

Note: You need to enable UTF-8 encoding even if you are using WAS Version 5.0 but your project uses J2EE level 1.2.

If you have not set this environment variable in the application server, you will receive an error when data is sent back to the server from the first WebFaced page, as shown in Figure 18.12.

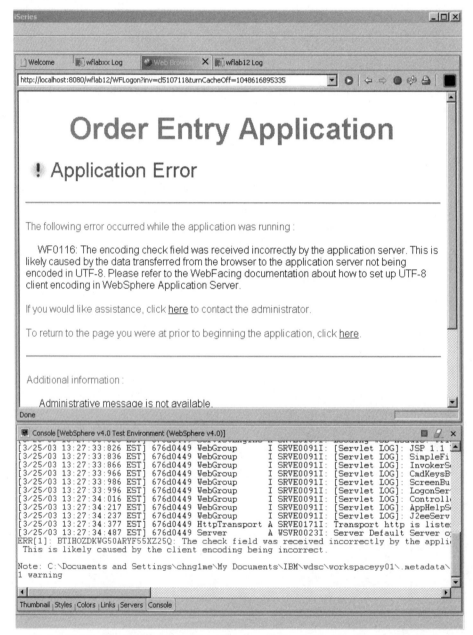

Figure 18.12: Error because UTF-8 setup is missing in the Version 4.0 application server

As you can see, the message clearly indicates that the problem is caused by the browser's failure to send a UTF-8 encoded data stream.

For J2EE level 1.2 projects,

■ The application server has to be set up to properly handle UTF-8 encoding. For every application server you use, you need to do the setup task once. If you use the WAS test environment on your workstation first and set up UTF-8 there, and then you move to your iSeries WAS production server, you will have to repeat the UTF-8 setup for this server as well.

■ Follow the instructions in the WebFacing Help, under: **Tasks → Configuring UTF-8 support in WebSphere Application Server**. You have to do this only once per application server that runs the WebFaced applications.

Note: You do not need to configure UTF-8 for WAS Version 5.0 when using J2EE level 1.3. It is set up automatically.

Application error in browser

If the application is started but then receives an exception that is not handled by the application, the browser will return an application error (see Figure 18.13). This application error is the equivalent to the same error that displays in a 5250 environment.

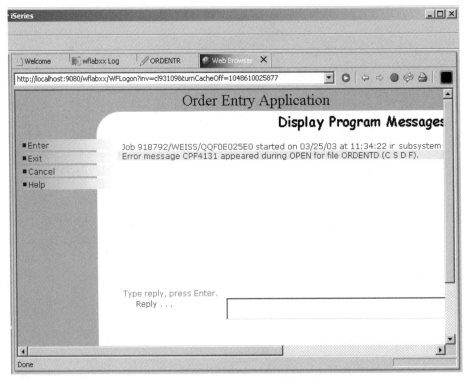

Figure 18.13: Level check exception message CPF4131 displayed in browser

You can reply with any of the valid options to the exception directly in the browser in the Reply entry field provided.

Conversion does not work in Development Studio Client Version 4.0

If you have trouble converting in Version 4.0, this might be related to the communications environment in CODE Designer. Although it is not obvious, the WebFacing Tool invokes the CODE Designer tool during WebFacing conversion. CODE Designer in Development Studio Client Version 4.0 uses the CODE communications layer and not the Remote System Explorer support that the WebFacing Tool normally uses.

Note: It is highly recommended that you use a host name and not an IP address when defining server identifications in the CODE communications layer. If you do not have a name server, use the *hosts* file under your Windows system directory to map the IP address to a host name.

One way to find out whether the CODE communications are causing a problem is to simply try starting CODE Designer from the Windows Start menu and try loading the DDS member from the iSeries server that you use for the WebFacing conversion. If this works, communications should not be a problem.

If it does not work,

- Close CODE Designer.

- Go to the **Windows Task Manager**.

■ Look in the Processes page for image names that start with evf. You can sort the list by clicking the header **Image Name**.

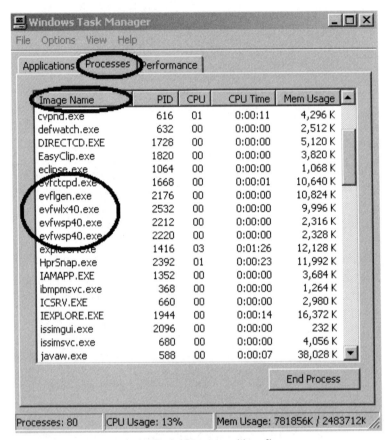

Figure 18.14: Windows Task Manager with evf* processes

End each of these evf processes by

■ Selecting the process

■ Clicking the **End Process** push button

After you end all evf processes, start CODE Designer again and access the DDS source member on your iSeries server.

If you are successful now,

■ Close CODE Designer and start the WebFacing conversion again.

Hopefully the WebFacing conversion now works. Otherwise, use the contacts listed in the beginning of this chapter to determine the cause for this problem.

Note: In Development Studio Client Version 5.0, the WebFacing conversion is changed so that CODE Designer does not use the CODE communications when performing WebFacing conversion.

CODE Designer Save dialog is visible indefinitely

In Development Studio Client Version 4.0, when you save members in CODE Designer, the message dialog box indicating that CODE designer is saving the source (Figure 18.15) often does not disappear after the save has been successful.

Figure 18.15: CODE Designer save dialog

If this message box still displays even after a reasonable time has been passed,

■ Click the **Stop** push button on the Save dialog.

■ Close the member in CODE Designer by pressing **command key 3**.

■ Reload the member to check that your changes have made it to the iSeries server.

Most likely the save was successful.

Note: This problem has been fixed in Development Studio Client Version 5.0 and Version 4.0 Service Pack 4. The Save dialog disappears after the save action is complete.

Summary

This chapter should help you resolve some of the problems you might encounter with the WebFacing Tool. If you still cannot resolve your problem, do not hesitate to use the newsgroups to ask for help. Chances are good that someone else has already encountered the same problem and can help you out.

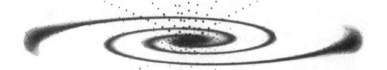

Exporting to iSeries WebSphere Application Server 5.0 or WebSphere Application Server Express 5.0

Until now you have only tested your application in the local WAS test environment. Now you are ready to test on an iSeries IBM WebSphere Application Server. In this exercise, you will export files created by the WebFacing Tool to a remote WebSphere Application server, to publish and deploy your application as you would in real-life development.

The goal of the exercise

This exercise shows you how to publish your WebFacing files to a remote Web-Sphere Application Server 5.0 environment on an iSeries host. The tasks described in this exercise are split for WebSphere Application Server Express 5.0, which is very easy, and WebSphere Application Server Version 5.0 for iSeries, which is a little more complex. If you are working with WebSphere Application Server Version 5.0 (and not Version 4.0 or 3.5), follow the instructions in this chapter to create the Web application from a WebFacing project in the workbench. The instructions for the other two versions of WAS are in Appendix A and Appendix B.

You will start the Export tool in Development Studio Client, specify files to export, and install and start the Web application using the WAS Administrative Console. At the end of this exercise, you should be able to

- Use the WebSphere Development Client wizards to specify the files to deploy to the application server

- Export the selected Enterprise Archive File (EAR) files to the server file system

- Install the WebFaced application on the remote application server through the WAS Administrative Console

- Use a browser to invoke the WebFaced application on the remote application server

- Learn how to copy selected files from a WebFacing project in the workbench to the application server, to apply small changes without having to copy the complete EAR file

Scenario

You have tested the WebFaced application in the WAS test environment and you are ready to move it to your iSeries WAS environment. You are running WAS Version 5.0 on your iSeries server. The first step is to copy your WebFacing project files to the iSeries file system, and the second step is to install the application in the application server.

The J2EE standard has the concept of an Enterprise Archive File (EAR). This file is a zip file that contains all information about your Web application. In the workbench, this file is built automatically for Web projects. Since your WebFacing project is a Web project, the wflabxxEAR file exists already. You only have to move it to the application server, point to it, and then install the application. There is no need to worry about the structure of the application; everything is taken care of in the workbench.

Exporting the files to the Web server

This section describes how to copy the WebFacing project files to a WebSphere Application Server, Version 5.0. These first steps are the same for WebSphere Application Server, Version 5.0 and the Express, Version 5.0. If you are using WAS Version 4.0 or 3.5.6, follow the instructions in Appendix A or Appendix B.

Before you export any files, you must map a network drive to the Root file system on the iSeries where WAS is installed.

- Right-click the **Network Neighborhood** (or **My Network Places**) icon on the desktop.

- Select **Map Network Drive** from the pop-up menu.

In the Folder field of the Map Network Drive dialog box (Figure 19.1),

- Enter two backslashes (\\) and the Netserver name of your Web server, and then **\root**, for example, **\\S400A\root.**

- Click the **Finish** push button.

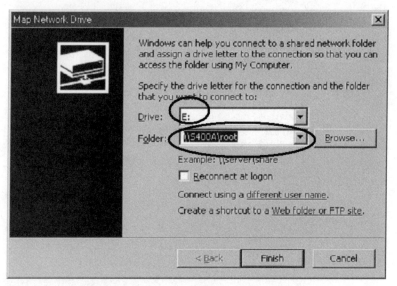

Figure 19.1: Map Network Drive *dialog*

You now have an additional drive available on your workstation, and you are ready to export your WebFacing project files.

Exporting your EAR file

Return to the Development Studio Client workbench. In the WebFacing perspective,

- Select the **File** option from the workbench menu bar.

- Select the **Export** option from the pull-down menu.

The Select page of the Export wizard opens (Figure 19.2).

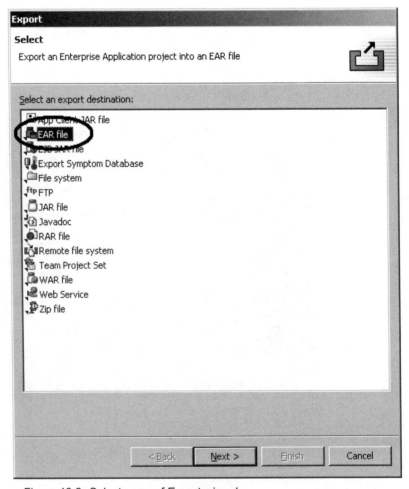

Figure 19.2: Select page of Export wizard

■ Select the **EAR file** icon.

An EAR file is a compressed Enterprise Application Archive, and it contains all the files needed for the Web application.

■ Click the **Next** push button.

The EAR Export page opens (Figure 19.3).

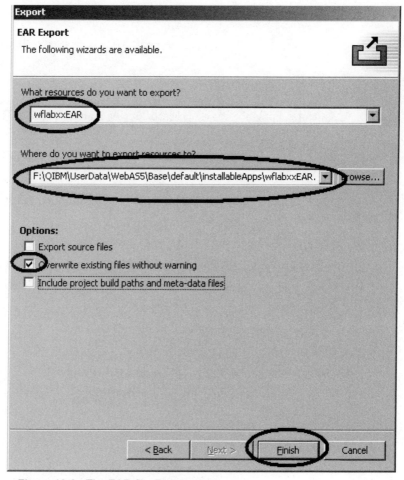

Figure 19.3: The EAR file Export dialog

- Select the name of the resources you used when creating your WebFacing project. This should be **wflabxxEAR**.

In the Where do you want to export the resources to? field,

- Specify where to put the EAR file by entering the drive and directory structure of the IFS drive you mapped in the earlier steps. For example, use the default WAS directory structure for installable applications:

  x:\QIBM\UserData\WebAS5\Base\default\installableApps\wflabxx.ear,

  where *x:* is the drive letter mapped from your iSeries host in the previous steps.

Note: For WebSphere Application Server Express, the default installation directory would be x:\QIBM\UserData\WebASE\ASE5\server_name\installableApps \wflabxx.ear

---

- Select the **Override existing resource without warning** check box.

- Click the **Finish** push button.

If you see a message asking you to create a directory or delete an existing file,

- Click the **OK** or **Yes** push button and continue.

Now you can install the application in WAS. Continue here if you use WAS Express; otherwise skip to Installing the Application to a Remote WebSphere Application Server (page 456).

WAS Express users: Installing the application to a remote WebSphere Application Server Express

At this point, you already need to have set up and started the WebSphere Application Server (WAS) Express and an associated HTTP server on your iSeries server.

Open any Web browser:

■ Type **http://servername:port#a/** in the URL entry field.

> **Note:** The default administrative port number for the HTTP server is 2001.

The Login dialog appears.

■ Type your iSeries **user ID**.

■ Type your iSeries **password**.

■ Click the **OK** push button.

In the browser,

■ Click the **IBM WebSphere Application Server - Express for iSeries** menu option (Figure 19.4).

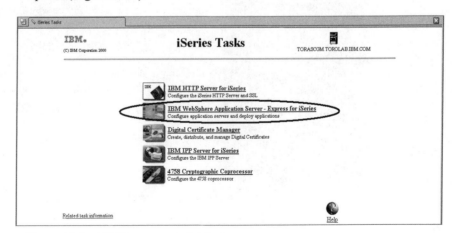

Figure 19.4: HTTP server administration menu

Note: You could also select the first option: *IBM HTTP Server for iSeries.*

The administration pages for the HTTP and application servers display.

■ Select the **Manage** Tab.

The Manage Application Server - Express page displays (Figure 19.5).

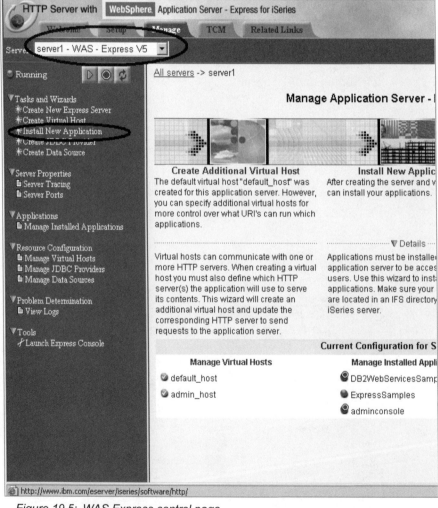

Figure 19.5: WAS Express control page

- Select your **WAS Express server instance** in the Server combination box.

- Click the **Install New Application** link in the Navigation tree.

The Install New Application page displays (Figure 19.6).

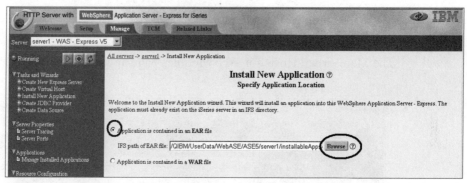

Figure 19.6: Install New Application *page*

- Select the **Application is contained in an EAR file** radio button.

- Specify the location of your EAR file (the file that you exported in the previous step). You can use the **Browse** push button to locate the file.

- Click the **Next** push button.

A page appears with options for application installation (Figure 19.7).

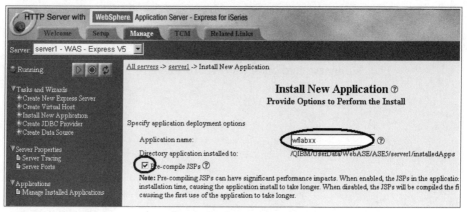

Figure 19.7: Specifying option for application installation

- Specify **wflabxx** in the Application name entry field.

- You can select the **Pre-compile JSPs** check box to speed up the process of showing the page the first time. (JSPs are compiled into servlets when first touched.)

- Click the **Next** push button.

The Map Virtual Hosts for Web Modules page appears (Figure 19.8).

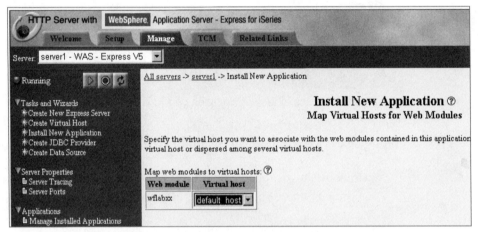

Figure 19.8: Selecting the virtual host to be associated with the Web modules

- Select a **Virtual host** of your choice, or leave the **default host** selected.

- Click the **Next** push button.

The Summary page displays (Figure 19.9).

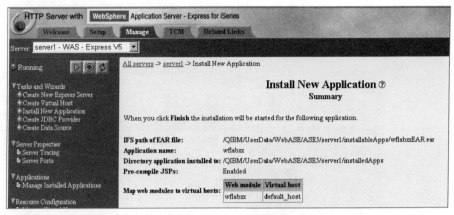

Figure 19.9: Summary page for application installation

- Check the information.

- Click the **Finish** push button.

After the successful installation you see a page where you can manage the installed applications (Figure 19.10).

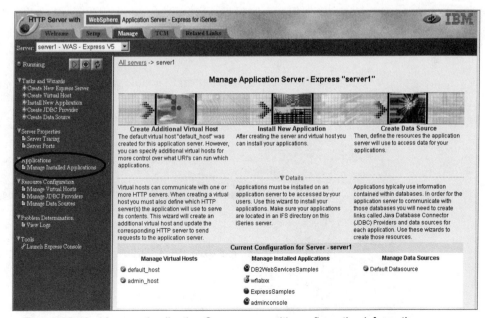

Figure 19.10: Manage Application Server page with configuration information

■ Click the **Manage Installed Applications** link in the Navigation bar.

A page with the installed applications displays (Figure 19.11).

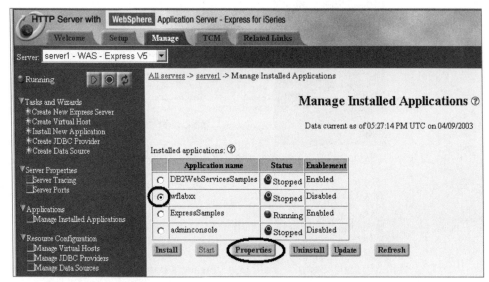

Figure 19.11: Selecting the application from the list

■ Select the **wflabxx** application radio button in the list of installed applications.

If the wflabxx application is disabled,

■ Click the **Properties** push button to enable the application.

■ Select **Enable** in the combination box, as shown in Figure 19.12.

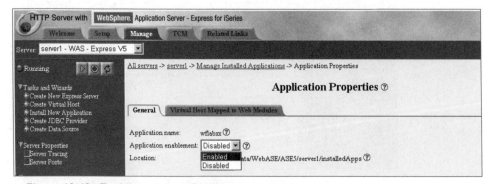

Figure 19.12: Enabling your application

- Click the **OK** push button.

Now with wflabxx in the Enabled state (Figure 19.13),

- Select the **wflabxx** application radio button.

- Click the **Start** push button.

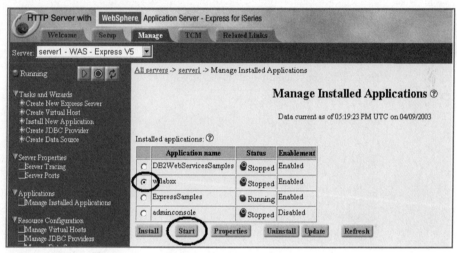

Figure 19.13: Starting the application

After the wflabxx application is in Running and Enabled state,

- Click the **Close** push button.

Now you are ready to test your application. Skip ahead to Running the Web-enabled Application (page 465).

Installing the application to a remote WebSphere Application Server

At this point, you need to have set up and started the WebSphere Application Server (WAS) and an associated HTTP server on a remote iSeries server.

Open any Web browser,

- Type **http://servername:port#a/admin** in the URL entry field

Port#a refers to the Application Server Administrative Console port number.

Note: The default Administrative Server port number is 9090.

The Login dialog appears (Figure 19.14).

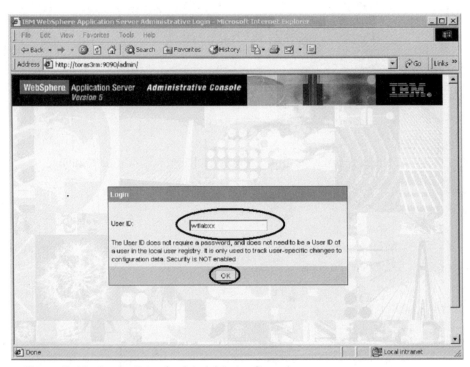

Figure 19.14: Login dialog for Administrator Console

■ Type any name in the user ID field.

■ Click the **OK** push button.

On the Administrative Console (Figure 19.15),

■ Expand the **Applications** node on the left-hand navigation bar.

Click the **Install New Application** link in the left-hand menu.

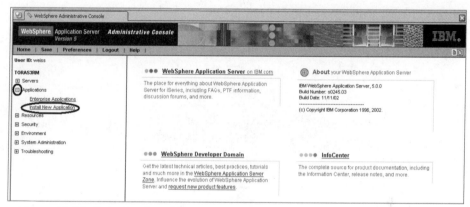

Figure 19.15: Selecting Install New Application

The Preparing for the application installation dialog appears (Figure 19.16).

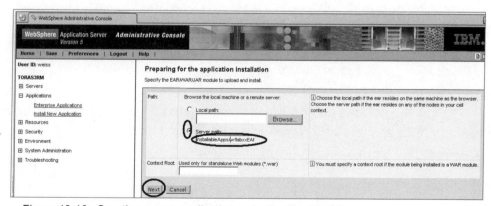

Figure 19.16: Creating a new application, selecting the EAR file

■ Select the **Server path** radio button.

■ Specify the location of your EAR file (the file that you exported in the previous step). Here you need only specify the directory hierarchy relative to the server directory. If you followed the naming previously used, it would be under the default directory: installableApps/wflabxxEAR.ear.

Note: You have to use forward slashes and not backslashes in the directory path.

■ Click the **Next** push button.

■ Accept the default **virtual host** unless you want to use a different one, as shown in Figure 19.17.

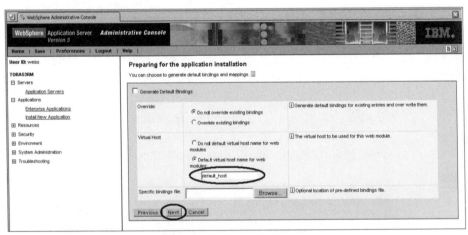

Figure 19.17: Selecting a virtual host

■ Enter the application name, **wflabxx**, in the Application name entry field on the Install New Application dialog (Figure 19.18).

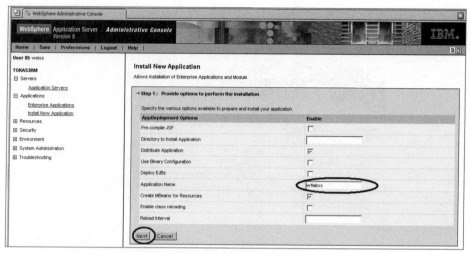

Figure 19.18: Specifying the application name

■ Click the **Next** push button.

■ Select the check box beside the wflabxx application name in the Map virtual hosts for web modules dialog (Figure 19.19).

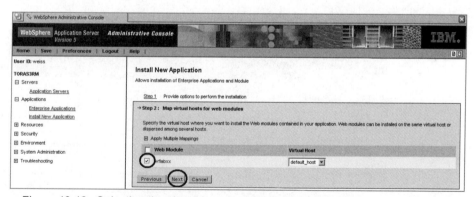

Figure 19.19: Selecting the virtual host for the wflabxx application

■ Click the **Next** push button.

■ Select the check box beside the application module name wflabxx to map it to your application server, as shown in Figure 19.20.

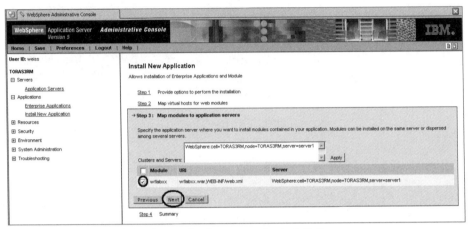

Figure 19.20: Specifying the application server for installation

■ Click the **Next** push button.

■ Now you can see the summary of the application you are going to create (Figure 19.21).

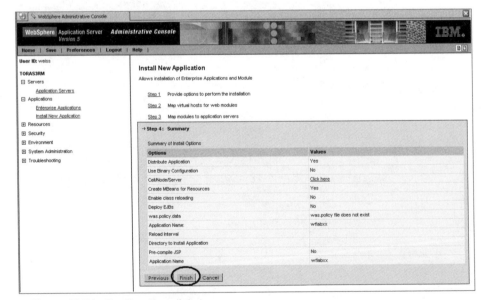

Figure 19.21: Confirmation dialog

- Verify that all of the information is correct.

- Click the **Finish** push button.

- Click the **Save to Master Configuration** link to save your changes (Figure 19.22).

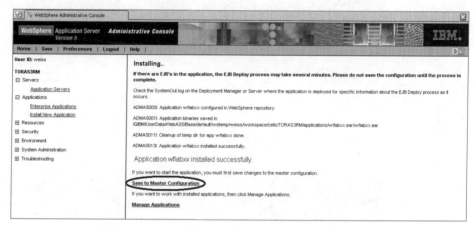

Figure 19.22: Final installation dialog in Administrative Console

- Click the **Save** push button to save the changes to the configuration (Figure 19.23).

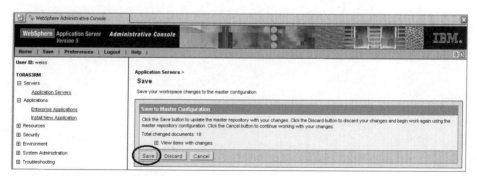

Figure 19.23: Save dialog

To start your application in the application server,

■ Click the **Enterprise Applications** link in the navigation area on the left, under Applications, as shown in Figure 19.24. You will see all the installed applications on this server (Figure 19.25).

Figure 19.24: Managing the installed application

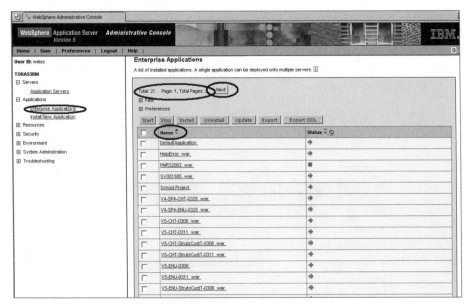

Figure 19.25: List of installed applications

If your application does not appear in the list, check to see whether there are multiple pages of installed applications. You can also sort the applications by name.

The page contains your wflabxx application in the list, as shown in Figure 19.26.

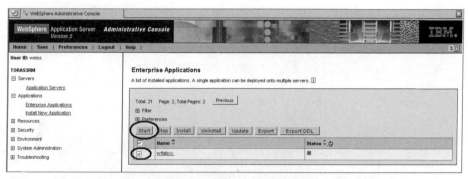

Figure 19.26: List with selected application to be started

■ Select the check box beside wflabxx, the newly installed application.

Notice the status of your application is indicated as stopped.

■ Click the **Start** push button.

You will notice that the Status indicator of the wflabxx application changes to running, as shown in Figure 19.27.

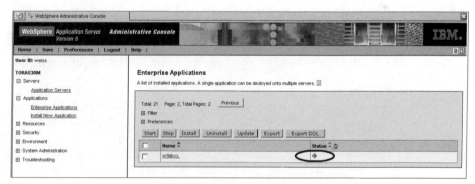

Figure 19.27: Status of wflabxx application is changed to running

You now have to enable the HTTP server to route requests for the wflabxx application to the application server. You have two choices. You can restart the HTTP server, which will automatically pick up a list of installed applications on the application server, or you can regenerate the information on the fly. You will regenerate the plugin information in this example.

- Expand the **Environment** node in the navigation tree, as shown in Figure 19.28.

- Select the **Update Web Server Plugin** link.

- Click the **OK** button on the Update web server plugin configuration page.

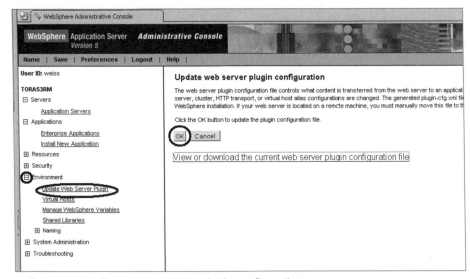

Figure 19.28: Page to update the plugin configuration

After a few moments, you will see a message as shown in Figure 19.29.

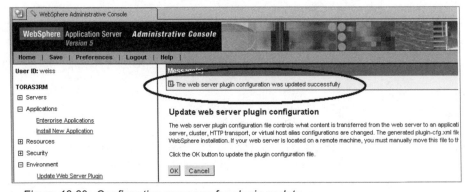

Figure 19.29: Confirmation message for plugin update

Now you can run your application.

Running the Web-enabled application

You are now ready to run the Web-enabled application.

- Open Internet Explorer.

- Type **http://servername:port#b/wflabxx** in the URL entry field.

Port#b refers to your HTTP Server port number.

Note: This is the http port name, most likely 80, not the application bootstrap port.

Your application index.html page should open. If it does not, double-check the URL and the port number. Also try restarting the HTTP server and the application server.

Refer to the Administrative Console Web site if you are having problems starting and running the HTTP server or the WebSphere Application Server.

If you still encounter problems, there are troubleshooting guides, FAQs, and newsgroups on the Web where you can find an explanation of your situation with more detailed information.

Updating the application server after reconverting selected record formats

You might wonder what to do if you change one record format in your DDS source and then reconvert it: How do you apply the changes to the remote application server? The easiest way would be to export the EAR file and perform an update of your application. If you have a large application and only a small change, this might seem to be a waste of time because the copy and update will take awhile for a large application.

A different approach is simply to update the files that you have changed. You can do this in WAS, which will pick up changed files as they are requested during run time. The only trick is to figure out where the changed files are located and where to copy them in the application server. Let's look at a way to do this.

When you reconvert a member, the conversion updates the .jsp and .xml files for this member as well. The directories containing these files have the same names as the members themselves, and the subdirectories in the directory structure actually have the names of the library and source file where the member is located.

In the WebFacing perspective, go to the Navigator view and locate these directories in the WebFacing project. Then copy them to the correct location in the application server's directory structure.

Inside the WebFacing project you have to follow the WebFacing project structure to locate the .jsp files. They are in the following directory structure: Web Content → RecordJSPs → library → source file, and members. In my example (see Figure 19.30), the path looks like this: *\wflabxx\Web Content\RecordJSPs\WFLABXX\QDDSSRC*.

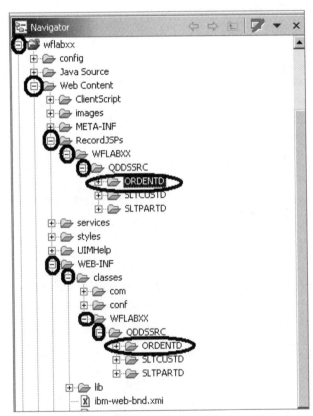

*Figure 19.30: Local drive directory structure for a
WebFacing project in the WDSC workspace*

You can copy the member directories that have been changed and paste them into the corresponding application server directories. Simply select member directories, right-click, and select **copy** from the pop-up menu.

You now need to find the corresponding directories on the application server to replace these. Use the Remote Systems view in the Remote System Explorer perspective to access the application server directories on the iSeries host.

Just specify a connection to your server and expand the **IFS Files** node in this connection tree. Inside the IFS tree, expand the **Root file system** node and drill down to the wflabxx.war directory, in a directory structure similar to this:

QIBM\UserData\WebAS5\Base\servername\installedApps\nodename\wflabxx.ear\wflabxx.war.

Inside the wflabxx.war directory structure (see Figure 19.31), you find the same directories as in the WebFacing project under the Web Content directory. Delete the directories you want to replace and then right-click the correct **source file directory** and select **Paste** on the pop-up menu.

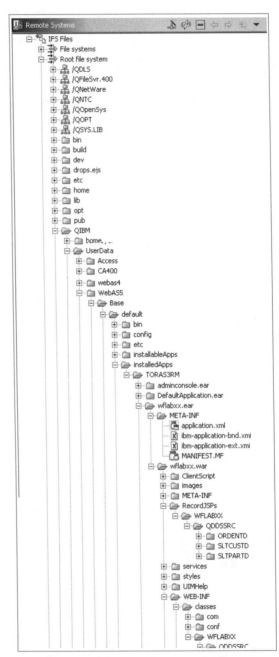

Figure 19.31: Sample WAS directory structure on iSeries IFS, shown in Remote Systems view

Now, after you have copied the directories containing the JSP files, you need to copy the directories with the XML files. The XML files contain the record buffer layout of the record formats.

Switch back to the WebFacing perspective from the Remote System Explorer perspective. In the Navigator view, find wflabxx and go to the following WebFacing project directory structure:

wflabxx\WebContent\WEB-INF\classes\WFLABXX\QDDSSRC

Here you find the directories with the XML files. Again, the names of the directories are the names of the corresponding DDS source members. Select the directories that contain the members you changed and converted, right-click the selected ones, and select the Copy option on the pop-up menu.

Now go down to the server IFS, delete the corresponding directories in the wflabxx.war directory, and Paste the new content in:

wflabxx.war\WEB-INF\classes\WFLABXX\QDDSSRC

Now when you run the WebFaced application, the new files are loaded.

These manual updates will save you time if your WebFacing projects are large because it takes a long time to copy the entire project. If you only work with a small project, however, it might be more efficient to just reexport the complete EAR file.

Analysis

You have completed the exercise Exporting to iSeries WebSphere Application Server 5.0. Here is what you accomplished:

- You exported the EAR file to a remote file system.

- You used the WAS console to install the application from the EAR file.

- You started the application in WAS.

■ You ran the application by pointing the browser to the remote server.

■ You learned how to update a remote application.

You are ready to move on; proceed to Chapter 20: Invocation of WebFaced Applications.

Invocation of WebFaced applications

Until now I have shown you only one way of invoking your WebFaced application, through the generated index.html file link.

In this chapter I will show you how to pass both static and dynamic parameters to your application. I will also show you how to invoke a WebFaced application from a different Web application. You will also have a chance to use the Java programming tools in the workbench.

The goal of this exercise

In this exercise, you will change the way you invoke the WebFaced application. I have split this chapter into three separate exercises:

1. Passing a fixed parameter value to the WebFaced program

2. Prompting for a parameter value and passing this value to the WebFaced program

3. Invoking the WebFaced application from a different program and determining the iSeries host name at run time

Scenario

The ORDENTR program that you used until now did not expect any parameters, thus illustrating the simplest case of invoking a program. I have provided an additional program that expects the customer number to be supplied at invocation. This program obtains the parameter value and prefills the Customer number entry field on the first panel. The first example in this chapter shows you how to supply a constant as a parameter to the program. The second example shows you how easy it is to prompt for a parameter and pass this value to the WebFaced application, because the WebFacing Tool actually generates the parameter entry fields for you on the initial Web page.

The third exercise assumes you need to invoke the WebFaced application from a different program or a different Web page. In that exercise, you build a simple servlet and a Web page that asks for the name of the iSeries host on which the user wants the WebFaced application to run. The servlet then invokes the WebFaced application using the server name provided.

Passing parameters in an invocation command

In previous exercises, no parameters were required to invoke the Order Entry Application. The WebFacing Tool, however, also provides capabilities to pass parameters to the program at invocation. In this situation, you have two choices:

1. Use fixed parameter values.

2. At run time, ask the user for parameter input on the index.html Web page.

If you have constants to pass, you would just specify the parameter as you do on a 5250 command line.

Using a fixed parameter value

The ORDENTRPAR program accepts one parameter. In this exercise, you add a program invocation with one parameter to the index.html page.

In the WebFacing Project view,

- Expand the **wflabxx** project.

- Right-click the **CL commands** node.

- Select the **Add** option from the pop-up menu.

The Specify CL commands dialog appears (Figure 20.1).

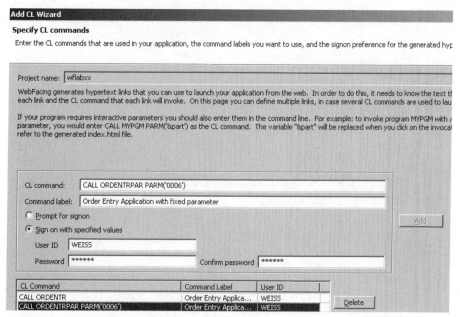

Figure 20.1: Adding a program invocation with one parameter to index.html *page*

- Enter the following CL command: **CALL ORDENTRPAR PARM('0006')**.

- Enter the following command label: **Order Entry Application with fixed parameter**.

- Specify your user authentication information.

- Click the **Finish** push button.

- Run the application.

- Select the new link in the browser.

Note that in Figure 20.2 the Customer number field is now prefilled with the parameter value you specified in the invocation command.

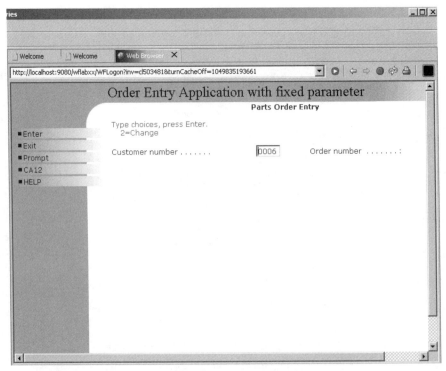

Figure 20.2: Customer number *field prefilled by value of fixed parameter*

Using a dynamic parameter value

You will use the same ORDENTRPAR program as before, but now instead of providing a fixed value, you will have the user specify a value on the index.html page.

In the WebFacing Project view,

- Expand the **wflabxx** project.

- Right-click the **CL commands** node.

- Select the **Add** option from the pop-up menu.

The Specify CL commands dialog appears (Figure 20.3).

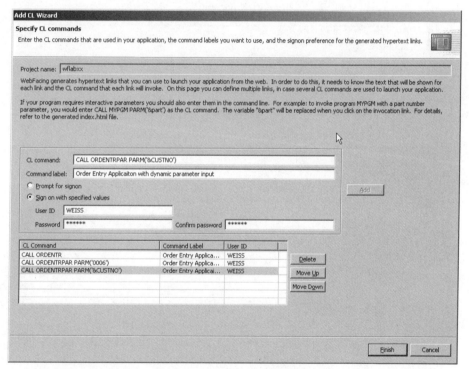

Figure 20.3: Adding a program invocation with one parameter to index.html *page*

- Enter the following CL command: **CALL ORDENTRPAR PARM('&CUSTNO')**.

- Enter the following command label: **Order Entry Application with dynamic parameter input.**

- Specify your user authentication information.

- Click the **Finish** push button.

- Run the application.

Note the &CUSTNO entry field on the index.html page (Figure 20.4).

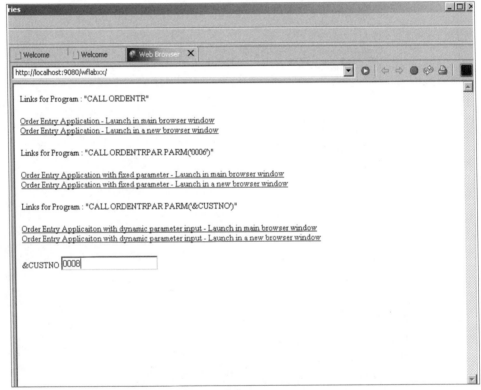

Figure 20.4: The index.html page with a parameter input field

---

Tip: You can improve the field heading text by editing the index.html file.

- Enter a valid customer number in the &CUSTNO entry field.

- Select the new link in the browser.

Note that in Figure 20.5 the Customer number field is now prefilled with the parameter value you entered on the index.html page.

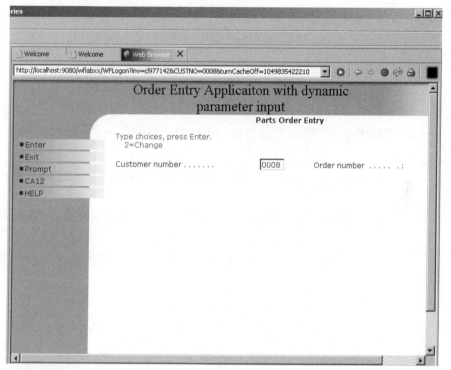

Figure 20.5: Customer number *field prefilled with input value from the* index.html *page*

Invoking the WebFaced application programmatically

If you have a separate Web application or Web page from which you want to start the WebFaced application, rather than from the default *index.html* page, you can do so by using the forward(..) or sendRedirect(..) methods in the standard servlet classes. These classes require you to provide a URL that will be used to determine the content to send back to the browser.

Don't worry if you have not performed any Java coding before; the Java code used here is very simple and the Web tools in the workbench do everything for you to set up the environment. I will guide you through all the steps to create this servlet. The servlet itself receives a server name from a form on a Web page. The server name is part of the URL that is sent to the server from the servlet. This URL is used to invoke the application on the correct server.

In this exercise, you build an HTML page with a form that contains one entry field for the server name. From this form you invoke a servlet, which obtains the server name and then uses the sendRedirect method with a URL passed as a parameter to invoke the WebFaced application.

More information on this topic and all the capabilities of dynamically invoking a WebFaced application are in the topic Programmatic invocation of WebFacing applications in the WebFacing Help documentation.

Creating a new Web project

To create a new Web project, you first need to open the Web perspective. Use **Window → Open Perspective** from the workbench menu bar.

In the Web perspective, create a new Web project with the name of SelectServer:

■ Use the project wizard on the workbench toolbar to invoke the Create a Web Project dialog.

Note: Make sure to create a Web project, and not a WebFacing project.

On the first page (Figure 20.6),

■ Enter the following project name: **SelectServer.**

■ Click the **Next** push button.

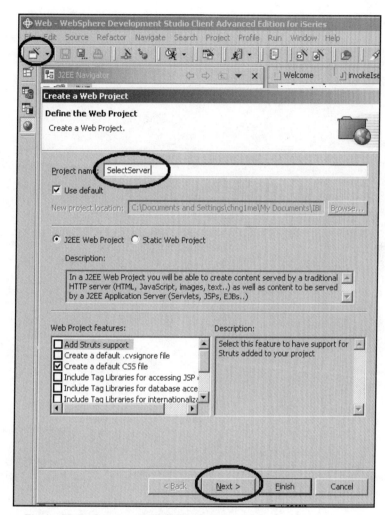

Figure 20.6: Create a Web Project dialog

On the second page of the Create a Web Project wizard (Figure 20.7),

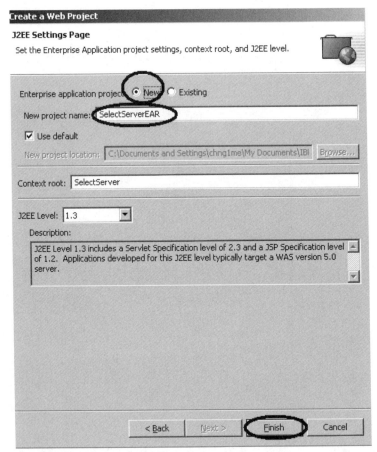

Figure 20.7: The second page of the Create a Web Project *wizard*

- Select the **New** radio button for the Enterprise application project.

- Enter **SelectServerEAR** in the New project name entry field.

- Click the **Finish** push button.

A new Web project is created.

Creating a servlet

Now that you have created a Web project, you can create a servlet. In the J2EE Navigator view, expand the **SelectServer** Web project you just created, as shown in Figure 20.8.

■ Select the **Java Source** directory.

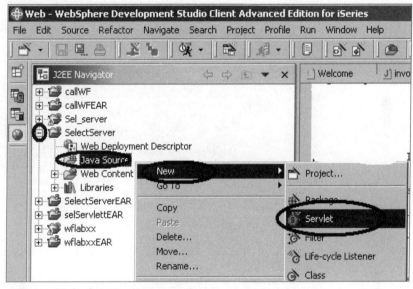

Figure 20.8: Creating a new servlet

■ Right-click **Java Source** and select the **New** option from the pop-up menu.

■ Select the **Servlet** option from the submenu.

The New Servlet wizard appears (Figure 20.9). Notice that the Folder information is prefilled.

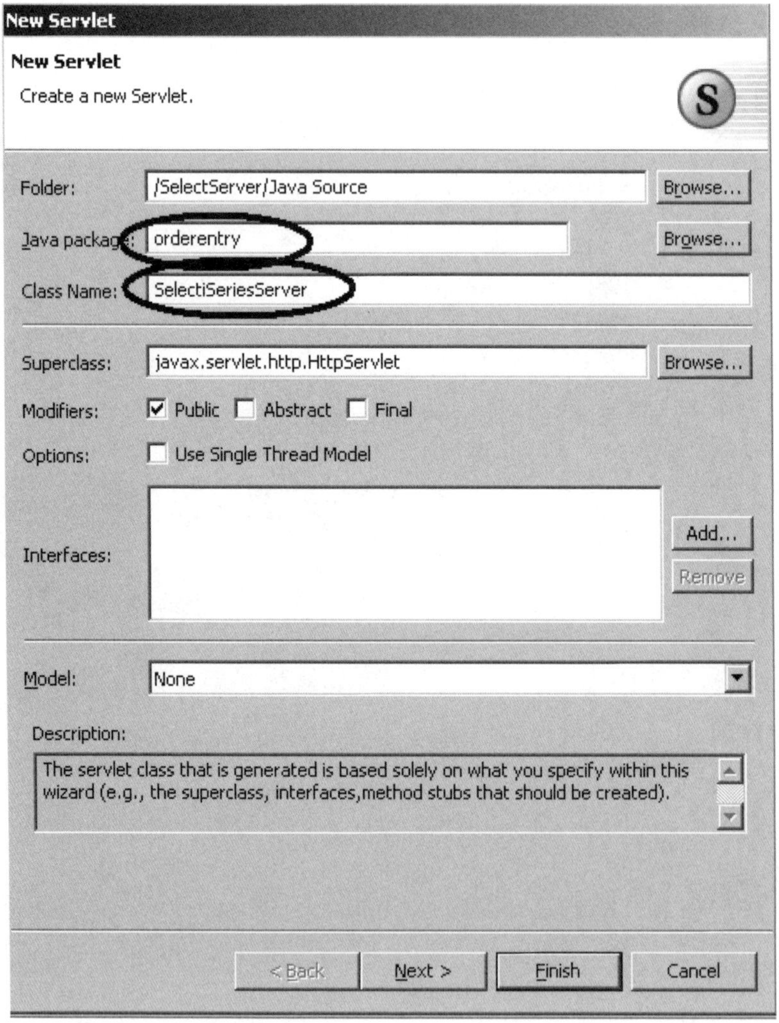

Figure 20.9: New Servlet wizard

■ In the Java package field, enter **orderentry**.

Note: A Java package is just a grouping mechanism for Java classes, similar to what a Service Program is for RPG procedures. For more information on the Java language, check out the book *Java for RPG Programmers,* 2nd edition, by Phil Coulthard and George Farr.

■ In the Class name entry field, enter the following servlet name: **SelectiSeriesServer**.

■ Click the **Finish** button.

The Java source editor opens, filled with a skeleton servlet.

In this servlet, you will create one method called invokeOrderEntry. The browser requests the servlet, which in turn invokes the method. By default, this request is invoked either by the doGet or doPost methods, as part of standard servlet behavior. The wizard has already created both of these methods; all you need to do is call your new invokeOrderEntry method from both of these predefined methods.

Add the new method to the source after the curly bracket, }, for the doPost method just before the ending curly bracket for the class, as shown in Figure 20.10.

```
package orderentry;

import java.io.IOException;
import javax.servlet.ServletException;

import javax.servlet.http.HttpServlet;
import javax.servlet.http.HttpServletRequest;
import javax.servlet.http.HttpServletResponse;
/**
 * @version     1.0
 * @author
 */
public class SelectiSeriesServer extends HttpServlet {

    /**
     * @see javax.servlet.http.HttpServlet#void (javax.servlet.http.HttpServletRequest, javax.servlet.http.F
     */
    public void doGet(HttpServletRequest req, HttpServletResponse resp)
        throws ServletException, IOException {

    }

    /**
     * @see javax.servlet.http.HttpServlet#void (javax.servlet.http.HttpServletRequest, javax.servlet.http.F
     */
    public void doPost(HttpServletRequest req, HttpServletResponse resp)
        throws ServletException, IOException {

    }

public void invokeOrderEntry(HttpServletRequest req, HttpServletResponse resp) {

}
```

Figure 20.10: Method invokeOrderEntry added to servlet

The method definition is the same for the doPost/doGet methods, so you can simply copy and paste one of them, changing the name to invokeOrderEntry.

Add two curly brackets, { and }, to indicate the beginning and ending of your method. You will add the logic that goes in between these brackets soon.

Now you have to call your new method from the doPost and doGet methods to run this code when a request comes from the browser.

- As shown in Figure 20.11, insert the following source to invoke inside the { } in both methods:

```
invokeOrderEntry(req, resp);
```

```
public class SelectiSeriesServer extends HttpServlet {

    /**
     * @see javax.servlet.http.HttpServlet#void (javax.servlet.http.HttpServletRequest, j
     */
    public void doGet(HttpServletRequest req, HttpServletResponse resp)
        throws ServletException, IOException {
        invokeOrderEntry(req, resp);
    }

    /**
     * @see javax.servlet.http.HttpServlet#void (javax.servlet.http.HttpServletRequest, j
     */
    public void doPost(HttpServletRequest req, HttpServletResponse resp)
        throws ServletException, IOException {
        invokeOrderEntry(req, resp);
    }
    public void invokeOrderEntry(HttpServletRequest req, HttpServletResponse resp) {

    }
}
```

Figure 20.11: Method calls in doGet and DoPost methods

The parameters to pass are the request and response objects, when the doGet and doPost methods are called.

Don't forget the semicolon (;) after the statement.

Tip: You can use CodeAssist to help you with the Java coding. Just type "i" for the first letter of the method and then press Ctrl and Space. This invokes the CodeAssist feature that lists all known valid Java constructs in your environment starting with i. It will list the invokeOrderEntry method, and you can select it from there to save you some typing.

Now you can add logic to your method to invoke the WebFacing application on the selected server.

In the invokeOrderEntry method , add the following code after the curly bracket ({):

```
// The url to use to invoke the application
String url = "http://localhost:9080/wflabxx/WFLogon?inv=cl208846&host=" ;
  // Getting the server name from web page
String serverName = req.getParameter("server_name");
  // adding servername to url
System.out.println("Host name: " + serverName);
url = url + serverName;
System.out.println("Invoking:" + url);
      try {
              // invoking the sendRedirect method to invoke the
applicaton
              resp.sendRedirect(url);
      }
      catch(Exception e) {
              System.out.println("Exception invoking application");
      }
}
```

Figure 20.12 shows the code in the editor.

Figure 20.12: Code in invokeOrderEntry method

You might wonder how I know which URL to specify for the WebFaced application. The information about the URL is documented in the WebFacing Help documentation. From that information, you can see that I use a URL which allows me to specify the server name with the rest of the connection information coming from the WebFacing project's invocation file.

> **Important:** You will need to change the name of the invocation file to your environment. To find the correct file name, you need to expand your WebFacing project according to the following path structure: wflabxx → Web Content → WEB-INF → classes → conf. Find the name of your .invocation file and use this name when specifying the **inv** keyword in the URL string in this servlet.

The lines that write information to System.out are not necessary for this servlet to function correctly, but they can help diagnose various problems. The text will appear in the application server's console when this servlet runs. Figure 20.13 shows a sample.

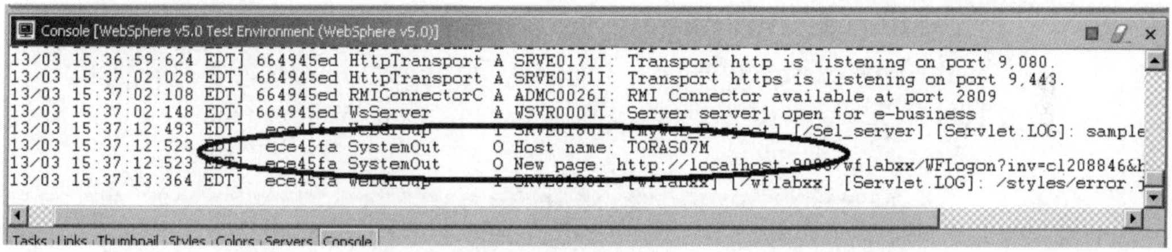

Figure 20.13: WAS console with messages from servlet

■ Save the Java file. If there are any error messages, fix the problem and save the file again.

> **Tip:** Java syntax and semantic errors are detected as you edit the code. A problem indicator displays in the editor: a little light bulb as shown in Figure 20.14.

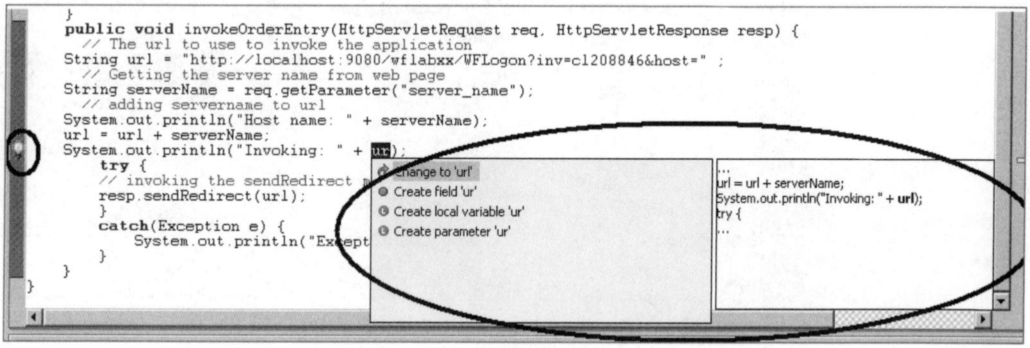

Figure 20.14: Java source editor with problem indicator showing error for nondefined variable

In the sample in Figure 20.14, the variable name *ur* is incorrect because it is not defined. Clicking on the light bulb (that displays on the line where an error is detected) will offer you assistance to fix the problem. In Figure 20.14, the choice would be to change the name to **url**.

Note: Java names are case sensitive; make sure you use the correct case.

You have completed the necessary Java coding. Now you can use the Page Designer tool to create the Web page that prompts for the server name.

Creating a Web page

In the Web perspective using the J2ee Navigator view (Figure 20.15), invoke the new HTML file wizard to create a Web page in your Web project.

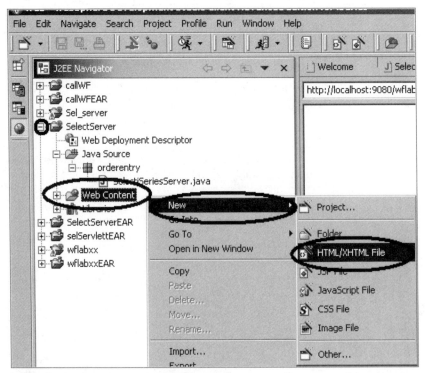

Figure 20.15: Invoking the HTML wizard

- Expand the **SelectServer** Web project.

- Select and right-click the **Web Content** directory.

- Select the **New** option from the pop-up menu.

- Select the **HTML/XHTML File** option from the submenu.

The New HTML/XHTML File wizard opens, as shown in Figure 20.16.

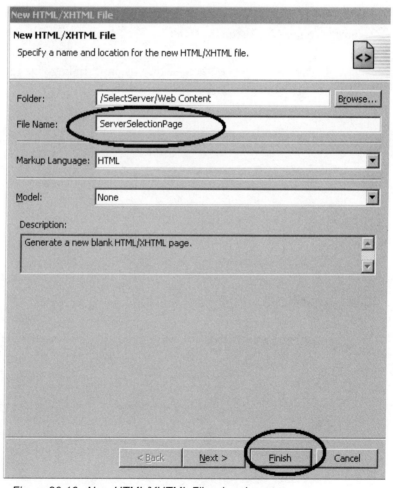

Figure 20.16: New HTML/XHTML File wizard

The Folder information should be correct since you started the wizard from the Web Content directory. If the information in this field is different, make sure to correct it.

- Enter **ServerSelectionPage** in the File Name entry field.

- Click the **Finish** button.

The file is created and the Page Designer tool opens.

You might want to drag a cascading style sheet onto the page to make it look more professional. The instructions in Chapter 13 tell you in detail how to accomplish this.

First I want you to create a header for this page. In Page Designer on the Design page (Figure 20.17),

- Erase the default text from the top of the page.

- Right-click the page background.

- Select the **Insert** option from the pop-up menu.

- Select the **Paragraph** option from the submenu.

- Select the **Heading 1** option from the submenu.

Figure 20.17: Creating the header

- In the area opened for the heading text, type in **Select Server For Order Entry Application**.

Now you need to add a form tag that allows you to send a request to invoke a servlet and pass parameter data to the server. Position the cursor underneath the header area.

- Right-click the page background.

- Select the **Insert** option from the pop-up menu.

- Select the **Form and Input Fields** option from the submenu.

- Select the **Form** option from the submenu.

A frame for a form is created on the page, as shown in Figure 20.18.

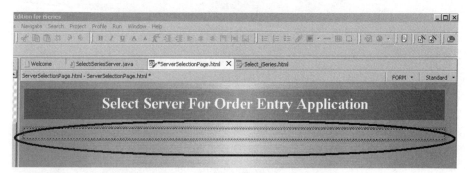

Figure 20.18: Page with form frame underneath the heading

Now you have to specify the program to call (your servlet), and you have to add the controls to enter the server name and a button to submit the request.

- Right-click inside the form frame.

- Select the **Attributes** option from the pop-up menu.

The Attributes [FORM] dialog appears in the bottom left area of the workbench, as shown in Figure 20.19.

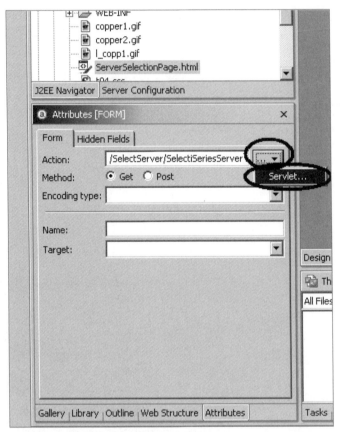

Figure 20.19: Form attribute dialog

- Click the push button to the right of the Action entry field.

- Select the **Servlet** option on the pop-up menu.

- Select the **SelectiSeriesServer** servlet from the list box.

- Click the **OK** push button on the Servlet list dialog.

In Page Designer in the form frame,

- Enter the following heading text for the selection entry field: **Specify the server name here**.

If you want to change the font or color of this text,

- Select the text on the Design page.

- Select the **Format** option on the workbench menu bar.

- Select the **Font** option from the submenu.

- Enter the required values in the Insert Font dialog box, as shown in Figure 20.20.

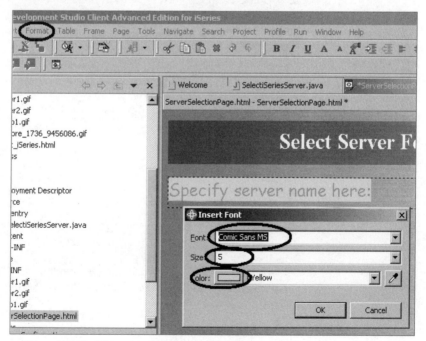

Figure 20.20: Changing font for heading text

You now need an entry field. I will explain how to add a combination box in which the user can select one of the available servers.

Inside the form frame,

- Position the cursor after the text you just entered and enter a **space**.

- Right-click at this position.

- Select the **Insert Input Fields** option from the pop-up menu.

- Select the **List Box** option from the submenu.

In the Insert List Box dialog (Figure 20.21),

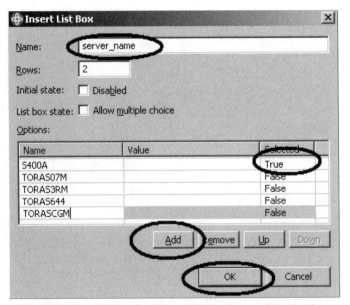

Figure 20.21: Setting up the values for the combination box

- Enter the list box name. This name has to be the parameter name you specified in the servlet to get the server name from. If you used the name I suggested, enter **server_name**; otherwise use the name you picked.

■ Add your valid server names to the list; the sample shows the names for my environment.

■ Make the most used server the selected one, by specifying **True** in the Selected column.

■ Click the **OK** push button when you finish adding valid server names.

In the list box Attributes [SELECT] dialog on the bottom left of the workbench (Figure 20.22),

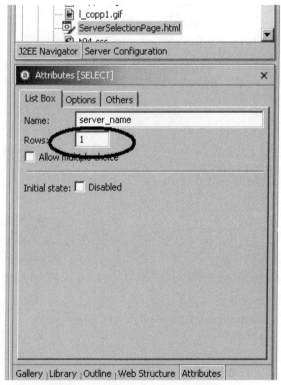

Figure 20.22: Changing the rows attribute of the list box to one

■ Change the Rows entry field to **1**.

Now you will add the push button. In Page Designer,

- Position the cursor behind the list box you just added.

- Press the **Enter** key twice to add some space.

- Right-click inside the form frame at the bottom left corner.

- Select the **Insert Input Fields** option.

- Select the **Submit** button option.

The Insert Submit Button dialog (Figure 20.23) appears.

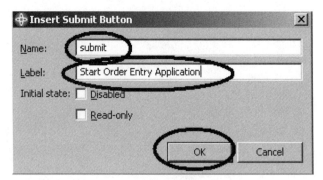

Figure 20.23: Insert Submit Button dialog

- Enter **submit** in the Name entry field.

- Enter **Start Order Entry Application** in the Label entry field.

- Click the **OK** push button.

You can add more content to the page to make it look more attractive, as you feel fit. I added, for example, a graphic to the bottom. To perform that task, just drag and drop the file onto the page.

Have a look at your page by using the Page Designer Preview tab at the bottom of the design pane. My page is shown in Figure 20.24.

Figure 20.24: The finished Server Selection page in preview mode

■ Save the page.

Running the application

In your Web project structure, find your Web page in the Web Content directory, as shown in Figure 20.25.

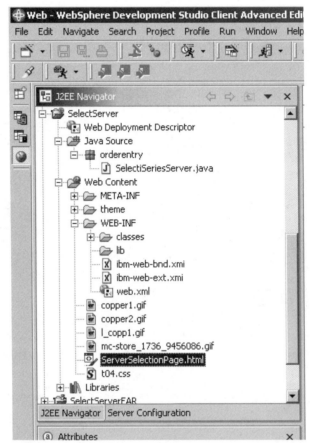

Figure 20.25: Selecting the ServerSelectionPage.html file

- Right-click the **ServerSelectionPage.html** file.

- Select the **Run on server** option.

Your page displays.

- Select a server and press the **Start Order Entry Application** push button.

The WebFaced Order Entry Application displays. If you experience any problems, check the console messages. Does the text from your servlet display? If not, that is an indication that the servlet is not being invoked.

If you receive "System.out" text from the servlet, check that the invocation file name is correct.

Analysis

In this exercise, you enhanced the startup of a WebFaced application by adding the capability of passing parameter values to the application. You also learned how to write a servlet and pass a value from a Web page to this servlet, and then invoke the Order Entry Application from this servlet. With this capability, you can invoke any WebFaced application from any other Web application or Web page and also control the authentication behavior and the server environment for the WebFaced application.

Hopefully this little excursion into Java servlet programming will help you expand your original 5250 applications to the Web.

In the next chapter, you will analyze how your DDS fits the WebFacing Tool's capabilities. Proceed to the Chapter 21: Checking Your DDS for WebFacing Support.

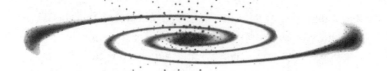

Checking your DDS for WebFacing support

You might want to know whether your DDS display file source is supported by the WebFacing Tool, and what keywords you can and cannot use without causing your conversion to fail. This would allow you to estimate what the success rate is in your environment and how much resource you might need to convert your applications with the WebFacing Tool.

The goal of this chapter

In this chapter I am introducing a tool that you can download from the IBM Web site. The tool is called the DDS Keyword Survey Tool. It works on your iSeries host: You can input DDS source files and the tool creates a report that is stored in a spool file. I want to make you aware of this tool and show you where to find it.

Scenario

You want to modernize the user interface of your 5250 application, and you want to know how much effort it would take and how many keywords in your DDS source are not supported by the WebFacing Tool. Once you know this information, you can decide whether or not to convert your application and how much resource you will need to rework your DDS source for full support.

Downloading the DDS Keyword Survey Tool

The CD for this book contains a copy of the tool. However, you might want to make sure that it is the latest version; there is a possibility that the WebFacing development team has added more support to the tool in various Service Packs. The copy included with the book is based on WebFacing Version 5.0 capabilities.

Appendix C contains the readme file that comes with the tool; it can also be downloaded from the IBM Web site.

To check for the latest version of the DDS Keyword Survey Tool, I suggest you go to the main iSeries Application Development Tools Web page, since URLs further down in the Web hierarchy are changed frequently: *ibm.com/software/awdtools/iseries*.

From this Web page,

- Go to the WebSphere Development Studio Client page.

In the left side bar, you should see a context-sensitive menu bar that contains a **support** link:

- Click the **support** link.

- On the page you are directed to, search for **Survey Tool**.

The Search result page should show a link to the download page for the Survey Tool. IBM Web pages change frequently, so these instructions might eventually be out of date. However, if you search for the Survey Tool, you should be directed to the correct place.

Check the newest version; if there is newer version than yours available, use the download page to find this new version. The page contains the instructions about how to install the tool, and it contains a link to download the readme file for this tool as well.

- Read through the readme file and follow the instructions to FTP the Savefile containing the tool to your iSeries.

■ Restore the **Survey** library.

■ Add the **Survey** library to your library list, as shown in Figure 21.1.

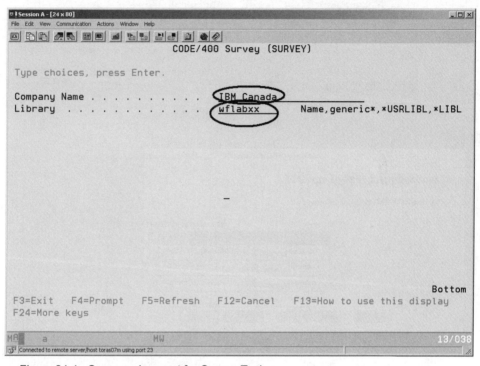

Figure 21.1: Command prompt for Survey Tool

■ Use the **Survey** command to point to the library containing your display file DDS source.

■ Run the tool and look at the spool file created by the tool, as shown in Figure 21.2:

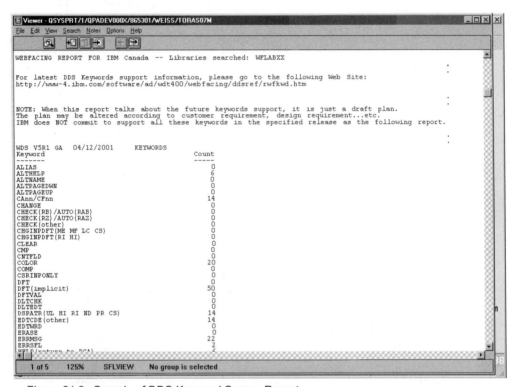

Figure 21.2: Sample of DDS Keyword Survey Report

The report will list

■ Supported keywords by version level

■ Support considered for future releases

■ Support not prioritized (most likely will not be supported unless feedback from customers indicates that support is needed)

■ Support not planned (IBM does not think these will ever be supported)

In general, the report shows you how much of your display file DDS is supported and what will and will not function after the WebFacing conversion is complete.

It also may give you an idea about different techniques you could use to change your DDS source yet still maintain the same results in a 5250 environment.

Many customers have told us they are not even aware that they use some of the keywords the Survey Tool lists. That is, the tool helps them clean up their DDS source to comply with internal standards before performing WebFacing conversion.

Summary

In this chapter, you learned that the WebFacing Tool is accompanied by a DDS Keyword Survey Tool. You also learned how to use this tool to investigate how the WebFacing conversion supports your DDS display file source in your specific environment.

This concludes the exercises in this book. I hope that you have enjoyed learning about the WebFacing Tool, and I also hope these exercises will help you modernize your 5250 applications.

Exporting to iSeries WebSphere Application Server Version 4.0

Until now you have tested your application only in the local WAS test environment. Now you are ready to test on an iSeries IBM WebSphere Application Server. In this exercise, you will export files created by the WebFacing Tool to a remote WebSphere Application server, to publish and deploy your application as you would in real-life development.

The goal of the exercise

This exercise shows you how to publish your WebFacing files to a remote WebSphere Application Server 4.0 environment on an iSeries host. It also explains how to create your Web application using the WebSphere Administrative Server Administrative Console.

If you are working with iSeries WebSphere Application Server Version 4.0 (and not Version 3.5 or Version 5.0), follow these instructions to create the Web application from an EAR file.

You will start the Export tool, specify files to export, start the WAS Administrative Console and use it to navigate through the server environment, create a Web application using the wizard, and start the application in a browser. The WebFacing project files are copied to a remote Web server so that the application server will be able to find and use them.

At the end of this exercise, you should be able to

■ Use the WebFacing Tool's wizards to specify the files to export

■ Copy specified WebFacing files to the Web server

You will also learn how to use the WebSphere Administrative Server Administrative Console of the WebSphere Application Server, so that you can define all the pieces needed to run on the server applications created with the WebFacing Tool. By the end of the chapter, you should be able to

■ Use the WebSphere Administrative Server Administrative Console

■ Navigate through the console environment

■ Use the console and its wizards to create the Web application that runs the WebFacing application

■ Use the console to start the Web application

Scenario

You have tested the application in the WAS test environment, and you are ready to move it to your iSeries WAS environment. You are running WAS Version 4.0 on your iSeries host, and you have the WAS Version 4.0 Administrative Console installed on your workstation.

Exporting the files to the Web server

In this section I describe how to export the WebFacing project files to a WebSphere Application Server Version 4.0. If you need to target Version 3.5, use the instructions in Appendix B.

Before you export your files, you must map a network drive to the root directory of your Web server iSeries IFS environment:

- Right-click the **Network Neighborhood** or (**My Network Places**) icon on the desktop.

- Select **Map Network Drive** from the pop-up menu.

- In the Folder field of the Map Network Drive dialog box (Figure A.1), enter two backslashes (\\) and the Netserver name of your Web server and then **root**, for example, **S400A\root**.

- Click the **Finish** push button.

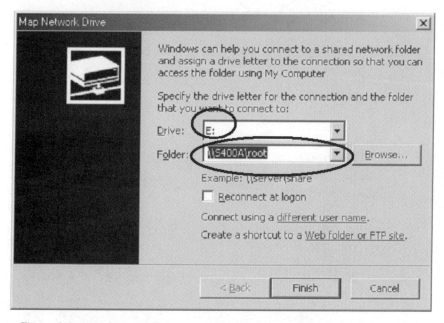

Figure A.1: Map Network Drive *dialog for Windows 2000.*

You are now ready to export your application.

Selecting the EAR file to export

- Return to the WebFacing perspective in WebSphere Development Studio Client.

- Select **File → Export** from the workbench menu bar.

The Select page of the Export wizard opens (Figure A.2).

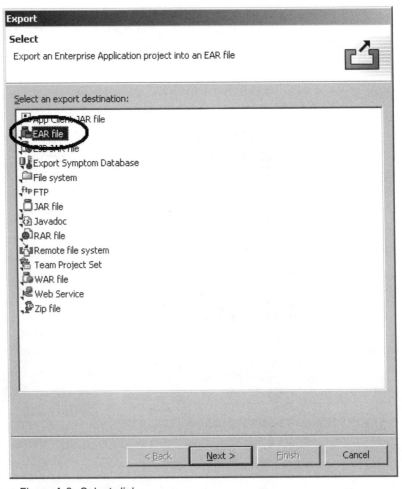

Figure A.2: Select *dialog.*

- Select the **EAR file** icon.

An EAR file is a compressed Enterprise Application Archive, and it contains all the files needed for the Web application.

- Click the **Next** push button.

Completing the EAR file export information

The **EAR Export** page opens (Figure A.3).

- Select the name of the resources you used when creating your WebFacing project from the combination box drop-down list. This should be wflabxxEAR.

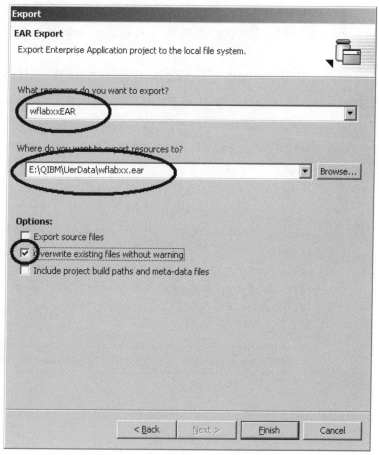

Figure A.3: EAR file export dialog.

- In the Where do you want to export the resources to? field, specify where to put the EAR file by entering the drive and directory structure of your Web server. It should look something like this: *x:\qibm\UserData\wflabxx*, where *x:* is the drive letter of the iSeries network drive that you mapped in the previous step.

- Select the **Override existing files without warning** check box.

- Click the **Finish** push button to copy the files to the EAR file.

If a message asks you to create a directory or delete an existing file,

- Click the **OK** push button or **Yes** to continue.

Creating a Version 4.0 Web application with the WebSphere Administrative Server Administrative Console

In this section, you will start the WebSphere Administrative Server Administrative Console. In the console, you can manage your server environment.

- To start the console, open a DOS command prompt on your workstation and type

adminclient <server_name> <port_number>

where <server_name> is the iSeries host that runs WebSphere Application Server and <port_number> is the port number for the WAS administrative server. 900 is the default port number for this server.

Important: The server name entry is case sensitive.

This will take a while; please be patient until the console opens.

Working with the WebSphere Administrative Server Administrative Console

Figure A.4 shows the view you should see after the console opens when it is connected to the default administration server.

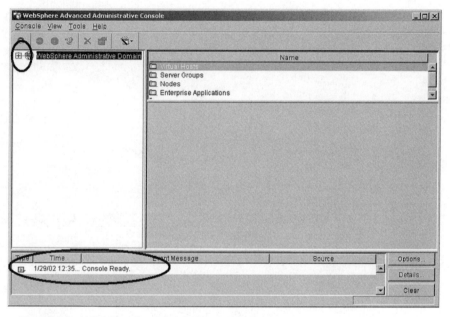

Figure A.4: WAS Version 4.0 Administrative Console.

If the console doesn't come up, make sure that

1. WAS is started on the iSeries.

2. The server name is spelled correctly and the correct case is used.

3. The port number is correct.

Make sure that the console message box at the bottom of the view contains the message Console Ready.

■ Expand **WebSphere Administrative Domain** by clicking the plus sign (+) beside it, if it is not already expanded.

■ Expand **Enterprise Applications** by clicking the plus sign (+) beside it, if it is not already expanded, as shown in Figure A.5.

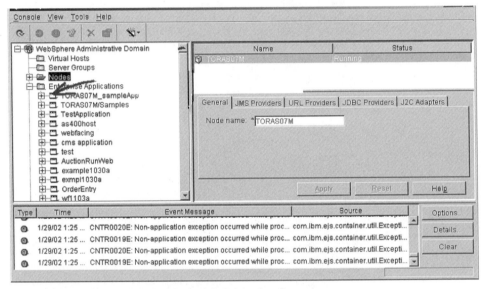

Figure A.5: Expanded tree view in Administrative Console.

Creating a new application

Now you are ready to create your WAS application:

■ Right-click the **Enterprise Applications** icon.

■ Select **Install Enterprise Application** from the pop-up menu.

The Install Enterprise Application Wizard opens, as shown in Figure A.6.

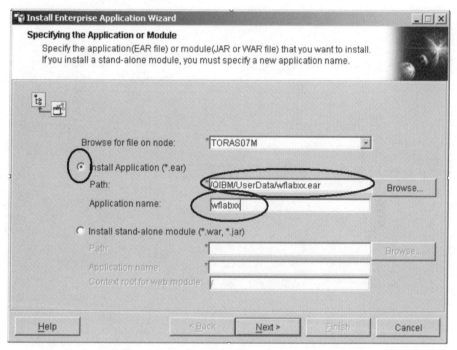

Figure A.6: Install Enterprise Application Wizard *dialog.*

- Select the **Install Application (*.ear)** radio button.

- Specify the name of the EAR file and the directory path that you exported the EAR file to. Do you still remember it?

- If not, click **Browse** to locate it. If you followed the instructions, it should be *x:/Qibm/UserData/wflabxx/wflabxx.ear*, where *x* is the directory in which you installed the product.

- Specify the application name: **wflabxx**.

- Click the **Finish** push button.

Note: If the Finish push button is disabled, click the **Next** push button until the Finish push button is enabled, accepting the default values on the other pages.

You should eventually see the completion message in Figure A.7.

Figure A.7: Completion message.

If you receive an error message, you might not be authorized to change the application server directories. In that case, make sure you are using the correct RWX authority.

Now you need to tell the HTTP server that this Web application exists, and what URL to use for the application. You can perform this task directly in the WebSphere Administrative Server Administrative Console:

- Expand the **Nodes** folder.

- Right-click the node that contains the iSeries system name you are working with, as shown in Figure A.8.

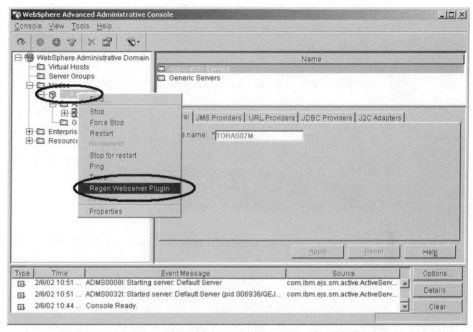

Figure A.8: Selecting Regenerate Webserver Plugin *from the Administrative Console.*

■ Select **Regen Webserver Plugin** from the pop-up menu.

Now the HTTP server knows about this new application.

Note: Another way to force the HTTP server to pick up this information is to restart the HTTP server.

Looking at application information

If you want to see where to find your application in the WAS environment, here are the steps to look for doing it.

In the console tree view, expand the system node that is the name of the iSeries host you are working with.

- Expand the **Application Servers** folder.

- Expand the **Default Server** folder.

- Click the **Installed Web Modules**.

In the top right list you can see all applications in the Web module of this application server, as shown in Figure A.9.

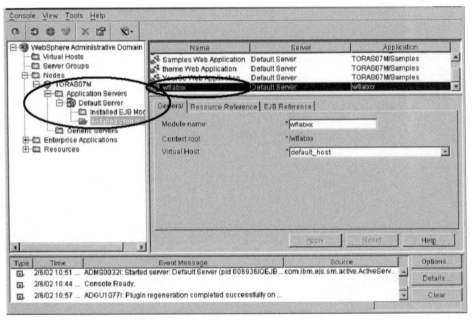

Figure A.9: Application details on Administrative Console.

- Scroll down the list of applications until you find your wflabxx application.

- Click **wflabxx**.

The notebook underneath the application list contains the detailed description of this application.

Note: Before you run the application, you need to change the application server settings to support UTF-8. The WebFacing Help documentation describes the steps required.

Running the Web-enabled application

You are now ready to run the Web-enabled application.

- Start Internet Explorer and enter **http://servername:portnumber/wflabxx**. Your application's index.html page should open. If it does not, check the URL. Also check that both the HTTP server and WebSphere Application Server have been started and are running.

Note: The port number is the HTTP server's port number; the default is 80. This is not the WAS administrative server port number

---

If the page still does not open, you might want to go back to the Administrative Console of WebSphere Application Server and try the following:

- Right-click your server instance.

- Select **Stop** from the pop-up menu.

A message confirms that the server is stopped.

- Right-click again on the server instance.

- Select **Start** from the pop-up menu.

If the application still does not work, there are troubleshooting guides on the Web, as well as FAQs and newsgroups where you might find more detailed information about your situation.

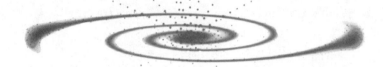

Exporting to iSeries WebSphere Application Server 3.5

Until now you have tested your application only in the local WAS test environment. Now you are ready to test on iSeries IBM WebSphere Application Server. In this exercise, you will export files created by the WebFacing Tool to a remote WebSphere Application server, to publish and deploy your application as you would in real-life development.

The goal of the exercise

This exercise shows you how to publish your WebFacing files to a remote WebSphere Application Server 3.5.6 environment on an iSeries host. It also explains how to create your Web application using the WebSphere Administrative Server Administrative Console.

If you are working with iSeries WebSphere Application Server Version 3.5 (and not Version 4.0 or Version 5.0), follow these instructions to create the Web application from a WAR file.

You will start the Export tool, specify files to export, start the WAS administrative console and use it to navigate through the server environment, create a Web application using the wizard, and start the application in a browser. The WebFacing project files are copied to a remote Web server so that the application server will be able to find and use them.

At the end of this exercise, you should be able to

- Use the WebFacing Tool's wizards to specify the files to export

- Copy specified WebFacing files to the Web server

You will also learn how to use the WebSphere Administrative Server Administrative Console of the WebSphere Application Server, so that you can define all the pieces needed to run on the server applications created with the WebFacing Tool. By the end of the chapter, you should be able to

- Use the WebSphere Administrative Server Administrative Console

- Navigate through the console environment

- Use the console and its wizards to create the Web application that runs the WebFacing application

- Use the console to start the Web application

Scenario

You have tested the application in the WAS test environment, and you are ready to move it to your iSeries WAS environment. You are running WAS Version 3.5 with the latest PTF level on your iSeries host, and you have the WAS Version 3.5 Administrative Console with the corresponding fix pack level installed on your workstation.

Exporting the files to the Web server

In this section I describe how to export the WebFacing project files to a WebSphere Application Server, Version 3.5. If you need to target Version 4.0, use the instructions in Appendix A.

Before you export your files, you must map a network drive to the root directory of your Web server's iSeries IFS environment:

■ Right-click the **Network Neighborhood** or (**My Network Places**) icon on the desktop.

■ Select **Map Network Drive** from the pop-up menu.

■ In the Folder field of the Map Network Drive dialog box (Figure B.1), enter two backslashes (\\) and the Netserver name of your Web server and then **\root**, for example, **\\S400A\root**.

■ Click the **Finish** push button.

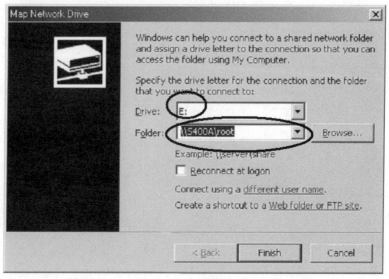

Figure B.1: Map Network Drive *dialog for Windows 2000.*

You are now ready to export your application.

Selecting the WAR file to export

- Return to the WebFacing perspective in WebSphere Development Studio Client.

- Select the **File** option from the workbench menu bar.

- Select the **Export** option from the pull down menu.

The Select page of the Export wizard opens, as shown in Figure B.2.

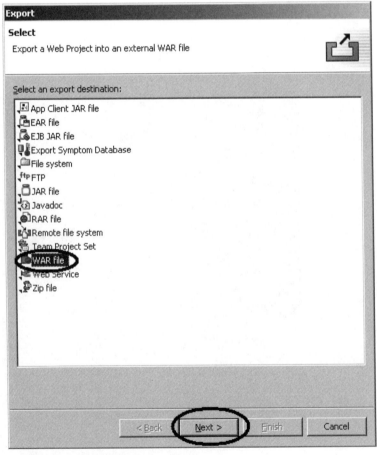

Figure B.2: Select dialog.

- Select the **WAR file** icon.

A WAR file is a compressed Web Application Archive, and it contains all the files needed for the Web application.

- Click the **Next** push button. The WAR Export page opens.

Completing the EAR File Export information

- On the War Export page (Figure B.3), select the name of the resources you used when creating your WebFacing project from the combination box drop-down list. This should be wflabxxWAR.

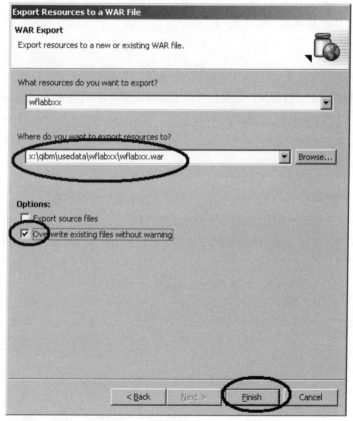

Figure B.3: WAR Export dialog.

- In the Where do you want to export resources to? field, specify where to put the WAR file by entering the drive and directory structure of your Web server. It should look something like this: *x:\qibm\UserData\wflabxx.war,* where *x:* is the drive letter of the iSeries network drive that you mapped in the previous step.

- Select the **Override existing files without warning** check box.

- Click the **Finish** push button to copy the file to the new location.

If a message asks you to create a directory or delete an existing file,

- Click the **OK** push button or **Yes** to continue.

Creating a Web application with the WebSphere Administrative Server Administrative Console

In this section you will start the WebSphere Administrative Server Administrative Console, Version 3.5. In the console, you manage your WebSphere application server environment.

Starting the WebSphere Administrative Server Administrative Console

To start the console:

- Open a DOS command prompt on your workstation and type **adminclient <server_name> <port_number>**, where <server_name> is the iSeries server that runs WebSphere Application Server and <port_number> is the port number for the WAS administrative server. 900 is the default port number for this server.

Important: The server name entry is case sensitive.

This will take awhile; please be patient until the console opens.

Working with the WebSphere Application Server Administrative Console

Figure B.4 shows the view you should see after the console opens up connected to the default administration server.

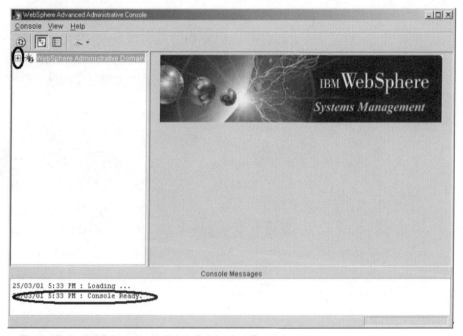

Figure B.4: WAS Version 3.5 Administrative Console.

Make sure that the console's message box at the bottom of the view contains the message Console Ready.

Expand the **Administrative Domain** by clicking the plus sign (+) beside it, if it is not already expanded.

Creating the Web application

The WAR file was generated in a WebSphere Application Server Version 5.0 environment, which is different from what is needed in Version 3.5. For this reason, the Version 3.5 WebSphere Administrative Server Admin Console has a tool to convert a WAR file into a Version 3.5-compatible structure. The next section takes you through this process.

On the WebSphere Administrative Server Admin Console (Figure B.5),

- Select the **Console** option on the console menu bar.

- Select the **Tasks** option from the pull-down menu.

- Select the **Convert a WAR file** option to start the tool.

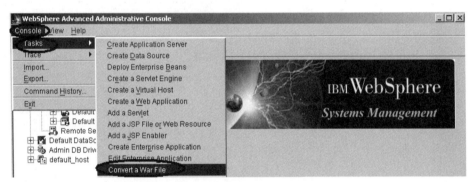

Figure B.5: Selecting the Convert WAR File option in the console.

On the Select Servlet Engine page (Figure B.6),

- Expand the nodes tree to the bottom.

■ Select the servlet engine to add your WebFacing application to. Most likely you are using the Default Servlet Engine.

■ Click the **Next** push button.

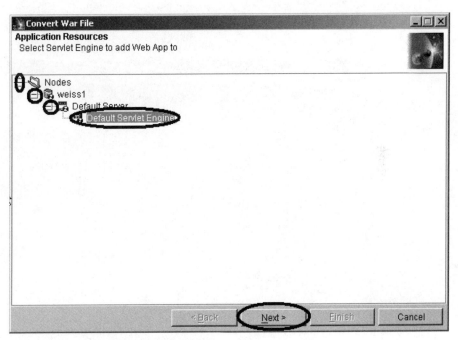

Figure B.6: Selecting a Servlet Engine.

On the Select Virtual Host page (Figure B.7),

- Select the virtual host that the application is to be run under. Most likely you are using default_host.

- Click the **Next** push button.

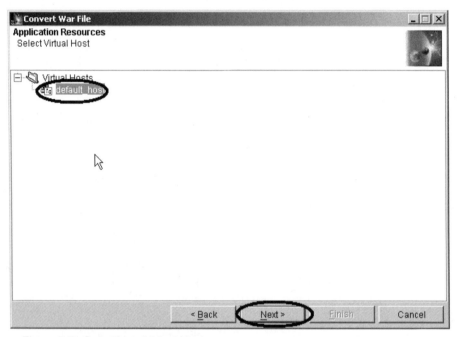

Figure B.7: Selecting a Virtual Host.

On the Select War File to Convert page (Figure B.8),

■ Browse to where you have exported the wflabxx.war file on the IFS.

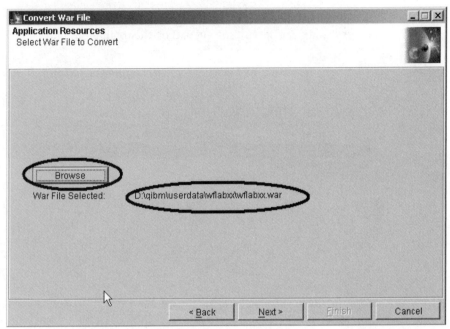

Figure B.8: Selecting WAR file to convert.

Tip: The **Browse** dialog lists the folder names in alphabetical order, but the collating sequence is case sensitive; this is different from the collating sequence that the Windows Explorer uses by default.

■ Select the **wflabxx.war** file.

■ Click the **Next** push button.

On the Select Destination Directory page (Figure B.9),

- Browse to the IFS directory where you want to install the application. If you are using the default instance, then this path would be

    /QIBM/UserData/WebASAdv/default/hosts/default_host/.

- Click the **Next** push button.

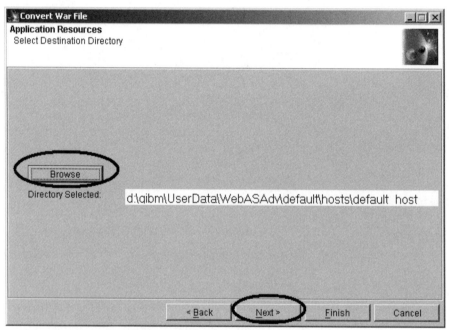

Figure B.9: Selecting destination directory for application.

On the Web Application Path and Web Application Name page (Figure B.10),

- Type **wflabxx** in the Enter a Web Application Web Path entry field. This value becomes part of the URL that will be used to access your WebFacing application.

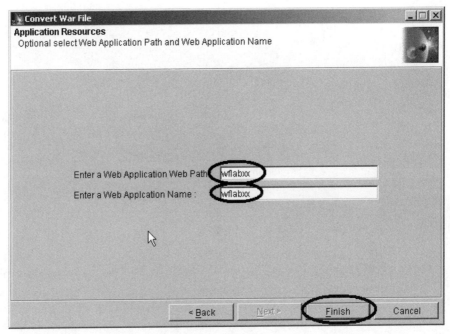

Figure B.10: Entering Web path and application name.

Example: If your server name is myserver and your instance of WebSphere Application Server is using the 9080 HTTP port, the first part of the URL to access your application would be *http://myserver:9080*. Using the Web path value, the complete URL to your application would be *http://myserver:9080/<web_application_web_path>*. When you enter the Web path value, include a forward slash at the beginning. In your example here, the full URL to the application would be *http://myserver:9080/wflabxx/*.

■ Type **wflabxx** in the Enter a Web Application Name entry field. After you finish installing the Web application from the WAR file, you will be able to administer, start, and stop the application with this name. An icon representing your application will be listed under the servlet engine that you chose for the application. In this exercise, it is Default Servlet Engine.

■ Click the **Finish** push button.

After the application is created, you will receive the message dialog shown in Figure B.11.

Figure B.11: WAR file conversion completed message.

■ Click the **OK** push button.

Setting up the application server to run the application

To work with the new application,

■ Locate the new application wflabxx icon under the Default Servlet Engine, as shown in Figure B.12.

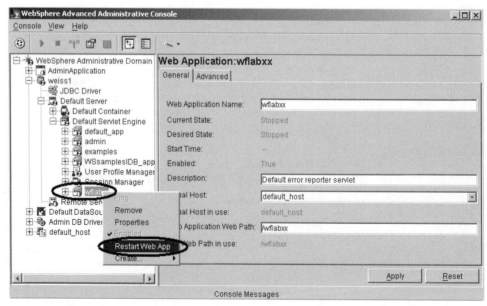

Figure B.12: Restarting the new application.

You will notice that the application is not active.

- Right-click on the application icon.

- Select the **Restart Web App** option from the pop-up menu.

You will see the completion message shown in Figure B.13.

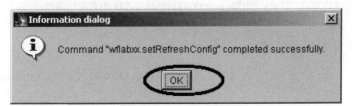

Figure B.13: Restart completion message.

- Click the **OK** push button.

If the Restart option is disabled, you need to stop the application server instance:

- Right-click the application server instance icon.

- Select the **Stop** option form the pop-up menu.

Wait until you see the message that the application has been successfully stopped.

- Right-click the application server instance icon.

- Select the **Start** option from the pop-up menu.

Wait until you see the message that the application has been successfully started.

- Click the **OK** push button.

Note: Before you run the application, you need to change the application server settings to support UTF-8. The WebFacing Tool Help documentation describes the steps required.

This is all you need to do in the WebSphere Administrative Server Administrative Console. Click the minimize button on the top right corner of the console.

Running the Web-enabled application

You are now ready to run the Web-enabled application.

■ Start Internet Explorer and enter **http://servername:portnumber/wflabxx**.

Your application's index.html page should open. If it does not, check the URL. Also check that both the HTTP server and WebSphere Application Server have been started and are running.

Note: The port number is the HTTP server's port number; the default is 80. This is not the WAS administrative server port number

---

If the page still does not open, you might want to go back to the Administrative Server Administrative Console of WebSphere Application Server and try the following:

■ Right-click your server instance.

■ Select **Stop** from the pop-up menu.

A message confirms that the server is stopped.

■ Right-click again the server instance.

■ Select **Start** from the pop-up menu.

If the application still does not work, there are WebSphere Application Server trouble-shooting guides on the Web, as well as FAQs and newsgroups where you might find more detailed information about your situation.

One other thing you can try to do is run the snoop application from your browser. Snoop is a sample application that is installed with WAS. If it displays in the browser, you are at least sure that the HTTP server and application server are set up correctly. Enter this URL in your browser to test the snoop application: **http://servername:portnumber/servlet/snoop**.

If snoop runs, then you know the application server set up is correctly and something is wrong with your newly installed application. If snoop does not run, then the application server or HTTP server might not be set up correctly.

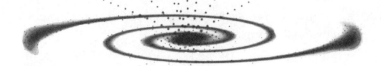

Readme for DDS keyword survey tool

This is a copy of the readme.html file for the DDS survey tool. This tool surveys your DDS source to determine

- What keywords in your application are supported in the current level of the WebFacing Tool.

- When you can expect support for the remainder of the keywords.

To use the SURVEY tool on a V4R5, V5R1, or V5R2 iSeries host, follow these steps:

1. If you have an older version of this tool, complete the next sub-steps to remove it. If you do not have an older version, skip to Step 2.
   a. Using the DSPLIBL command, check the library list to ensure there is no SURVEY library in your library list.
   b. If there is a SURVEY library listed, use the CHGLIBL command, then press F4 to remove SURVEY from the list.
   c. Delete the SURVEY library using the command:
      DLTLIB SURVEY.

2. Download the file survey.savf to your workstation.

3. FTP the save file to the iSeries host.

    a. Create an empty Save File on your host with the following command:
```
CRTSAVF FILE(SURVEY) LIBRARY(your_library_name)
```

    b. From a Windows command prompt, CD to the directory where you downloaded survey.savf file.

    c. To begin a new FTP session, enter:
```
FTP your_host_name
```

    d. In the FTP session, enter BIN to switch to binary mode. CD to the library you created the empty Save file in:
```
CD your_library_name
```

    e. Transfer the Save file with the PUT command:
```
PUT SURVEY.SAVF SURVEY
```

    f. When the transfer is completed, enter QUIT to exit the FTP session.

4. Restore the SURVEY library from the save file using the command:
```
RSTLIB LIB(SURVEY) DEV(*SAVF)
SAVF(your_library_name/SURVEY)
```

5. Add the SURVEY library in your library list or make SURVEY your current library.

    a. To add SURVEY to your library list, use the command:
```
ADDLIBLE LIB (SURVEY)
```

    b. To make SURVEY your current library, use the command:
```
CHGCURLIB CURLIB (SURVEY).
```

6. Use the SURVEY command to run this tool. In the Prompt screen, fill in your company name as the first parameter, and provide the name of the library containing your DDS source as the second parameter. This command will check all the DSPF members in every Physical File and count the DDS Keywords.

7. Use the WRKSPLF command to check the result. The spool file name is QSYSPRT and the user-specified data of that file is WEBFACING.

Index

C

Note: Boldface numbers indicate illustrations.

O

online help, 27–31
Opt heading, hiding, 107–111
Options column, hiding, 105–106
ORDENTD member
  converting, 355–356
  opening with CODE Designer, 384–385
ORDENTR member
  changing, 348–355
  creating a module from, **352**
ORDENTR module, **353**
Order Entry application, 138, 499
  first panel, **27**
  running, 189
  starting, 26
Order Entry Application panel, **145**
Order Entry Application properties dialog, **166**
Order Entry Application properties page, **166**
Order Entry Application screen
  customer details, with, **91**
  quantity specified, with, **93**
Order entry panel
  detailed customer data, with, **33**
  Part selection list, 34
  specify parts quantity, **34**–35
Order number field help, exiting, 31
Overview page, **68**
  areas of information on, **68**–69

P

Page Designer
  adding a heading 1 tag, 238–239, 269–270
  adding a heading to the Logon page,
    170–173
  adding moving text, 241–248, 272–279
  attributes editor, **175**
  changing the background color of the Logon
    page, 174–179
  changing the text color in, 247–249,
    279–281
  creating a header, **490**–491
  creating a Web page, 488–497
  design page, **216**
  invoking, 170–171

linking a style to the Web page, **220**
opening, 215–216
pop-up menu, **174**
resizing the logo in, **268**
saving space with, 277
Source editor window in, **178**
Source view, 177
starting in Development Studio Client
  Version 4.0, 254–256
views of, **255**–256
WebFacing logon, 171
Page Designer tool, creating a Web page,
  488–497
page properties
  working with, 217–219
  working with in Development Studio Client
    Version 4.0, 257–258
Page Properties dialog, **218**
parameters, passing in an invocation command, 472–477
parameter value
  using a dynamic, 474–477
  using a fixed, 473–474
parts selection list, **92**
pop-up calendars, 375–383
  added files for, **378**
  adding the cascading style sheet information,
    379–380
  CODE Designer and, **381**
  displayed on the Web page, **383**
  prerequisites to displaying, 377
project properties dialog, **153**
  changing the logon page with, **180**
  providing run-time properties for the project,
    165–166
  using, 164
  Window properties page, **153–154**
Properties Style dialog, 119
  invoking, 120–123
  opening, 121
PTF, 10
Publishing failure message, handling,
  209–212
push button, adding, 496

Note: Boldface numbers indicate illustrations.

Note: Boldface numbers indicate illustrations.

Note: Boldface numbers indicate illustrations.